SYMPHONIA

Saint Hildegard of Bingen

SYMPHONIA

A Critical Edition of the *Symphonia armonie celestium revelationum* [Symphony of the Harmony of Celestial Revelations]

WITH INTRODUCTION, TRANSLATIONS, AND COMMENTARY BY

BARBARA NEWMAN

SECOND EDITION

Cornell University Press
Ithaca and London

CORNELL UNIVERSITY PRESS GRATEFULLY ACKNOWLEDGES
A GRANT FROM THE ANDREW W. MELLON FOUNDATION
THAT AIDED IN BRINGING THIS BOOK TO PUBLICATION

First edition published 1988 by Cornell University Press.
Second edition published 1998.

Printed in the United States of America

Cornell University Press strives to use environmentally responsible suppliers and materials to the fullest extent possible in the publishing of its books. Such materials include vegetable-based, low-VOC inks and acid-free papers that are also either recycled, totally chlorine-free, or partly composed of nonwood fibers.

Library of Congress Cataloging-in-Publication Data

Hildegard, Saint, 1098–1179.
[Symphonia armonie celestium revelationum. English and Latin.] Symphonia : a critical edition of the Symphonia armonie celestium revelationum [Symphony of the harmony of celestial revelations] / Saint Hildegard of Bingen ; with introduction, translations, and commentary by Barbara Newman. 2nd ed.
p. cm.
Includes bibliographical references and index.
English and Latin.
ISBN 0-8014-8547-9 (pbk. : alk. paper)
1. Hymns, Latin (Medieval and modern) 2. Chants (Plain, Gregorian, etc.)
I. Newman, Barbara, 1953– . II. Title.
782.25'0268—dc21 98-9609

Paperback printing 10 9 8 7 6 5 4 3 2 1

Omnis caelestis harmonia speculum divinitatis est,
et homo speculum omnium miraculorum est Dei.

All celestial harmony is a mirror of divinity,
and man is a mirror of all the miracles of God.

SAINT HILDEGARD, *Causes and Cures*

Contents

Preface

Twenty years ago only a handful of medievalists knew the name of Saint Hildegard of Bingen. But no sooner do contemporary tastes change than the past takes on new contours. Names from the margins of our historical awareness are rediscovered, illumined, shifted toward center. So it was that, with the help of a few art historians, the forgotten Georges de la Tour suddenly became a painter of the first rank. So it was that Felix Mendelssohn "discovered" Johann Sebastian Bach; Franz Pfeiffer discovered Meister Eckhart; and a sisterhood of nuns discovered Hildegard of Bingen.

Hildegard, whose personal fame reached from England to Byzantium during her lifetime (1098–1179), has always had admirers in her native Germany. But her reputation suffered eclipse not long after her death. Though celebrated throughout the Middle Ages as an apocalyptic prophet, she was all but forgotten as a versatile writer, composer, and scientist. Between the Reformation and the early twentieth century, an occasional author hailed her as a great woman, a great saint, or a great German. Flurries of publication marked the 750th anniversary of her death in 1929 and the octocentennial in 1979. But her belated emergence as a major representative of twelfth-century civilization owes most to two factors: the feminist quest for a canon, and the critical scholarship of the nuns at St. Hildegard's Abbey in Eibingen. Sister Maura Böckeler, who was attempting to revive and modernize Hildegard's distinctive theology, published a German translation of her most famous work, the *Scivias,* in 1928. Böckeler's *Scivias,* reprinted many times, became the first of a series; all of Hildegard's major works are now available in abridged German versions published by Otto Müller Verlag of Salzburg. In the meantime two other Eibingen nuns, Marianna Schrader and Adelgundis Führkötter, broke ground in 1956 with an important historical and paleographic study, establishing the long-contested authenticity of Hildegard's works beyond doubt.[1] Together with Angela Carlevaris, Führkötter also published a critical edition of the *Scivias* for the series *Corpus Christianorum: continuatio mediaevalis* (Turnhout, 1978). But the rest of Hildegard's works, which are extensive, remain in limbo. Most of the printed texts are poor, and for the English-speaking reader, only brief excerpts are available in trustworthy versions.

Yet despite these problems, popular interest in Hildegard is burgeoning. Herbalists have begun to use her prescriptions and diets in their medical practice. A fashionable Catholic guru salutes her, generously but falsely, as the prophet of everything from ecological justice to global ecumenism. Novels and films about her life are under way, and illustrations from her works have been cast in ceramics and needlework for Judy Chicago's mammoth exhibition *The Dinner Party.* Her music in particular has received fresh attention, thanks to several fine recordings by English and Continental ensembles. Peter Dronke, the author of many perceptive essays on Hildegard, finds in her songs "some of the most unusual, subtle, and exciting poetry of the twelfth century."[2] I believe he is right, and I present this edition of Hildegard's lyrics to make this extraordinary body of work available both to the scholar and to the general reader.

[1]Marianna Schrader and Adelgundis Führkötter, *Die Echtheit des Schrifttums der heiligen Hildegard von Bingen* (Cologne and Graz, 1956).

[2]Peter Dronke, "Hildegard of Bingen as Poetess and Dramatist," in *Poetic Individuality in the Middle Ages* (Oxford, 1970): 151.

This volume contains a critical text of Hildegard's poetic cycle, the *Symphonia armonie celestium revelationum* [Symphony of the harmony of celestial revelations], together with two sets of facing-page translations, one in plain prose and the other in free verse. It is recommended that the general reader begin with the verse translations. The prose versions are offered partly as a corrective to my poetic license, but principally as an aid to the student who is trying to decipher Hildegard's rewarding but peculiar and often bewildering Latin. These prose versions are quoted in the examples throughout the introduction. The commentary at the end of the book includes manuscript information along with a discussion of each individual poem. For the benefit of musicologists and singers, it also provides cross-references to the German edition of Hildegard's music.[3] All biblical citations refer to the Vulgate.

I thank the librarians at the Hessische Landesbibliothek in Wiesbaden and the Bibliotheek der St.-Pieters-&-Paulusabdij in Dendermonde, Belgium, for their hospitality and for providing the manuscript photographs that appear on pages 52 and 53. I am also grateful to the Württembergische Landesbibliothek in Stuttgart and the Österreichische Nationalbibliothek in Vienna. Oxford University Press has graciously permitted me to reprint the stanzas by Charles Williams which appear on p. 282; they are taken from Williams's play *The House of the Octopus* (London: Edinburgh House Press, 1945), as reprinted in his *Collected Plays* (London: Oxford University Press, 1963). Twelve of the poems in this volume have previously appeared, in slightly different form, as an appendix to my earlier study, *Sister of Wisdom: St. Hildegard's Theology of the Feminine* (Berkeley: University of California Press, 1987). Parts of the introduction have appeared in *Arts & Sciences,* a magazine published by Northwestern University (Fall 1987).

This project would not have been possible without a travel

[3]Pudentiana Barth, M.-I. Ritscher, and Joseph Schmidt-Görg, eds., *Hildegard von Bingen: Lieder* (Salzburg, 1969).

grant from Northwestern University, for which I am deeply grateful

As a literary scholar with no claim to expertise in music, I offer my observations on Hildegard's musical style with some trepidation. My particular thanks are due to the musicians and musicologists who have saved me from many errors and offered helpful suggestions: Theodore Karp, Barbara Lachman, William Mahrt, Therese Schroeder-Sheker, and Barbara Thornton. Marianne Richert Pfau Kindly agreed, when this project was near completion, to let me include her essay on Hildegard's music. My husband, Richard Kieckhefer, has read the manuscript, as always, with vigilance as well as tender loving care. I thank Lieven Van Acker for sharing his ideas on the thorny manuscript problems discussed in the Appendix. Finally, I am grateful to David Myers for nerving me to "write *poems*" instead of pallid academic facsimiles of Hildegard's Latin. The infelicities that remain are all my own.

A Note on the Second Edition

Ten years after the original publication of the *Symphonia*, I am pleased to offer the reader this second, revised edition. The bibliography and discography have been updated to include more recent editions, translations, studies, and recordings of Hildegard's works. In addition, I have thoroughly revised the prose translations for the benefit of readers and listeners who do not read Latin. Without departing from strict fidelity to Hildegard's texts, I now offer more fluent and elegant versions that do less violence to normal English syntax. Finally, in the case of a single poem (no. 29), I have changed my interpretation of the last three lines and modified my translation and comments accordingly. The other verse translations and all the Latin texts are unaltered.

BARBARA NEWMAN

Evanston, Illinois

SYMPHONIA

Introduction

Biographical Sketch

Hildegard's biography is well documented, and the outlines of her eventful life are well known.[1] The scion of an ancient and noble family, she was born in 1098 in the town of Bermersheim near Alzey, in the diocese of Mainz. As the tenth and last child of her parents, Hildebert and Mechtild, Hildegard was offered to God as a tithe. A noblewoman named Jutta, daughter of the count of Sponheim, had chosen a life of religious seclusion near the recently founded monastery of St. Disibod, and the eight-year-old Hildegard was given to this anchoress as a companion in 1106. Jutta, whom Hildegard would later characterize as an "unlearned" woman, was nonetheless literate enough to teach the girl elementary reading and singing. Their textbook was the Latin Psalter, the centerpiece of monastic prayer. Hildegard undoubted-

[1]The main source is a hagiographic life by the monks Gottfried of St. Disibod and Dieter of Echternach, *Vita Sanctae Hildegardis,* in J.-P. Migne, ed., *Patrologiae cursus completus: series latina,* 221 vols. (Paris, 1841–1864; hereafter PL), 197: 91–130; German translation by Adelgundis Führkötter, *Das Leben der heiligen Hildegard von Bingen* (Düsseldorf, 1968); English translation by Anna Silvas, "Saint Hildegard of Bingen and the *Vita Sanctae Hildegardis,*" *Tjurunga: An Australasian Benedictine Review* 29 (1985): 4–25; 30 (1986): 63–73; 31 (1986): 32–41; 32 (1987): 46–59. There is a biography in German by Eduard Gronau, *Hildegard von Bingen* (Stein-am-Rhein, Switzerland, 1985).

ly became familiar with other books of the Bible and with the monastic liturgy at an early age, although she was always keenly aware that she lacked "education." She took to the religious life easily, yet by her own account she was a peculiar child: her health was always frail and she was touched from infancy by her exceptional gift of *visio*.

This condition involved unusual and sometimes painful perceptions—such as her vision at the age of three of "a brightness so great that [her] soul trembled"—combined with a kind of clairvoyance. Without losing consciousness or ordinary perception, the girl was able to see hidden things, such as the color of a calf in its mother's womb, and to foretell the future. Hildegard retained this *visio* throughout her life. In her seventies, she characterized it as a nonspatial radiance that filled her visual field at all times, without impairing her natural vision. She called this radiance "the reflection of the living Light," and in it she saw both the "living Light" itself and the complex symbolic forms that fill her visionary writings.[2] She interpreted these forms with the assistance of a "voice from heaven" which addressed her in Latin, sometimes speaking for God in the first person and sometimes about him in the third. It was this voice, Hildegard maintained, which dictated her books and letters.

Vision, illness, and prophetic authority were inextricably bound together in Hildegard's life. Some of her physical symptoms, together with certain structural elements in her visions—flashing and scintillating lights, concentric circles, and recurrent "fortification figures"—led a historian of medicine to conjecture in 1917 that she suffered from a form of migraine.[3] She was extremely sensitive to the weather, especially storms and wind; in her own view, this susceptibility or "airiness" also made her re-

[2]Letter to Guibert of Gembloux, Ep. 2 in J.-B. Pitra, ed., *Analecta sacra* 8 (Monte Cassino, 1882; hereafter Pitra): 332–33.

[3]Charles Singer, "The Scientific Views and Visions of Saint Hildegard," in *Studies in the History and Method of Science* 1 (Oxford, 1917): 1–55; rpt. in *From Magic to Science: Essays on the Scientific Twilight* (New York, 1958): 199–239. The theory has been popularized by Oliver Sacks in *Migraine: Understanding a Common Disorder* (Berkeley, 1985): 106–8.

ceptive to the mighty wind from heaven, the Holy Spirit.[4] Other attacks of illness, however, were brought on by acute conflict between the commands of her divine voice and the limitations imposed by her gender and her own anxiety. Serious illnesses preceded or accompanied all the most important and frightening decisions of her life: to begin writing, to found her own monastery, to obtain financial independence for it, to undertake her first preaching tour. Nevertheless, her determination to obey God always prevailed over her frailty, and the healings that followed action both reinforced her own conviction and helped to persuade opponents that her call was genuine.

Despite her lifelong visionary experience, Hildegard did not emerge as a public figure until the age of forty-three. From adolescence through her twenties and thirties, she lived an apparently unremarkable life in a community of women, suppressing the marks of her singularity. Jutta's hermitage, like many similar retreats, had become the nucleus of a monastery as like-minded women gathered around the anchoress, and at some point they were formally incorporated as Benedictine nuns under the supervision of the abbot of St. Disibod. Hildegard herself took monastic vows in her teens and received the veil from Otto, bishop of Bamberg. We have no further record of her until 1136, the year of Jutta's death, when Hildegard was chosen abbess (*magistra*) in Jutta's stead. Her election may bear witness to her family's high social position as well as to her own spiritual gifts and her emerging talent for leadership.

Five years later, the abbess was stunned by a divine call that commanded her to "tell and write" what she saw and heard in her visions.[5] Although she resisted at first "on account of humility" and took to her bed in pain, the call persisted, and at last she accepted the challenge. Two close friends—the nun Richardis von

[4]Hildegard of Bingen, *De operatione Dei [Liber divinorum operum]* 3.10.38, in PL 197: 1038a.

[5]Hildegard of Bingen, *Scivias,* ed. Adelgundis Führkötter and Angela Carlevaris in *Corpus Christianorum: continuatio mediaevalis,* vols. 43–43a (Turnhout, Belgium, 1978): 3. The two volumes are paginated continuously.

Stade and the monk Volmar of St. Disibod, provost of her convent—provided moral support as well as physical assistance with the act of writing. In addition, Volmar served as her copyeditor, correcting her untutored and in some ways defective Latin without substantially altering her work. Hildegard was to remain dependent on Volmar's services until his death in 1173, six years before her own.

The *Scivias,* fruit of these initial labors, took Hildegard ten years to complete. Based on a series of twenty-six visions, it is divided into three books that set forth the grand scheme of creation, redemption, and sanctification. Visual descriptions, often brilliantly original, alternate with much longer allegorical passages in which Hildegard's—or God's—doctrinal teaching is expounded by means of the visionary images. In 1147/48, when this book was about half-finished, Hildegard had a stroke of extraordinary good fortune. It happened that Pope Eugenius III, a Cistercian who had been a disciple of Bernard of Clairvaux, was attending a synod of bishops at Trier, not far from Hildegard's monastery. Less than a year earlier, Hildegard had written to Bernard, the outstanding saint of her age, to seek confirmation of her prophetic call. Bernard had encouraged her, and as he was also present at Trier, he suggested to the pope that so great a light as hers should not remain hidden under a bushel.[6] Meanwhile a delegation of clergy led by Heinrich, archbishop of Mainz—a weak prelate but a strong supporter of Hildegard—had already approached the pontiff with news of his remarkable visionary nun. On Heinrich's urging, Eugenius sent two legates to St. Disibod to visit Hildegard and procure a copy of her writings. Having obtained it, Eugenius himself, it is said, read from the *Scivias* before the assembled prelates, after which he sent the abbess a letter of apostolic blessing and protection.

The Synod of Trier marked the second major turning point in Hildegard's life. After her official recognition by the highest authority in the Church, she found that she had become a celebrity. Not only was her writing vindicated but her counsel was sought

[6] *Vita S. Hildegardis* 1.5 in PL 197: 94–95; Ep. 29 in ibid.: 189–90.

by clergy and laity alike, ranging from ordinary matrons to the emperor Frederick Barbarossa to Odo of Soissons, master of theology at Paris. A letter from this Odo, written in 1148, indicates that Hildegard was already famous halfway across Europe, not only for her visions but also for her novel poems or songs (*modos novi carminis*).[7] Thus even before she finished her *Scivias,* which ends with a collection of liturgical songs, we know that Hildegard was already at work on the music that she later collected in her *Symphonia*.

In the years immediately following Trier, Hildegard's fame created new opportunities as well as new conflicts. Her sudden prestige brought a steady stream of pilgrims, and hence of revenue, to St. Disibod. At the same time it brought new aspirants to her community, and evidently Hildegard felt that she and her nuns had both physically and spiritually outgrown the double monastery. Hence she determined to start an independent foundation on a site revealed to her in a vision—the Rupertsberg, a desolate mountain slope where the river Nahe flows into the Rhine. Hildegard felt spiritually drawn to Saint Rupert, a ninth-century nobleman whose mother had founded a monastery on this site; it had lain in ruins for centuries, but the abbess resolved to rebuild it. Her decision provoked strong opposition, however, perhaps stronger and more widespread than she had anticipated. Kuno, the abbot of St. Disibod, did not want to lose his monastery's latest source of distinction; nor did he want to lose the nuns' rich endowments; nor was he willing to let Volmar go. The nuns themselves grumbled, reluctant to leave their comfortable quarters for a life of penury in the wilderness. And some of the local families thought Hildegard was quite simply mad, if not possessed.

In this crisis she resorted to a twofold strategy. On the one hand, she went to her two staunchest supporters, Heinrich of Mainz and the countess Richardis von Stade, mother of her favorite nun. With their help, she managed to secure permission for the move and entered into protracted negotiations for the Rupertsberg land. On the other hand, she met the monks' resistance with

[7]Ep. 127 in PL 197: 352a.

a paralyzing illness. Lying in bed like a stone, she remained immobile even when Kuno tried to lift her bodily from the spot—a "miracle" that convinced him that he was indeed resisting God's will. Upon his conversion, she rose from her sickbed at once.

Construction of the new monastery apparently began in 1148; the nuns moved in 1150, and Heinrich of Mainz consecrated their church in 1152. But despite this triumph, the early 1150s were also a time of deep loss for Hildegard. Because of the Rupertsberg's initial poverty, a few disgruntled nuns left, or refused to enter, the new foundation. And in 1151 her beloved Richardis departed to become abbess of a distant community near Bremen. Hildegard's memoirs indicate that she felt abandoned and deeply betrayed, like Moses wandering in the desert. Although she appealed to the countess von Stade as well as to two archbishops and the pope himself, she was unable to prevent Richardis's defection. She did make the young woman feel guilty enough to agree to return to the Rupertsberg, but before Richardis could actually do so, she fell sick and died, leaving Hildegard penitent and grieving.[8] In 1153 the abbess lost three more protectors. Heinrich of Mainz was deposed from his see on the charge of embezzling church funds—despite Hildegard's intervention on his behalf—and in the same year Saint Bernard and Pope Eugenius died. Thus Hildegard's life was by no means serene and carefree while she was composing the jubilant songs of the *Symphonia*. An ailing woman in her fifties, bereaved and ridiculed, she was embroiled in a long struggle for property rights with the monks of St. Disibod, while attempting at the same time to secure the well-being of her fledgling convent.[9]

Composition and Dating of the Symphonia

Hildegard had finished the *Scivias* in 1151, and it was not until seven years later that she began her second visionary work, the

[8]Marianna Schrader and Adelgundis Führkötter, *Die Echtheit des Schrifttums der heiligen Hildegard von Bingen* (Cologne and Graz, 1956): 131–41; Peter Dronke, *Women Writers of the Middle Ages* (Cambridge, 1984): 154–59.

[9]Letter to her congregation, printed as part of an *Explanatio symboli Sancti Athanasii* in PL 197: 1065b–67a.

Book of Life's Merits. It is most unlikely that, during the turmoil of the 1150s, the abbess envisaged a sequel to the *Scivias,* much less the trilogy that she eventually produced. (The third and greatest volume, *On the Activity of God,* was the work of her old age; she finished it in 1173 at the age of seventy-five.) But once she had taken up the heroic labor of writing—which she believed to be unprecedented for a woman—she never ceased. During the 1150s she engaged in a vast correspondence and, with astonishing energy, turned her creative gifts to two widely diverse fields: natural science and music. It is in this period that she began her encyclopedia, variously known as the *Physica,* the *Book of Simple Medicine,* or *Nine Books on the Subtleties of Different Kinds of Creatures.* These creatures include herbs and trees, mammals, reptiles, fishes and birds, "elements," gems, and metals, each described with reference to its wholesome or toxic properties and its medicinal uses. The work attests to a mind at once systematic, boundlessly inquisitive, and well versed in traditional but not academic medical lore. Its companion volume, the *Book of Compound Medicine* or *Causes and Cures,* deals with physical and mental diseases; it also includes extensive material on sexuality, introduced through discussions of Adam and Eve. These two works are unique in Hildegard's corpus in that they claim no visionary inspiration. Nor did the abbess make any attempt to publish them, although they are listed in several contemporary accounts of her works. These peculiarities may explain their weak manuscript tradition and the confused state of the texts.

Far different is the *Symphonia,* a work that would scarcely be ascribed to the same author if the historical record left room for doubt. As Odo of Soissons's letter reveals, Hildegard was already composing music in the 1140s, and it seems likely that all her songs written before 1151 were incorporated in the *Scivias.* The last "vision" recorded in that work is not really a vision at all: it is the transcription of a celestial concert that the visionary heard when the heavens were opened to her. In the preface to this concluding segment of her work, Hildegard wrote that she had seen a "most luminous sky" in which she heard a "sound like the voice of a multitude singing in harmony, in praise of the celestial hierarchy."[10] There follow fourteen songs in honor of the Virgin Mary, the angels, and the saints, although the *Scivias* manuscripts do not include their notation. After the songs comes a dramatic sketch representing a pilgrim soul torn between the devil and a choir of personified Virtues. This sketch is the kernel of an engaging morality play, the *Ordo virtutum* (*Play of Virtues*), which Hildegard at some point expanded and set to music. It is not clear whether she intended the complete *Ordo,* a sort of cantata, as an independent work or as the final portion of her cycle. It follows the *Symphonia* in only one of the two manuscripts. I have not included the play here because a critical edition of the text, a good translation, and a performance edition are all readily available.[11]

After completing the *Scivias,* Hildegard continued to compose. In the preface to her *Book of Life's Merits* she says that, when she began working on that book in 1158, she had already spent eight years writing the *Symphonia,* the *Subtleties,* a great many epistles, and several minor works.[12] It is usually assumed, therefore, that the *Symphonia* was substantially finished by 1158, although some pieces may have been added later. But its history is not so simple. The *Symphonia* exists in two manuscripts representing very different versions, which will be described in greater detail below (pp. 51–60). The earlier was prepared under Hildegard's supervision around 1175 as a gift for the monks of Villers and contains fifty-seven songs. A revised and enlarged edition, which includes seventy-five songs, was produced at the Rupertsberg scriptorium in the 1180s, not long after the composer's death. To complicate matters, twenty-six of the *Symphonia* pieces also appear, without their music, in a prose miscellany that has hitherto gone unnoticed. Cardinal J.-B. Pitra published this text in his *Analecta sacra* (1882) under the misleading title of "Epilogue to

[10]*Scivias* III.13, pp. 614–15.

[11]"The Text of the *Ordo virtutum,*" ed. Peter Dronke in *Poetic Individuality in the Middle Ages* (Oxford, 1970): 180–92; trans. Peter Dronke in record liner for *Hildegard von Bingen: Ordo virtutum,* recorded by Sequentia (Harmonia mundi 20395/96); music ed. Audrey Davidson, *The "Ordo virtutum" of Hildegard of Bingen* (Kalamazoo, 1985).

[12]Hildegard of Bingen, *Liber vitae meritorum* [*Book of Life's Merits*], Pitra 7–8.

the Life of St. Rupert," because the first three pieces in it are addressed to that saint and it follows his *vita* in the manuscripts. In a footnote to this compilation, however, Pitra shrewdly characterized it as a "varied and dramatic program of lyrics, songs, and colloquies which the virgins of Bingen, led by Hildegard in ecstatic fervor, were accustomed to perform outside of choir on their titular feast day."[13]

Ecstasy aside, this description is a plausible one. We know that the *Ordo virtutum* was intended for performance by Hildegard's nuns, and after that artistic triumph, she may well have prepared additional if less ambitious "dramatic programs" to enhance the monastic liturgy. I suggest that she composed her songs not to fulfill a conceptual scheme but to suit particular occasions, integrating them with suitable homilies, prophecies, and dramatic exchanges. Such liturgical programs could have been recorded by someone at the time, perhaps by Volmar or one of the nuns, and later arranged in a rather haphazard compilation by an editor who wished to assemble Hildegard's "collected works." Another little-known text, her series of homilies on the Gospels, appears to have had a similar genesis.[14] Because the so-called "Epilogue" miscellany has received virtually no attention to date, I have offered some further speculations about its construction and dating in an appendix (pp. 68–73 below).

To summarize my findings, I believe the miscellany indicates at least four new conclusions about the *Symphonia*. In the first place, it suggests that Hildegard did not initially plan to compose a song cycle any more than she planned to write a trilogy. Her music had its origins in the concrete liturgical life of the Rupertsberg, and only when she had composed a substantial body of lyric—probably in the late 1150s—did she decide to collect all her songs and arrange them in a systematic order. After making this decision, she continued to compose new pieces that were incorporated in the cycle only after her death.

Secondly, the miscellany may enable us—very tentatively—to

[13] *Ad Vitam S. Ruperti Epilogus,* Pitra 358–68; quotation, p. 358.
[14] *Expositiones quorumdam evangeliorum,* Pitra 245–327.

distinguish early, middle, and late periods in Hildegard's oeuvre. By 1151 she had written the fourteen pieces that appear in the *Scivias* and all or part of the *Ordo virtutum*. This earliest layer of composition, including twelve songs in honor of the celestial hierarchy (nos. 29–34, 37–40, and 55–56), shares with the *Scivias* its cryptic and elliptical style. There is no overlap between these fourteen pieces and the twenty-six recorded in the miscellany. Since various segments in the latter suggest a date in the late 1150s, these twenty-six pieces may define a middle period that includes most of the Marian songs and a hymn and sequence to the Holy Spirit. There remain over thirty pieces that appear in one or both of the *Symphonia* manuscripts. Among these pieces are several long and masterful compositions honoring local saints (Matthias, Eucharius, Maximin, and Ursula) which can plausibly be assigned to Hildegard's latest period. It should be stressed, however, that the evidence does not permit conclusive dating of any individual piece.

In the third place, the song-texts in the miscellany differ in significant ways from those in the *Symphonia*. Not only are they embedded in a prose context and copied without notation; they also lack textual cues, such as doxologies and alleluias, which would assign them to particular liturgical genres. It is possible that, if the miscellany segments were transcribed from actual celebrations, this information was omitted as superfluous to a worshiping community that already knew the music and the appropriate rubrics from performance. On the other hand, it may be that Hildegard formalized the genre designations—and tidied up her texts—only when she had her music copied out for a distant community that would have been unfamiliar with the Rupertsberg's distinctive liturgical style.

This possibility leads me to a final speculation. When Hildegard's collected songs were arranged in the final version of the *Symphonia,* did her editors include *all* her lyrical compositions, or were some of them left out? It is a peculiar fact that the second *Symphonia* manuscript (c. 1180–1190) adds twenty pieces to the first, but omits the short antiphons "O frondens virga" (no. 15) and "Laus Trinitati" (no. 26). These two lyrics may have been deleted for artistic reasons, as Peter Dronke suggests.[15] But at the time this manuscript was prepared the abbess was no longer alive to delete them, and it may be that their music had simply been lost or forgotten. In fact, it is unlikely that the two *Symphonia* manuscripts, since they differ widely in structure and content, were copied from the same bound exemplar. (The second could not have been copied from the first, which was already at Villers.) Perhaps the texts—with or without their music—had previously been transcribed only on loose sheets of parchment. If the compiler of the miscellany strung some of these sheets together more or less awkwardly, producing an impromptu record of Hildegard as liturgist, the compiler of the second *Symphonia* manuscript may have sifted through them more judiciously to isolate her songs.

In that case, however, a few songlike compositions could have escaped notice, as "O frondens virga" evidently did. This possibility becomes more likely if we assume that the music was not originally written above the text, but learned orally and performed by the nuns from memory.[16] The miscellany, in fact, contains at least four lyrical passages that are thematically and stylistically very close to the *Symphonia* pieces, although no music for them is extant. I propose that these passages represent either "lost" songs or lyrics that Hildegard had originally meant to set to music, but never did. Because of their poetic quality, I have chosen to edit them at the end of the *Symphonia* as "songs without music." The four compositions are "O Verbum Patris," "O Fili dilectissime," "O factura Dei," and "O magna res."

Finally, a word on the title is in order. *Symphonia* and [*h*]*armonia* are overlapping terms, and there is no modern English equivalent that has the same range. The word *symphonia* was used very freely in the Middle Ages and could mean either melody or harmony or simply music in general, whether vocal or instrumental. For late antique theorists such as Cassiodorus and for

[15]Peter Dronke, "The Composition of Hildegard of Bingen's *Symphonia,*" *Sacris Erudiri* 19 (1969–1970): 389.

[16]Cf. Leo Treitler, "Oral, Written, and Literate Process in the Transmission of Medieval Music," *Speculum* 56 (1981): 471–91.

Isidore of Seville, a *symphonia* was a consonant interval (fourth, fifth, or octave) as opposed to a dissonant one; the term was later applied to organum or early harmonized chant. It could also indicate at least two different instruments: a kind of timbrel or hand drum and, more commonly, the hurdy-gurdy used by minstrels.[17] In Hildegard's title, however, the most general meaning is probably the one intended. *Symphonia armonie celestium revelationum* might be rendered as "The Harmonious Music of Heavenly Mysteries."

The Symphonia *in the Monastic Liturgy*

There is no doubt that Hildegard intended her music for Mass and the Divine Office at her monastery. Guibert of Gembloux, her friend and secretary after Volmar's death, wrote that after she had enjoyed the sweetness of celestial harmony in her visions, she would "make the same measures—more pleasing than ordinary human music—to be sung publicly in church, with sequences (*prosis*) composed in praise of God and in honor of the saints."[18] Some of this liturgical singing even took place beyond the Rupertsberg. Abbot Kuno, once he had forgiven Hildegard for leaving St. Disibod, showed his good will toward her by soliciting revelations about his monks' patron saint: "If God has shown you anything about our patron, blessed Disibod, I ask you to let me know, so that my brethren and I may not hesitate to give him fervent praise for it."[19] In a similar way Heloise had tried to make peace with Abelard after their quarrel by asking him to compose hymns for her nuns. Like Abelard, Hildegard met the request, supplying an antiphon, a responsory, and a sequence (nos. 41, 42, 45). It also seems likely that the pieces honoring saints Matthias, Eucharius, Maximin, and Boniface (nos. 50–54) were written on commission, as all these saints were venerated in the nearby city of Trier,

[17]Edgar de Bruyne, *Etudes d'esthétique médiévale* (Bruges, 1946), 1: 323–31; Giulio Cattin, *Music of the Middle Ages,* vol. 1, trans. Steven Botterill (Cambridge, 1984): 127, 168–69, 171, 174, 178–79.

[18]Ep. 16, Pitra 385–86.

[19]Ep. 38 in PL 197: 203b.

where Hildegard had many connections and where she gave a public sermon in 1160.[20] Some of her music may even have been sung at the distant monastery of Villers in Brabant. Around 1175 the abbess sent these Cistercians a copy of her *Book of Life's Merits* as a gift, and she attached the oldest text of the *Symphonia* complete with neumes.[21]

Monastic worship is ordered around the Divine Office, which consists of seven daily "hours" or services of common prayer plus the night service of matins. The basic structure of these services is set forth in chapters eight through eighteen of the Benedictine Rule. Each hour consists in varying proportions of psalmody, lessons from Scripture, and assorted texts of prayer and praise set to music—canticles, antiphons, responsories, and hymns.[22] The three Gospel canticles are fixed texts, but the other items vary with each day and hour and constitute a vast corpus of medieval chant. The genre most fully represented in the *Symphonia,* as in the chant repertoire generally, is the *antiphon*. Forty-three of Hildegard's compositions, well over half, belong to this category, which is related to the practice of psalmody.

In standard medieval usage an antiphon, or freely composed text with melody, would be sung before and after each psalm in the Office. Because the Office was designed by Saint Benedict so as to cover the full cycle of 150 psalms every week, this style of psalmody required an enormous number of antiphons. Matins in the monastic usage includes as many as twelve psalms, each with its antiphon. Vespers has up to five, as does the early morning office of lauds; and each of the lesser hours has three. As the antiphon is liturgically subordinate to the psalm, it is usually a brief, unpretentious composition suited to the scriptural theme or the feast of the day. It takes its name from the practice of antiphonal singing: psalm verses would be chanted alternately by two

[20]Dronke, "Composition" 390.

[21]Letter from the monks of Villers, Ep. 20, Pitra 394.

[22]For the discussion of liturgical genres I am indebted to Willi Apel, *Gregorian Chant* (Bloomington, 1958): 13–23; Richard Hoppin, *Medieval Music* (New York, 1978): chap. 4; and Andrew Hughes, *Medieval Manuscripts for Mass and Office* (Toronto, 1982): 26–43, 50–80.

half-choirs, while the antiphon was sung by the full choir to a simple tune related to the reciting tone. (In more elaborate performance, it might be sung between verses as well as before and after the psalm.) In Hildegard's cycle, the simple psalm antiphon is best represented by a series for matins on the feast of Saint Ursula (no. 63). Other examples are "Karitas habundat" (no. 25), "O mirum admirandum" (no. 41), and a group of short antiphons for the Virgin (nos. 11–15).

Not all antiphons were tied to psalmody, however. It became customary to insert somewhat longer, more elaborate antiphons after the Gospel canticles that concluded the major hours, especially the Magnificat at vespers and the Benedictus at lauds. The Marian devotion of the Middle Ages expressed itself richly in these longer antiphons, a few of which are still in use (such as the "Salve regina" and "Alma Redemptoris Mater"). Hildegard's most complex antiphon to the Virgin, "O tu illustrata" (no. 23), belongs to this category of "free" or votive antiphons. Still others, such as "O gloriosissimi lux vivens angeli" (no. 29) and "O spectabiles viri" (no. 31), although not addressed to Mary, are also independent devotional pieces. Of Hildegard's forty-three antiphons, fourteen appear to be votive antiphons, for in the manuscripts they lack the *differentia* or cadence that would connect them with a psalm tone.

The second most frequent item is the *responsory,* represented by eighteen pieces and intended primarily for matins. This service, in the most solemn monastic usage, consists of three sections called nocturns, each nocturn including a group of psalms or canticles with their antiphons followed by four lessons from Scripture. After each lesson is sung a responsory—a freely composed, musically complex piece that alternates solo verses with choral response. Unlike antiphons, responsories tend to give several notes and sometimes highly embellished melodic phrases to each syllable so that the trained soloists and choirs can display their skill. The textual form is also complex and allows for many structural variants. One very common form can be illustrated by Hildegard's solemn responsory, "Rex noster promptus" (no. 59). In the diagram below, R represents the *respond,* composed of three sections or periods (a, b, and c); its final period, R_c, is called the *repetenda* or refrain. V signifies the verse, and D is the short form of the doxology ("Glory be to the Father"). V and D are sung to the same melody.

choir R_a with solo intonation to*	Rex noster* promptus est suscipere sanguinem innocentum.
choir R_b	Unde angeli concinunt et in laudibus sonant.
choir R_c	Sed nubes super eundem sanguinem plangunt.
solo V	Tirannus autem in gravi somno mortis propter maliciam suam suffocatus est.
choir R_c	Sed nubes super eundem sanguinem plangunt.
solo D	Gloria Patri et Filio et Spiritui sancto.
choir R_c	Sed nubes super eundem sanguinem plangunt.

Thus the overall form is R_{abc}–V–R_c–D–R_c, a form that characterizes the last responsory in each nocturn. In simpler forms the doxology may be omitted, giving the pattern R_{abc}–V–R_c, as in "O quam preciosa" (no. 22) and "O vos angeli" (no. 30).

In addition to antiphons and responsories, the *Symphonia* includes fourteen longer pieces that are artistically among Hildegard's most accomplished. According to the manuscripts, four of these pieces are hymns (nos. 17, 27, 50, and 65), although in its musical form "Mathias sanctus" (no. 50) is actually a sequence. Medieval hymns and sequences were normally two distinct genres. *Hymns,* which grew out of early Christian congregational singing, were sung at various points in the Office but never at Mass. A typical twelfth-century hymn was a song in which each stanza followed the same metrical pattern and rhyme scheme and was sung to the same relatively simple tune. *Sequences* developed in the Carolingian period and underwent a complex musical and poetic evolution.[23] Composed by the thousands, they were to be sung between the Alleluia and the Gospel at Mass. Classical sequences, like those of Notker, are composed of paired versicles rather than stanzas. Following the principle of *strophic responsion,* the two versicles in each pair have the same number of syllables and are sung to the same tune, but the melody and the textual form change from pair to pair. The Easter sequence "Victimae paschali" is a well-known example. By the twelfth century, however, most new sequences were being composed in stanzaic form and followed a set meter and rhyme scheme, even though their music retained the older strophic responsion.

Hildegard, a maverick, preferred the archaic nonmetrical sequence, but exceeded the Carolingian composers in irregularity. In fact, her forms are so free that it is often hard to tell a sequence from a hymn. The *Symphonia* rubrics identify seven pieces as sequences: nos. 20, 28, 45, 49, 53, 54, and 64. But if we add "Mathias sanctus" (no. 50) to the list, on musical grounds we would have to delete "O Ecclesia" (no. 64), as it shows no sign of strophic responsion. In these two exceptional cases, the musical form may have been at odds with the liturgical use. "O Ierusalem" (no. 49) begins stanzaically like a hymn, continues with paired strophes like a sequence, and ends in totally free form.[24] Three other pieces—"O viridissima virga" (no. 19), "O dulcissime amator" (no. 57), and "O Pater omnium" (no. 58)—follow neither the hymn nor the sequence form but are through-

[23]On origins of the form see Richard Crocker, "The Troping Hypothesis," *Musical Quarterly* 52 (1966): 183–203; Peter Dronke, "The Beginnings of the Sequence" (1965), rpt. in *The Medieval Poet and His World* (Rome, 1984): 115–44; Stephen Ryle, "The Sequence—Reflections on Literature and Liturgy," in Francis Cairns, ed., *Papers of the Liverpool Latin Seminar 1976* (Liverpool, 1977): 171–82. Richard Crocker offers more sustained treatment in "The Sequence," in Wulf Arlt, Ernst Lichtenhahn, and Hans Oesch, eds., *Gattungen der Musik in Einzeldarstellungen* (Bern, 1973), 1: 269–322, and *The Early Medieval Sequence* (Berkeley, 1977).

[24]Ludwig Bronarski, *Die Lieder der heiligen Hildegard* (Leipzig, 1922): 31–36.

composed, that is, without melodic repetition. Numbers 57 and 58 are designated in the manuscripts as "Symphonia virginum" and "Symphonia viduarum"—love songs to Christ meant to be sung respectively by virgins and widows, the two types of women in the nunnery. Hildegard may have composed these songs as independent devotional pieces, not connected directly with the Mass or Office.

Finally, the *Symphonia* includes two short pieces for Mass: a setting of the Kyrie and the alleluia-verse "O virga mediatrix" (no. 18), to be sung in place of a sequence before the Gospel. The cycle thus includes a total of seventy-seven pieces. All are reproduced here except for the Kyrie, which of course has no independent text. Under no. 63, however, I have grouped together the eight short antiphons for matins of Saint Ursula, because textually they make up a single narrative. This grouping explains the discrepancy between the seventy-seven pieces listed in the older edition and the sixty-nine numbered in this volume.

Aesthetics and Theology of Music

In her memoirs Hildegard recalled, with her characteristic blend of diffidence, pride, and wonder, how she began to compose: "untaught by anyone, I composed and chanted plainsong in praise of God and the saints, although I had never studied either musical notation or any kind of singing."[25] Contemporaries who knew her music were taken with its beauty and its strangeness. Dieter of Echternach, one of her hagiographers, marveled at the "chant of surpassingly sweet melody" that she created "with amazing harmony" (*mirabili symphonia*).[26] And Volmar delighted in her *vox inaudite melodie*—strange and unheard-of music, with a gesture toward those unheard melodies which Keats would claim are sweetest.[27] Hildegard could say of her musical gift, as she said of the *Scivias*, that she acquired it "not through human

[25] *Vita S. Hildegardis* in PL 197: 104a; Dronke, *Women Writers* 232.
[26] *Vita* 2.14 in PL 197: 101b.
[27] Ep. 8, Pitra 346.

lips, nor through human intelligence and ingenuity, nor through a desire for human composition," but through God alone.[28] Because of such direct claims to divine inspiration, the *Symphonia* is to medieval hymnography what "Kubla Khan" is to Romantic poetry. Whatever conscious artistry has done or left undone, the inspiration is avowed as Other.

Both Volmar and Dieter, as well as Hildegard herself, mentioned her music in connection with another project, the *Lingua ignota* or "Unknown Language," which also engaged her during the 1150s.[29] This exceptional work, a glossary of some nine hundred invented names for earthly and celestial beings, has its own "unknown alphabet" of twenty-three characters. It includes both a liturgical vocabulary and terms for every aspect of daily life in the monastery, such as the names of all objects in the wardrobe, the herb garden, and the scriptorium. The *Lingua ignota* might have been a kind of secret language for the initiated, used to create an atmosphere of mystical intensity in the convent. The fact that Hildegard and her associates spoke of it in the same breath with her music suggests that these works served a common function. Both were revealed from heaven and had arcane significance, and both could be shared by the privileged congregation that was striving to imitate the life of heaven on earth. A few words from the *Lingua* appear in Hildegard's antiphon "O orzchis Ecclesia" (no. 68), and in one manuscript the letters of the unknown alphabet are written on musical staves along with her Kyrie and "O virga mediatrix" (no. 18).[30]

Hildegard understood music in what would now be called a mystical context, although in the twelfth century hers was a widely shared understanding. When she wrote, in a celebrated apologia for music, that the very soul is symphonic (*symphonialis est anima*),[31] she was appealing to an insight as old as Pythagoras, transmitted to the medieval world through Boethius's treatise *On*

[28] *Scivias*, Protestificatio, p. 3.

[29] *Liber vitae meritorum*, preface, Pitra 7; letter to Pope Anastasius IV, Ep. 2 in PL 197: 152d.

[30] Vienna, Nationalbibliothek Cod. 1016, fols. 118v–119r (13th c.).

[31] Ep. 47 in PL 197: 221c.

Music. According to Boethius, the Pythagoreans had taught that "the whole structure of soul and body is united by musical harmony."[32] Boethius added that there are three kinds of music: *musica mundana,* or music of the spheres, which is produced by the motion of celestial bodies and serves to order the elements and the four seasons; *musica humana,* which binds the rational to the irrational part of the soul and both to the body; and finally *musica instrumentalis,* which is made by human beings. Because the human microcosm is so subtly and sensitively tuned to the cosmos, art-music cannot fail to affect it. Thus the ancient world held the emotional power of music to be a moral and spiritual power that could be used either for good or for ill. If music could heal, soothe, and inspire, it could also arouse the soul to erotic frenzy or savagery. To make dangerous music was immoral; conversely, to be immoral was to be unmusical.

In the words of Cassiodorus, another schoolmaster to the Middle Ages, "if we perform the commandments of the Creator and with pure minds obey the rules he has laid down, every word we speak, every pulsation of our veins, is related by musical rhythms to the powers of harmony. . . . If we live virtuously, we are constantly proved to be under its discipline, but when we commit injustice we are without music."[33] For Hildegard, following a similar logic, the ultimate unmusical spirit was the devil. In one of her most powerful myths she tells how Satan was moved to despair by the voice of Adam singing in paradise, because it reminded him of the sweet songs of heaven; so in his envious cunning he has never ceased "to disturb or destroy the affirmation and beauty and sweetness of divine praise and spiritual hymns."[34] In the *Ordo virtutum* only the devil has a speaking (or more precisely a shouting) part. The soul and all the Virtues sing.

A distinctly "romantic" strain in Hildegard's aesthetics is revealed by her strong interest in the expressive rather than the

[32]Boethius, *De institutione musica* 1.1, ed. Gottfried Friedlein (Leipzig, 1867); trans. Oliver Strunk, *Source Readings in Music History* (New York, 1950): 83.

[33]Cassiodorus, *Institutiones* 5.2, ed. R. A. B. Mynors (Oxford, 1937); trans. Strunk, *Source Readings* 88.

[34]Ep. 47 in PL 197: 220d–21a, as emended in Dronke, *Women Writers* 315.

formal qualities of music. Most academic writers on the art, following Boethius, treated it as a branch of applied mathematics and despised mere singers.[35] Hildegard's view, on the other hand, is closer to a Neoplatonist tradition that can be traced back to Pseudo-Dionysius and Erigena, and may have reached her through the Carolingian theorist Regino of Prüm. Regino and his followers assimilated the *musica humana* with singing and drew their essential distinction between "artificial" and "natural" music. Artificial music "is contrived by human skill and ingenuity, and exists in certain instruments," whereas natural music "is made by no instruments nor by the touch of fingers, nor by any touch or instigation of man: it is modulated by nature alone under divine inspiration" and exists in the heavens and the human voice.[36] Thus vocal music is both natural and inspired, and Regino explicitly identifies it with chant composed in the eight liturgical modes. There is an obvious resemblance between his conception of plainsong and the language Hildegard used to describe her inspiration.

To the classical *musica mundana* and *musica humana,* Christian theorists added the notion of *musica celestis:* the singing of the angels in heaven.[37] It was a monastic commonplace that "the office of singing pleases God if it is performed with an attentive mind, when in this way we imitate the choirs of angels who are said to sing the Lord's praise without ceasing."[38] Music was both duty and joy, the continual and sometimes arduous discipline of a monastic community, but also the sign of its angelic and supra-

[35]This medieval approach is strangely echoed in the work of Pozzi Escot, a contemporary composer and theorist who treats Hildegard's music in purely mathematical terms. See "The Gothic Cathedral and Hidden Geometry of St. Hildegard," *Sonus* 5 (1984): 14–31.

[36]Regino of Prüm, *Epistola de harmonica institutione,* ed. Martin Gerbert, *Scriptores ecclesiastici de musica* (1784; rpt. Milan, 1931), 1: 232, 236; Calvin Bower, "Natural and Artificial Music: The Origins and Development of an Aesthetic Concept," *Musica Disciplina* 25 (1971): 17–33; Nino Pirrotta, "'Musica de sono humano' and the Musical Poetics of Guido of Arezzo," *Medievalia et Humanistica,* n.s. 7 (1976): 13–27.

[37]de Bruyne, *Etudes* 2: 120–22.

[38]Aurelian of Réôme, *De musica disciplina* 1, ed. Lawrence Gushee, *Corpus scriptorum de musica* 21 (Nijmegen, 1975): 59.

mundane life. Hildegard liked to contrast human beings, who were composed of soul and body so as to express God's image in both praise and work, with the angels, who were pure spirit and therefore pure song.[39] It is the privilege of the blessed, here and hereafter, to sing harmony with them:

In te symphonizat Spiritus sanctus,	In you the Holy Spirit makes symphony,
quia angelicis choris associaris	for you are joined to the angelic choirs
et quoniam in Filio Dei ornaris. (no. 49, 5)	and adorned in the Son of God.

Thus Hildegard honors her patron, Saint Rupert. And of the Virgin she sings:

Venter enim tuus gaudium habuit	For your womb held joy
cum omnis celestis symphonia de te sonuit,	when all the harmony of heaven resounded from you;
quia virgo Filium Dei portasti. (no. 17, 5)	for as a virgin, you bore the Son of God.

Because it is Christ whom the angels praise, wherever he is music must also be.

Christ himself, in certain ancient writings, is portrayed as musician, minstrel, lord of the dance. In the second century the apologist Clement of Alexandria, desiring to convert the Pythagoreans, set himself up as mystagogue to elaborate on this theme. Orpheus, he allowed, could move stones and wolves with his music, but Christ, the New Song, had done more: he has turned stony minds and wolvish hearts into men. It is he who created the cosmos and the microcosm and "makes melody to God on this instrument of many tones. . . . A beautiful, breathing instrument of music the Lord made man, after His own image. He Himself, . . . the supramundane Wisdom, the celestial Word, is the all-harmonious, melodious, holy instrument of God." What is more,

[39] *De operatione Dei* 3.10.14, PL 197: 1016bc; *Prooemium Vitae S. Disibodi,* Pitra 352.

his worship provides a pleasing alternative to pagan initiatory rites. On the mountain of God "there revel [not the Maenads] . . . but the daughters of God, the fair lambs, who celebrate the holy rites of the Word, raising a sober choral dance. The righteous are the chorus; the music is a hymn of the King of the universe. The maidens strike the lyre, the angels praise, the prophets speak; the sound of music issues forth, they run and pursue the jubilant band."[40] Here is a programmatic description of the *Symphonia* one thousand years *avant la lettre*. Hildegard even echoes the theme of Christian versus pagan when, in the sequence to Saint Rupert, she contrasts the symphonies of the Holy Spirit with an antithetic pagan rite, "the dance of the ancient cave." Again, in a song to the virgin martyr Ursula, she pits the powerful music (*magna symphonia*) sung in mockery by the persecutors against the supreme harmony of the celestial choirs.

The theology of music included, at least in theory, instrumental as well as vocal performance. Both psalm commentaries and their illustrations seem to afford evidence for instrumental praise, and in many manuscripts—including one from an illuminated *Scivias* produced at the Rupertsberg—angels or saints are shown playing instruments.[41] But this music, like everything else in the Middle Ages, had a "spiritual sense" that could overwhelm the literal. It has been convincingly argued that the evidence of manuscript paintings must be referred to medieval ideas about ancient Hebrew worship, not to contemporary practice; for although the psalter commends musical instruments, medieval churchmen disliked them and tried to explain the biblical references away.[42] Augustine and the Carolingians sanctioned a tradition of alle-

[40]Clement of Alexandria, *Protreptikos* 1 and 12, in *Ante-Nicene Fathers* (New York, 1880–1899), 2: 172, 205.

[41]Illustration to *Scivias* II.3 from Wiesbaden, Hessische Landesbibliothek, Hs. 1 (now lost); reproduced in *Scivias,* vol. 43, facing p. 134. Cf. Reinhold Hammerstein, *Die Musik der Engel: Untersuchungen zur Musikanschauung des Mittelalters* (Bern, 1962).

[42]Edmund Bowles, "Were Musical Instruments Used in the Liturgical Service during the Middle Ages?" *Galpin Society Journal* 10 (1957): 40–56; James McKinnon, "Musical Instruments in Medieval Psalm Commentaries and Psalters," *Journal of the American Musicological Society* 21 (1968):3–20.

gorizing the various instruments mentioned in the psalms, particularly Psalm 150. The tambourine, for example, stands for asceticism, because the skin stretched over the wood must be taut and dry, like the body purified by fasting and continence.[43] The organ represents the communion of saints united in charity, as its several pitches are harmonized in the diapason.[44] The trumpet recalls the voice of the prophets, and among stringed instruments, psaltery and lyre (cithara) symbolize heaven and earth, because the one is plucked from above and the other from below. The psaltery also has ten strings to remind us of the Ten Commandments.[45] Following this tradition, Hildegard writes that, in the ensemble of Psalm 150, "outer realities teach us about inner ones—namely how, in accordance with the material composition and quality of instruments, we can best transform and shape the performance of our inner being towards praises of the Creator."[46] She also mentions instrumental music in several other places, for instance in her hymn to the Holy Spirit, who plays "upon the timbrel and the lyre" (no. 27, 1).

This spiritual understanding of music reached its height in Hildegard's own writings and those of her contemporary Wolbero, Benedictine abbot of St. Pantaleimon in Cologne (1147–1167). In a commentary on the Song of Songs, written for the edification of nuns, Wolbero interpreted the entire mystical love song with the aid of musical analogies.[47] For him every preacher and exegete is a cantor who sings to calm the impassioned (like Saul) or to arouse the sluggish (like Elisha). The Song of Songs is a *spiritualis harmonia* in four parts, or a canticle to the Lord "modulated" in the seven tones by the seven gifts of the Holy Spirit. Virgins sing the new song of the heavenly bridegroom, widows the song of gladness, and married folk the song of praise. The three estates

[43] Augustine, *Enarrationes in Psalmos* 150.7, in *Corpus Christianorum: series latina* (Tournai, 1953– ; hereafter CCSL), 40: 2195.

[44] Otloh of St. Emmeran, *Dialogus de tribus quaestionibus* 45, PL 146: 125c.

[45] Théodore Gérold, *Les Pères de l'église et la musique* (Paris, 1931): 126–30.

[46] Ep. 47 in PL 197: 219d–20a; Dronke, *Women Writers* 197–98.

[47] Wolbero, *Commentaria in Canticum canticorum*, PL 195: 1005–1278; David Chamberlain, "Wolbero of Cologne (d. 1167): A Zenith of Musical Imagery," *Mediaeval Studies* 33 (1971): 114–26.

of virginity, widowhood, and marriage are like workshops wherein the instruments of praise are fashioned. Wolbero's extensive musical imagery shows how intimately this art could be bound up with spiritual realities, as one would expect among monks and nuns who devoted their lives to choral praise. Hildegard may well have known Wolbero personally, as she had several correspondents in Cologne and preached in that city during his abbacy. In any case, his commentary shows that contemporary Benedictines shared Hildegard's passion for music, if not all of her ideas about it.

Hildegard's dedication to her art was put to the test in the last year of her life when, at the age of eighty, she found herself and all her sisters laid under interdict, the ultimate ecclesiastical sanction.[48] The issue was apparently trivial: she had buried a nobleman, formerly excommunicate, in her monastic churchyard, and the prelates of Mainz demanded that his corpse be exhumed as unworthy of Christian burial. The abbess and her daughters maintained that they were in the right—that the deceased had in fact been reconciled to the Church—and it is likely that some political grudge lay behind the sanction. Be that as it may, the nuns held out for several months before the interdict was lifted. In the meantime they could not hear Mass, receive the sacraments, or chant the monastic Office, which they were simply to recite. This penalty deprived the abbess of music for the first time since her childhood, and during the long silence of the choir she reflected on the meaning of music, its charismatic nature, and its place in the divine scheme of things.

The result was an extraordinary appeal to the prelates of Mainz in which she not only protested the interdict but also expounded her theology of music, concluding with a prophetic warning to its enemies. Not for her the doctrine that, when actual music is silent, its spiritual essence will suffice. Instead she warns the prelates to "beware, before you use an interdict to stop the mouth of any church of God's singers . . . lest you be ensnared in your

[48]Adelgundis Führkötter, *Hildegard von Bingen* (Salzburg, 1972): 45–47; Dronke, *Women Writers* 196–97.

judgments by Satan, who lured man away from the celestial harmony and the delights of paradise." If the erring clerics do not repent, "they will forego the fellowship of angelic praise in heaven, for they have unjustly despoiled God on earth of the beauty of his praise."[49] To silence music in the Church is to create an artificial rift between earth and heaven, to put asunder that which God has joined together.

The abbess made her most original contribution to the theology of music in reflecting on the fall of Adam. In her view, the first human beings enjoyed extraordinary graces—omniscience, prophecy, converse with angels, direct vision of God—and Adam, among his other perfections, possessed a voice that rang with "the sound of every harmony and the sweetness of the whole art of music. And if he had remained in the condition in which he was formed, human frailty could never endure the power and the resonance of that voice."[50] Thus music, for Hildegard, was not the province of a gifted elite, but a thing quintessentially human; mankind was never meant to live without it. So to compensate for the voice that Adam lost, "the holy prophets . . . invented various musical instruments," and others came after and imitated them. For Hildegard, not only inspired canticles but all music was associated with prophecy and the nostalgia for Eden. That is why, she says, "a person often sighs and moans upon hearing some melody, recalling the nature of the celestial harmony." And that is why David, the inspired psalmist, commanded us to make a joyful noise unto the Lord. For music could not only express the prophetic spirit; it might even awaken that spirit. Regino of Prüm had recalled the story of Elisha: the man of God once recognized that the spirit of prophecy was not in him, so he called for a minstrel and, as soon as he heard the music, "the Spirit suddenly descended upon him and he prophesied" (2 Kings 3:15).[51]

The relationship of music and text is of particular interest in the *Symphonia,* although this whole subject is fraught with problems. It is important to recall that poetry, in the medieval curriculum,

[49]Ep. 47 in PL 197: 221a–c; Dronke, *Women Writers* 315.
[50]Ep. 47 in PL 197: 220cd; Dronke, *Women Writers* 198.
[51]Regino of Prüm, *Epistola,* ed. Gerbert, 1: 236.

was not a discipline unto itself. Literary criticism was considered an aspect of grammar and figures of speech a part of rhetoric, while versification came under the art of music. Thus, according to Isidore of Seville, music theory has three parts of which only one, harmonics, deals with musical pitch and melody. The other two concern verbal music: rhythmics, or syllabic versification, and metrics, or classical prosody.[52] Guido of Arezzo, an eleventh-century theorist, drew analogies between metrical verse and the composition of chant. In poetry, one or more speech sounds make up a syllable, two or three syllables a foot, and a set number of feet compose a metrical line. So also in music: one or two syllables are sung to a *neuma* or cluster of related notes, and one or more neumata make up a *distinctio* or musical phrase.[53] A little later, John (of Afflighem?) made a similar comparison between the phrasing of plainsong and the syntactic units in liturgical prose.[54] Such analogies suggest that the relationship of words and music was conceived in primarily formal terms: both embody the *armonia* or structural pattern in closely related media. Words need not be set to music that will express their meaning or even their emotional quality; rather, words and music together are "set" to a third thing, a formal idea, which in turn expresses the harmony of the cosmos.[55]

This principle, so unfamiliar to modern listeners, helps to explain some seeming anomalies in Hildegard's music and in the chant repertoire generally. For instance, the placing of musical stress through *melismas* (long melodic phrases sung to one syllable) is not firmly correlated with either the natural speech accent of a word or its importance in the text.[56] Examples in Hildegard's

[52]Isidore of Seville, *Etymologiae* 3.18, PL 82: 164b.

[53]Guido of Arezzo, *Micrologus de disciplina artis musicae,* ed. Joseph Smits van Waesberghe, *Corpus scriptorum de musica* 4 (Nijmegen, 1955): 162–77; Pirrotta, "'Musica de sono humano'" 17–21.

[54]See Marianne Richert Pfau, "Music and Text in Hildegard's Antiphons," p. 82 below.

[55]John Stevens, *Words and Music in the Middle Ages: Song, Narrative, Dance and Drama, 1050–1350* (Cambridge, 1986): 499. Chapters 8 and 11 are very helpful on the problem of words, meaning, and expression in chant.

[56]Apel, *Gregorian Chant* 279–89.

repertoire include melismas on the unstressed syllables in *an*tiqui (an*cient,* no. 31), sens*u*um (sens*es,* no. 33), and castiss*i*me (ve*ry* chaste, no. 35). Rhymes and other figures of speech are seldom accentuated by the melodic line. This lack of correlation does not imply that music and text are independent. On the contrary, the two sonorities can work in a kind of counterpoint, unpredictable and rich, as delineated below in the essay of Marianne Richert Pfau.

For Hildegard, the duality of word and song was itself patient of theological interpretation. Unlike many patristic and Cistercian writers, she was untroubled by the sensual beauty of music and its potential for distracting worshipers from the text. Augustine had once tried, in the anguished self-searching of his *Confessions,* to analyze his response to psalmody, distinguishing between the wholesome text and the dangerously seductive melody.[57] But, unable to separate the profits of the one from the perils of the other, he had to give up the effort as fruitless. Hildegard never made the attempt. For her, liturgical song was a medium that perfectly united soul and body, rational praise and spiritual melody, just as Christ had united the human nature with the divine. "Thus the word designates the body, but music manifests the spirit. For the harmony of heaven proclaims the divinity of God's Son, and the word makes known his humanity."[58]

Musical Style and Performance

Hildegard's creations, compared with a contemporary hymn by Abelard or a sequence by Adam of St. Victor, will sound either primitive or unnervingly avant-garde. In a sense they are both. As a Benedictine, she was acquainted with a large repertoire of chant, but she lacked formal training and made no attempt to imitate the mainstream poetic and musical achievements of her day. Various scholars have hypothesized that she was influenced by German folksong, yet her compositions lack the two essential traits of a

[57]Augustine, *Confessiones* 10.33, CCSL 27: 181–82.
[58]*Scivias* III.13.12, p. 631.

popular tune: it must be easy to remember and easy to sing. The difficult music of the *Symphonia* is sui generis. In M.-I. Ritscher's words, it is "gregorianizing but not Gregorian" and impossible to classify in terms of any known contemporary movement.[59]

One useful way of discussing the style of plainsong is to locate items on a spectrum ranging from simple *syllabic* pieces, in which each syllable is sung to a single note, to ornate *melismatic* chant, in which one syllable may be embroidered with a figure of several notes or even several phrases. In general, the more melismatic a piece, the more solemn, elaborate, and difficult it is, and the more the text is dominated by the music. Hildegard's sequences and hymns fall into the intermediate range sometimes called *neumatic*, in which there are seldom more than two or three notes to a syllable. Her antiphons and responsories, however, can be melismatic in the extreme, with the longest melismas falling at the beginning and end of songs as a kind of musical punctuation. The style can be florid, almost rococo, and demands a skillful and well-trained choir. In her most outstanding example, "O vos angeli" (no. 30), Hildegard achieves an average ratio of more than six notes per syllable, and in the final word of the respond there is a melisma of some eighty notes.[60]

Another eccentric feature of Hildegard's style is the wide vocal range she employs. Many songs have an ambitus of two octaves and some even of two and a half, placing a considerable strain on the voice of the average singer. The composer liked to use the extreme upper and lower ranges of the voice for emphasis, and a few of her flights are unmistakably meant as tone-painting, as in the rising, hovering, and then sharply plummeting figure on *qui volare voluit* ("who wished to fly") in "O gloriosissimi lux vivens angeli" (no. 29).[61] Satan's ascent and fall could not be more forcefully represented. But this device is not consistently used;

[59]M.-I. Ritscher, "Zur Musik der heiligen Hildegard von Bingen," in *Hildegard von Bingen, 1179–1979,* ed. Anton Brück (Mainz, 1979): 200–201.

[60]Joseph Schmidt-Görg, "Die Sequenzen der heiligen Hildegard," in *Studien zur Musikgeschichte des Rheinlandes: Festschrift Ludwig Schiedermair,* ed. Willi Kahl, Heinrich Lemacher, and Joseph Schmidt-Görg (Cologne, 1956): 115.

[61]Bronarski, *Lieder* 102.

more often than not, such figures have a purely ornamental purpose. Also notable are the wide melodic leaps, especially the frequent ascending and descending fifths. Hildegard had a way of scurrying rapidly up and down the octave, like an angel on Jacob's ladder, several times in the space of a word. Ludwig Bronarski has characterized her melodic lines as angular and "gothic"—full of the sharply pointed arches that, in the architectural realm, still lay several decades into the future.[62]

The eight church modes or scales, as Hildegard used them, tend to collapse into three different tonalities, on d, e, and c. One tonality resembles our major and another our minor scale, the third being the medieval Phrygian mode.[63] In each mode, however, Hildegard drew on a relatively small number of motifs which she repeated, with ingenious variation, in every piece composed in that mode. This quality of repetition restores some of the musical stability she sacrificed in abandoning strophic construction. But even in her more or less regular hymns and sequences, the repeated melodies are never exactly the same because the text itself is not regular. So to accommodate the uneven numbers of syllables, small melodic motifs are continually interpolated and omitted. As a result, nothing is ever musically predictable. This extreme liberty of construction is the counterweight to Hildegard's motivic style of composition.

There is no answer to the usual vexed question of whether the *Symphonia* was performed "rhythmically." As few chant notations supply note values, singers must use their discretion. Nor is there evidence that the songs were accompanied with instruments, although performers are free to experiment, and several fine recordings make use of them. Despite our maddening ignorance about medieval performance practice, it is nonetheless tempting to imagine how the *Symphonia* sounded in situ at the Rupertsberg. Literary evidence can provide a few tantalizing clues, if not hard facts, about Hildegard's own taste and practice.

In her sequence to Saint Disibod (no. 45), there is an interesting

[62]Bronarski, *Lieder* 108.

[63]I thank William Mahrt of Stanford University for this observation.

reference to antiphonal singing. Among other praises of the saint, the abbess exclaims:

O Disibode,	O Disibod,
in tuo lumine	in your light,
per exempla puri soni	with exemplars of pure sound,
membra mirifice laudis edificasti	you built up a body of wondrous praise
in duabus partibus	in two parts
per Filium hominis.	through the Son of man.

(4b)

These two parts suggest the division of the monastic choir, both musically and architecturally, for antiphonal chant.[64] The saint through his music is building the body of Christ, who in a different sense has "two parts" because he is both divine and human. Although the "exemplars" could be mere songbooks, antiphonaries, the context indicates something more mystical and Platonic. I believe that Hildegard was projecting her own experience of inspired music onto the saint, imagining the musical light and luminous sound of her visions as the exemplar of liturgical song in the Church.

Given her visionary conception of music, it is hard to believe that the rhapsodic quality of her lyrics did not call forth a similarly rapt, uninhibited performance style. The vocal timbre that Hildegard praises is always the sweet, clear, ringing tone (*dulcissima, clara, sonans*). Mary is said figuratively to deliver fallen man by crying out "with a clear voice" (no. 14), and with the same kind of voice Saint Eucharius intercedes for his people (no. 53) and Saint Ursula and her companions greet martyrdom (no. 65). Hildegard would probably have agreed with Isidore of Seville that "the perfect voice is high, sweet, and loud (*clara*): high, to be adequate to the sublime; loud, to fill the ear; sweet, to soothe the minds of the hearers."[65] The abbess compared her own voice

[64]Pudentiana Barth, M.-I. Ritscher, and Joseph Schmidt-Görg, eds., *Hildegard von Bingen: Lieder* (Salzburg, 1969): 247.

[65]Isidore of Seville, *Etymologiae* 3.20.14, PL 82: 166a; trans. Strunk, *Source Readings* 96.

(allegorically) to that of a trumpet resounding by the breath of God.[66] And when Adam sang with the angels, she wrote, he had "a resonant voice like the sound of a monochord."[67]

This choice of instruments is striking, for the monochord (already known to Pythagoras and Euclid) was a simple, one-stringed instrument used, throughout antiquity and the Middle Ages, for teaching the elementary laws of harmonics and singing. By Hildegard's day, however, it had come to be used as a solo instrument, with additional strings and hence a greater sonority.[68] So this passage may refer either to the power or, more likely, to the natural harmony in Adam's voice. It also indicates that the Rupertsberg may have possessed a monochord on which Hildegard could pick out her melodies in order to teach them. Regino of Prüm had written that although natural music or song is superior to artificial music, the former can only be appreciated by means of the latter.[69]

In a second text on Adam, Hildegard says that the wise men who invented the various kinds of organum (early harmonized chant) "adapted their singing to the bending of the finger-joints, as it were recalling that Adam was formed by the finger of God, which is the Holy Spirit."[70] This bit of allegory alludes to the Guidonian hand, another pedagogic device of medieval choir directors. Promoted by Guido of Arezzo in the eleventh century, the Guidonian hand enabled a cantor to lead his or her choir in unfamiliar music by pointing to the finger-joints on the left hand, which were correlated with the notes of the scale.[71] This is another method Hildegard might have used to teach new pieces to her nuns.

References to organum, here and perhaps also in a sequence to the Virgin (no. 20, 4b), indicate that the abbess was at least

[66]Letter to Elisabeth of Schönau, Ep. 45 in PL 197: 217d.

[67]Hildegard of Bingen, *Causae et curae,* ed. Paul Kaiser (Leipzig, 1903): 148.

[68]David Munrow, *Instruments of the Middle Ages and Renaissance* (London, 1976): 17–18.

[69]Regino of Prüm, *Epistola,* ed. Gerbert, 1: 236.

[70]Ep. 47 in PL 197: 220c; Dronke, *Women Writers* 198.

[71]The device is illustrated in Gustave Reese, *Music in the Middle Ages* (New York, 1940): 151.

acquainted with this type of harmony. In a letter of 1153/54 to Pope Anastasius, she described her musical inspiration in these words: "He who is great without failing has now touched a little dwelling-place [i.e., herself] . . . so that it resounds with melody in many tones, yet concordant with itself" (*multimodam, sed sibi consonantem, melodiam sonaret*).[72] This wording recalls Augustine's definition of harmony as a "sweet concord of different but not mutually clashing sounds" (*diversis quidem sed non inter se adversis sonis*).[73] If Hildegard's phrase is not purely formulaic, it might indicate harmonized rather than monodic chanting, although one cannot make direct inferences from what Hildegard heard in her visions to what her nuns performed in their choir. *Multimodam* could also mean various or wide-ranging or simply "composed in many modes." Listeners may wish to compare the a capella, unison recording by the nuns of St. Hildegard's Abbey with the more variegated performances by Gothic Voices and Sequentia, which employ instruments and a vocal drone.

Poetic Style

Hildegard's poetic world is like the Sibyl's cave: difficult of access, reverberating with cryptic echoes. The oracle's message, once interpreted, may or may not hold surprises. But the suppliant emerges with a sense of initiation, and the voice itself is unforgettable.

No formal poetry written in the twelfth century, and none that Hildegard might have known, is very much like hers. For models one must look, rather, to the rich corpus of liturgical prayer. It is not surprising that, until the advent of modern vers libre, scholars were reluctant even to dignify Hildegard's songs with the title of poetry.[74] In style they are much closer to *Kunstprosa,* a highly

[72]Letter to Pope Anastasius IV, Ep. 2 in PL 197: 152d.

[73]Augustine, *Enarrationes in Psalmos* 150.6, CCSL 40: 2196.

[74]G. M. Dreves calls them "mere sketches, the rough drafts of hymns and sequences"; see *Analecta hymnica medii aevi,* ed. Dreves and Clemens Blume (Leipzig, 1886–1922), 50[2]: 484. Cf. the assessments of F. J. E. Raby, *A History of Christian-Latin Poetry from the Beginnings to the Close of the Middle Ages*

wrought figurative language that resembles poetry in its density and musicality, yet with no semblance of meter or regular form. Nowadays we would call it free verse. The source of this "freedom" lies not only in Hildegard's visionary inspiration but also in the character of the monastic Office itself. As Jean Leclercq has observed, texts for the Office were "obliged to conform to the laws of a special rhythm which is not like that of ordinary or even of artistic prose nor yet that of recited poetry."[75] Before the advent of the rhymed sequence, liturgical chants other than hymns were generally nonmetrical, influenced primarily by the Vulgate Psalms. Hildegard's originality, then, lies less in the invention of new forms than in the audacious and luxuriant elaboration of old ones.

It is the repertoire of votive antiphons and responsories, rather than the classical or the new accentual sequence, which provides the closest analogues to her composition. To sense the disparity between her idiom and the mainstream liturgical poetry of her day, we need only compare a few lines of hers with a strophe on the same subject by Adam of St. Victor, a highly regarded contemporary poet. The subject, than which no more conventional can be conceived, is the opposition of Eve and Mary. Here are Adam's neat rhyming trochaics:

Eva prius interemit,	Eve once destroyed us,
Sed Maria nos redemit	But Mary redeemed us
Mediante filio;	By means of her Son.
Prima parens nobis luctum,	One mother bore sadness;
Sed secunda vitae fructum	The other with gladness
Protulit cum gaudio.[76]	Fruit second to none.

(Oxford, 1927): 294; Joseph de Ghellinck, *L'Essor de la littérature latine au XIIe siècle* (Paris, 1946), 1: 198; Joseph Szövérffy, *A Concise History of Medieval Latin Hymnody* (Leiden, 1985): 86.

[75]Jean Leclercq, *The Love of Learning and the Desire for God*, trans. Catharine Misrahi (New York, 1961): 299.

[76]"Sequentia V in nativitate Domini," in *Adam von Sankt Viktor: Sämtliche Sequenzen*, ed. Franz Wellner (Munich, 1955): 48.

And here is Hildegard on the same theme:

O clarissima mater sancte medicine, tu ungenta per sanctum Filium tuum infudisti in plangentia vulnera mortis, que Eva edificavit in tormenta animarum. (no. 9)	O most radiant mother of sacred healing! Through your holy Son, you poured ointments on the sobbing wounds of death that Eve built into torments for souls.

Adam's sequences are regular, highly finished, and easy to memorize. Hildegard, on the other hand, brought to her songs a directness, an imagistic bravura, that does away with the boundary between dogmatic statement and rhapsodic expression. Her sentences are not concisely crafted like Adam's, but their irregular flow has a rhythm of its own. Whereas Adam preferred succinct parallel clauses, Hildegard reveled in periodic sentences spun from strings of relative clauses, participial and prepositional phrases.[77] Compare the beloved Marian anthem "Alma Redemptoris Mater":

Alma Redemptoris Mater, quae pervia caeli
Porta manes et stella maris, succurre cadenti
Surgere qui curat populo; tu quae genuisti,
Natura mirante, tuum sanctum Genitorem;
Virgo prius ac posterius, Gabrielis ab ore
Sumens illud Ave, peccatorum miserere.[78]

The Carolingian antiphon is written in hexameters, of course. But its melody hardly stresses the fact, and Hildegard—who had

[77]On the traditional rhetoric and syntax of prayer see Ricarda Liver, *Die Nachwirkung der antiken Sakralsprache im christlichen Gebet des lateinischen und italienischen Mittelalters* (Bern, 1979).

[78]*Corpus antiphonalium officii,* vol. 3, *Invitatoria et antiphonae,* ed. R.-J. Hesbert (Rome, 1968), no. 1356.

not studied grammar or rhetoric—might have "heard" something more like this:

Alma Redemptoris Mater,	Gracious Mother of the Redeemer,
quae pervia caeli porta manes	heaven's ever-open door
et stella maris,	and star of the sea,
succurre cadenti,	assist your falling people
surgere qui curat, populo:	who struggle to rise;
tu quae genuisti,	you who were mother,
natura mirante,	while nature marveled,
tuum sanctum Genitorem,	to your holy Father,
virgo prius ac posterius,	a virgin before and after,
Gabrielis ab ore	receiving from Gabriel's lips
sumens illud Ave,	that greeting "Hail":
peccatorum miserere.	Have mercy on us sinners.

Sprung from its meter, "Alma Redemptoris Mater" yields a syntactic structure close to that of Hildegard's lyrics, though somewhat more sophisticated. To take the comparison a step further, the tension between meter and speech rhythms in quantitative verse—even without the addition of music—affords an analogue for the counterpoint between verbal and melodic structures in the *Symphonia*.

Hildegard's lyrics, like her prose, are rich in allusions but sparing in quotations. As Morton Bloomfield once said of Langland, she too "spoke Bible." She was so deeply immersed in the sacred page that her language rings with echoes from the Vulgate, especially from the Psalter and the Song of Songs. Yet these are seldom more than echoes, verses recalled or paraphrased rather than quoted:

macula non est in te (Song 4:7)	nullam maculam habes (no. 49, 5).
despiciens per fenestras, prospiciens per cancellos (Song 2:9)	columba aspexit per cancellos fenestre (no. 54, 1).
exultavit ut gigans ad currendam viam suam (Ps. 18:6)	ipse pre gaudio sicut gygas in viribus suis surrexit (no. 50, 1b).

Hildegard had a tenacious memory for images and ideas, but no penchant for exact citation.

Some of her strongest effects are achieved through clustered allusions that carry with them whole structures of meaning. Take the fifth stanza of "O viridissima virga" (no. 19):

Unde celi dederunt rorem
  super gramen
et omnis terra leta facta est,
quoniam viscera ipsius
  frumentum protulerunt
et quoniam volucres celi
nidos in ipsa habuerunt.
	So the skies rained dew
	  on the grass
	and the whole earth exulted,
	for her womb brought forth
	  wheat,
	and the birds of heaven
	made their nests in it.

To appreciate this stanza the reader must be at least subliminally aware of the Advent antiphon "Rorate celi desuper" ("Drop dew, ye heavens, from above," based on Isa. 45:8) and of Christ's parable of the mustard seed (Matt. 13:32). The rest of the poem is similarly laced with allusions that presuppose an audience familiar with the Bible, its traditional glosses, and the Catholic liturgy. Footnotes can supply mere information: Mary is the grass and the green earth, the dew is the Spirit that made her fruitful, Christ is both the wheat for eucharistic bread and the tree to which he likened the kingdom of heaven. Yet, even though allegorical values like these shape the sense of the poem, spelling them out in cold prose is like trying to explain a joke: "meaning" can be supplied but all resonance is lost.

Hildegard's poems, at their best, are not simply vehicles for the immense common stock of symbols. One can take these symbols as a kind of bass continuo to ground the more fluid, unexpected meanings that constitute the "melody" of the poem. In the stanza just cited, what is most impressive is the absence of any direct reference to Mary, so that the supernatural event is implied by purely natural images. Yet even so, there is something miraculous about the swiftness and suddenness of the progression from grass to wheat to the suggested tree with birds in its branches. These birds trace one arc of a parabolic sweep down from heaven to earth and back again to the skies, and the birth of Christ takes place just at the midpoint of this cosmic motion.

Nonscriptural borrowings are rare and derive most often from the liturgy. In "O Ierusalem" (no. 49, 1a), the line "ornata regis purpura" is lifted from Venantius Fortunatus's hymn, "Vexilla regis prodeunt," where it describes not the heavenly city but the cross. Many allusions to the Song of Songs evoke not only the biblical text but also its liturgical adaptations for feasts of the Mother of God and the virgin martyrs. More intriguing is the case of "O splendidissima gemma" (no. 10), which probably takes its title from an exquisite poem by Bruno of Segni:

Quis est hic	Who is this
qui pulsat ad ostium,	that knocks at the gate,
noctis rumpens somnium?	troubling the dreams of night?
Me vocat:	He calls me:
O virginum pulcherrima,	O fairest of maidens,
soror, coniunx,	sister and bride,
gemma splendidissima.[79]	resplendent gem.

Bruno's song may also be a source for Hildegard's "O choruscans lux stellarum" (no. 69), in which she celebrates the Church as "splendidissima . . . gemma" and bride of Christ. His poem ends with the line "quo in regis inducar palatium"; hers with "et veniens veni in palatium regis." But the echoes are distant; it is notoriously hard to pin down Hildegard's sources, because she made everything she touched her own.

Yet, although hers was a character of exceptionally strong will and individuality, our poet made no use of the first person singular. The *Symphonia* is poetry of public worship; no matter how distinctive the idiom, its content is monumentally objective, almost impersonal.[80] We hear in it the voices of communal prayer:

Nunc igitur obsecramus,	Now then we beseech,
obsecramus te	we beseech you
per Verbum tuum	by your Word
(no. 6)	

[79]Szövérffy, *Concise History* 66.

[80]Cf. Hennig Brinkmann, "Voraussetzungen und Struktur religiöser Lyrik im Mittelalter," *Mittellateinisches Jahrbuch* 3 (1966): 39–40.

and exposition:

Quia ergo femina mortem instruxit, clara virgo illam interemit (no. 12)	Because a woman constructed death, a bright virgin demolished it.

and unabashed praise:

O gloriosissimi lux vivens angeli! (no. 29)	O most glorious angels, living light!

On occasion Hildegard took up the erotic voice that had filtered from the Song of Songs, by way of the Apocalypse, into the mainstream of liturgical poetry. Affiliated with the cult of chastity, this voice has a paradoxical ring:

O dulcissime amator, o dulcissime amplexator: adiuva nos custodire virginitatem nostram. (no. 57)	O sweetest lover, o giver of sweetest embraces, help us keep our virginity.

It is this tone which pervades the "Symphonia virginum" just cited, the great song to Saint Ursula (no. 64), and some of the Marian pieces (nos. 17, 22). But it would be a mistake to overstress its importance or singularity. Here, as everywhere else, in Hildegard's voice we are hearing one of the many voices of the medieval Church, however strange the intonation.

Much of the strangeness is due to her diction, which has acquired a reputation for difficulty. But her language is not at all precious or studied. The problem is that her basic vocabulary—like that of the Provençal troubadours—was quite small, and she relied heavily on certain polyvalent key words. *Virtus* is virtue, power, grace, divine emanation; the *virtutes* are moral qualities, but also an order of angels and a choir of celestial maidens who figure in Hildegard's *Ordo*.[81] *Viriditas,* literally "verdure,"

[81]Barbara Newman, *Sister of Wisdom: St. Hildegard's Theology of the Feminine* (Berkeley, 1987): 16–17, 58–60.

evokes all the resilience and vitality of nature and its source, the Holy Spirit. Words such as *radix* and *materia* almost always have a metaphysical sense; the literal meanings of "root" and "matter" or matrix (womb) suggest something very like the Tillichian "ground of being." *Instrumentum* and *ornamentum* stand broadly for utility and beauty, but beauty of the imperishable kind that Yeats called the artifice of eternity. *Peregrinatio,* the classical word for "travel," has a distinctive medieval sense that combines the negative connotation of "exile" with the positive concept of "pilgrimage." In keeping with the rhetoric of medieval prayer, Hildegard's language also shows a marked tendency toward abstraction: *prophetia* in lieu of *propheta, divinitas* for *Deus, formatio* for *forma.*[82] Some of her verbs appear in contexts that suggest more general meanings than they normally have: *edificare, suffocare,* and *ungere* mean "to build," "to choke," "to anoint," but in her usage they can metaphorically represent any form of creation, destruction, or healing. There is no English equivalent for her *sudare:* "perspire" and "exude" are limp analogues. Hildegard's verb calls forth the image of a sun-drenched tree yielding balm, with the same generous abundance by which holy thoughts and deeds flow from a sanctified heart.

Some of the constraints imposed by limited vocabulary are turned to advantage through rhetorical figures. Hildegard was partial to the trope of *polyptoton,* or the use of different inclined forms of the same word:

O virtus Sapientie,	O energy of Wisdom,
que circuiens circuisti	you who circled circling.
(no. 2)	

A related figure is *annominatio,* which links etymologically related words—*mistico misterio* (no. 21), *vivificans vita* (no. 24), and the like.[83] These figures chime pleasantly in Latin but drive translators to despair. The English language was not meant to

[82]Cf. Liver, *Nachwirkung* 99–101; Christine Mohrmann, *Etudes sur le latin des chrétiens* (Rome, 1965), 3: 213–14.
[83]Bronarski, *Lieder* 16–18; Liver, *Nachwirkung* 302.

render lines such as "qui in ardore ardentis / effulsisti, radix" (no. 36). Other tropes are used sparingly, for instance *anaphora,* or the repetition of initial words (nos. 32, 57), and *prosopopoeia,* or direct speech (nos. 64, 65).

Among the more salient features of Hildegard's style is her fondness for the grand gesture. No less than fifty of her songs, or about two-thirds, begin with a solemn apostrophe: "O virga ac diadema," "O victoriosissimi triumphatores," "O felix apparicio." Here we can detect some influence from the great "O" antiphons of Advent, which are among the most exalted seasonal compositions in the liturgy.[84] Hildegard had a corresponding zeal for superlatives and sudden outbursts. The ecstatic "O" can surface even in the middle of a line or strophe:

O tener flos campi et o dulcis viriditas pomi et o sarcina sine medulla (no. 49)	O tender flower of the field, O sweet green of the apple, O burden without pith.

Another mark of grandiloquence, echoing the Psalter, is the "O quam" construction.[85]

O quam magna est benignitas Salvatoris! (no. 1)	O how great is the Savior's kindness!
O quam magnum miraculum est! (no. 16)	O what a great miracle it is!
O quam preciosa est virginitas virginis huius! (no. 22)	O how precious is the virginity of this virgin!

Less often, clauses are linked with a string of parallel *et*s to create a psalmlike, incantatory texture, as in the first stanza of "O Ecclesia" (no. 64).

The feature for which Hildegard's poetry is best known is its

[84] Bronarski, *Lieder* 26. These are the antiphons, beginning with "O Sapientia," which underlie the English hymn "O come Emmanuel."

[85] Liver, *Nachwirkung* 217–18.

unusual imagery, which can seem outlandish insofar as it reflects her compressed, synesthetic mode of perception. It is not simply that Hildegard used multiple metaphors to characterize a single object; this is a common trait of devotional writing. We find it, for instance, in Saint Bernard's famous sermon on the Name of Jesus:

> But the name of Jesus is more than light, it is also food. . . . Every food of the mind is dry if it is not dipped in that oil; it is tasteless if not seasoned by that salt. Write what you will, I shall not relish it unless it tells of Jesus. Talk or argue about what you will, I shall not relish it if you exclude the name of Jesus. Jesus to me is honey in the mouth, music in the ear, a song in the heart.
>
> Again, [his name] is medicine. Does one of us feel sad? Let the name of Jesus come into his heart, from there let it spring to his mouth, so that shining like the dawn it may dispel all darkness and make a cloudless sky.[86]

Beginning with his metaphor of the holy name as light, Bernard runs quickly through the images of food, oil, salt, honey, music, and medicine before circling back to the light of dawn. But confusion cannot arise because all these metaphors are logically and grammatically discrete; they are not mingled but juxtaposed.[87] The resultant sensual richness contributes to an impression of spiritual and intellectual richness, but each element is singled out for separate analysis. Contrast the very different use of metaphor in Hildegard's responsory for the patriarchs and prophets (no. 32):

O vos felices radices	O you happy roots,
cum quibus opus miraculorum	with whom the work of miracles
et non opus criminum	was planted—
per torrens iter	and not the work of crimes—
perspicue umbre	in a rushing course
plantatum est.	of translucent shadow.

[86]Bernard of Clairvaux, *On the Song of Songs* 15.6, trans. Kilian Walsh (Kalamazoo, 1976), 1: 110.

[87]Patrick Diehl observes that in medieval religious lyric "it is rare for a series of metaphors to establish a continuity of vehicle, precisely because continuity of tenor is assured from the start" (*The Medieval European Religious Lyric: An Ars Poetica* [Berkeley, 1985]: 124).

The images in these lines mix freely and unself-consciously. Roots evoke the lineage of Christ, and bright shadow, the chiaroscuro of prophetic vision. But although the two images are grammatically linked, their unity is intuitive rather than logical; the reader who sets out to construct a single coherent picture can go badly astray. As in Bernard's sermon, the signs refer vertically to the signified and not horizontally to each other. Yet where Bernard's syntax discriminates, Hildegard's unites, creating possibilities both for confusion and for extraordinary richness. Each image is an independent unit of meaning, a motif, that can appear in a variety of contexts. Just as she combined many short, formulaic musical phrases to spin a long melody, Hildegard could vary and recombine units of textual meaning to create unexpected wholes.

One must admit that, as a craftsman, she had her faults. She could be prolix, obscure to the point of opacity, or, more rarely, banal to the point of dullness:

vos estis inter illos qui hec faciunt (no. 40)	you stand among them who do these things.
ut et in te factum est (no. 17, 6)	so it was in you also.

Her diction is sometimes caught uneasily between visionary élan and the more prosaic discourse of exegesis. Logical connectives (*unde, ideo, ita quod*) serve in her prose works to introduce exhortations and allegories; in the *Symphonia* they can seem intrusive. Nor is the promised logic always apparent. Yet this feature reminds us that even in her lyrics, part of Hildegard's literary purpose was didactic. The exegetical background of her work is especially striking in the hymn "O ignee Spiritus" (no. 27), in which seven of the thirteen stanzas begin with argumentative conjunctions: *Cum vero, Sed et cum, Quando autem,* and so forth. Such connectives occur more frequently in the songs incorporated into the prose miscellany; in the *Symphonia* manuscripts many of them have been edited out.

Another peculiarity, typical of medieval religious lyric but disconcerting to modern readers, is the instability of pronoun reference. Some lyrics (nos. 1, 21) open with direct address in the second person and subside into third-person statement, while "O virga ac diadema" (no. 20) vacillates between the two. Patrick Diehl remarks of such shifts that, "in the speech of everyday life, we treat animals, prisoners, spouses, and children in this way, now speaking to them as persons, now speaking past them as if they were objects, but one would not expect God and the saints to receive the same treatment."[88] One might reply that the holy ones are, like beasts, not expected to reply; like prisoners, a captive audience; and like family, so intimate that the worshiper can take unusual liberties. More seriously, it is important to recall that while a liturgical text is directed "vertically" in prayer, it is also directed "horizontally" to inspire and edify the congregation.

A more shocking example of pronoun shift occurs in "Nunc gaudeant" (no. 67), in which the second person refers to Satan in lines 6–9 and to God in lines 11–12.

Unde, o turpissime serpens,
confusus es,
quoniam quos tua estimatio
in visceribus suis habuit
nunc fulgent in sanguine
   Filii Dei,
et ideo laus tibi sit,
rex altissime.
	So you, shameful serpent,
	are confounded,
	for those your jealousy
	held in its maw
	now gleam in the blood of
	   God's Son.
	Praise then be yours,
	O King Most High!

Here the change of reference suggests a dramatic context, and the prose miscellany confirms this hypothesis. "Nunc gaudeant" is part of a brief scenario in which a voice from heaven rebukes Satan, the Spirit rejoices, and the wretched earth laments.[89]

Given that the *Symphonia* lyrics were meant to be sung, it may seem perverse to consider their sonority as purely verbal constructs. But even from this perspective, some of them have a

[88]Diehl, *Religious Lyric* 167.
[89]Pitra 361.

pronounced musicality, based on assonance, alliteration, *annominatio,* and occasional rhyme. Like everything else in the songs, however, these four ornaments resist the lure of regularity. "O Ierusalem" (no. 49) demonstrates all of them:

Et ita turres tue,	So your towers,
o Ierusalem,	O Jerusalem,
rutilant et candent	gleam ruddy and bright
per ruborem	with the rosy glow
et per candorem sanctorum	and the sparkling white of the
(9)	saints
. . .	. . .
Unde vos, o ornati	O you adorned ones
et o coronati . . .	and O you crowned ones...
succurrite nobis famulantibus	help us who serve
et in exilio laborantibus.	and labor in exile.
(10)	

Most writers of artistic prose were careful to follow the rules of *cursus,* or cadence, which medieval rhetoricians had adapted from antiquity. According to this convention, every sentence or important clause had to end in one of four patterns of stressed and unstressed syllables as follows:

planus – u u – u
tardus – u u – u u
velox – u u u u – u
dispondaicus – u u u – u

A review of the sixty-nine *Symphonia* lyrics shows that forty-six, exactly two-thirds, end with some form of cursus. The *cursus planus* is the most common with twenty examples, the *velox* least frequent with only two. Within the longer pieces, seven of the ten strophes in "O Ecclesia" (no. 64) have proper cursus endings, as do eight of the nine in "Columba aspexit" (no. 54), and nine of the twelve in "O presul vere civitatis" (no. 45). Cursus rhythms are natural to the structure of Latin, and if Hildegard had been following the rules systematically, there would no doubt be fewer exceptions. Nevertheless, her strong predilection for these cadences marks the lyrics as less "raw" than has sometimes been argued.

As a verbal artist, Hildegard did not have the craftsmanship of a Notker or a Peter Abelard. But neither was she the inept, negligible figure that the standard histories of hymnography would have us believe. Often conventional in her subjects, she was wholly original in her treatment and style. Her poems, even apart from their musical settings, leave an indelible impression of freshness and power. What she lacked in fluency, Hildegard made up in sheer immediacy. Not words but images formed her native idiom, and in her lyrics these images can leap out of their verbal wrappings to assault the mind with all the force and inevitability of a Jungian dream. Startling at first, even incoherent, they slowly or suddenly explode into sense, revealing the lineaments of a pattern that—if one is a twelfth-century Christian—one has always known.

Themes of the Symphonia

Like all that Hildegard wrote, the *Symphonia* celebrates the mystery of God-become-man in the child of Mary. Virtually everything in her sphere of discourse is in some way a condition, a consequence, or an analogue of this event. In the beginning God created the heavens and the earth, that is, angels and human beings, but in his eternal wisdom he was already looking forward to the incarnation of the Word. Thus, in the first and thematically very significant lyric, "O vis eternitatis," Hildegard slips with astonishing speed from the ideal creation in the mind of God to the coming of Christ. Adam's fall, which presumably occasioned the Redeemer's birth, is merely implied in passing.[90] When the Savior was born, our poet says in her elliptical way, the first man's "garment"—or mortal body—was "cleansed from the greatest suffering." The figure of Adam fascinated Hildegard, who

[90] I have argued elsewhere (*Sister of Wisdom* 55–64) that Hildegard believed in the absolute predestination of Christ—the doctrine that the Incarnation was God's purpose in creating the world rather than a consequence of Adam's sin.

saw him both as a historical person and as an exemplar of the human race, as well as the precursor of Christ. In "O quam mirabilis" (no. 3) he appears at the center of creation as God's consummate work, in which all others are integrated, while "O eterne Deus" (no. 7) reveals Christ, the second Adam, as the cosmic man who in turn integrates the scattered limbs of humanity into a single body, which God created "in the primal dawn / before all creation."

In the short first section of her cycle, Hildegard dramatizes all the preconditions for Christ's coming: the creation of the world, God's "ancient counsel" of salvation, the making of man, and (obliquely) the Fall. The first three songs are pure celebrations praising the Creator under many names—"strength of eternity," "energy of Wisdom," "foreknowledge of the divine heart." There follow four prayers to the Redeemer in which the poet, now pleading on behalf of fallen humanity, invokes both the goodness of creation (no. 6) and the blood of Christ (no. 5). It is noteworthy that, however strange her expressions, Hildegard remains entirely orthodox in her theology. For instance, she does not simplistically identify God the Father as Creator and Christ as the Redeemer. In both cases the initiative comes from the Father but the act is accomplished by the Son, in keeping with patristic views of the Trinity.

The Virgin Mary holds the next place after God because her role in history is not just chronologically but also logically prior to the other great events of salvation—the gift of the Holy Spirit, the building of the Church, and the deeds of the saints—which Hildegard exalts in the last two thirds of her cycle. The meaning of Mary for the abbess can be gauged in part by what she does *not* say: in her lyrics there is no sign of interest in the Virgin's psychology, no sentimental devotion, no apocryphal legends or miracles—in short, nothing at all about Mary's life before, after, or apart from the Incarnation.[91] Three motifs occur time and again (although, like Hildegard's melodic formulas, they are ceaselessly

[91]Newman, *Sister of Wisdom* 159–60. See also Peter Walter, "*Virgo filium dei portasti:* Maria in den Gesängen der heiligen Hildegard von Bingen," *Archiv für mittelrheinische Kirchengeschichte* 29 (1977): 75–96.

varied): the divine motherhood, the virginity of Mary, and the comparison with Eve. The first theme needs no comment, but the second lends itself to misunderstanding. Mary's virginity meant more to Hildegard than an absence of sexual contact or a proof of Christ's divine paternity. It is deeply bound up with her traditional idea of paradise, in which sex as we know it did not exist and Eve, had she remained as she was, would have borne children without loss of virginity.[92] By remaining inviolate yet divinely fruitful, Mary regains the lost heritage of Eve. Her body becomes the emblem of paradise regained as well as the path to it:

Unde dulce germen,	Thus the tender shoot
quod Filius ipsius est,	that is her Son
per clausuram ventris eius	opened paradise
paradisum aperuit.	through the cloister of her womb.
(no. 22)	

For this reason Hildegard constantly associates Mary images of growth, greenness, flowering: she is the "shining lily" (no. 17), "the greenest branch" (no. 19), and so forth. Of course these images are scriptural and carry their full typological weight, but Hildegard chose them in preference to innumerable others that she could equally well have used.

The other striking feature in her treatment of Mary is the way she handles the ancient *Ave/Eva* motif—the notion that Mary's purity and obedience reversed the corruption and rebellion of Eve, thus redeeming womankind per se. This theme occurs in at least half the Marian songs. But alongside it runs another current of thought which asserts that, just as Christ not only redeems but also *is* Adam, so Eve in a sense is Mary. This idea is memorably expressed in no. 16, where Hildegard says that woman "beautified heaven / more than she formerly marred the earth" (cf. no 12 and no. 20, 4a). Ultimately, once salvation has been accomplished, the fallen Adam and Eve are at one with the redeemed human race.

[92]Heinrich Schipperges, ed., "Ein unveröffentlichtes Hildegard-Fragment," IV.29, *Sudhoffs Archiv für Geschichte der Medizin* 40 (1956): 72.

Union with God and its corollary, the communion of saints, are the themes on which the rest of the *Symphonia* spins variations. Holiness and oneness become possible through the Holy Spirit, the source of all unity in creation: the Spirit gives life to elements, souls, and bodies, and binds all nature into one (no. 28, 4a–4b). With respect to human beings, the Spirit is the one who infuses desire for God, vanquishes sin, and (most emphatically) heals the wounds it has caused:

Sanctus es vivificando formas. Sanctus es ungendo periculose fractos, sanctus es tergendo fetida vulnera. (no. 28, 1a–1b)	Holy are you, giving life to the Forms. Holy are you, anointing the dangerously broken; holy are you, cleansing the fetid wounds.

This tendency to see evil in terms of the suffering it inflicts on the sinner is typical of Hildegard. However, she looks on the saints less as forgiven sinners than as beings in whom the Spirit already dwells in glory. They are lights, mirrors, flames, epiphanies of Christ or of his bride, the Church.[93] But above all, Hildegard loved the imagery of Apocalypse 21 in which all the saints coalesce into a single double-natured vision, the bride of Christ and City of God. Each saint becomes a living stone in the walls of Jerusalem (cf. 1 Pet. 2:5):

Fenestre tue, Ierusalem, cum topazio et saphiro specialiter sunt decorate. In quibus dum fulges, o Ruperte . . . (no. 49, 3a–3b)	Your windows, Jerusalem, are specially embellished with topaz and sapphire, in which...you gleam, O Rupert...
Iste, turris excelsa de ligno Libani et cipresso facta,	He, a lofty tower built from the wood of Lebanon and cypress,

[93]Peter Walter, "Die Heiligen in der Dichtung der heiligen Hildegard von Bingen," in Brück, *Hildegard von Bingen* 211–37.

iacincto et sardio ornata est,	is adorned with jacinth and ruby,
urbs precellens artes	a city surpassing the arts
aliorum artificum.	of other artisans.
(no. 54, 2a)	

The image of the City allowed Hildegard to set each individual saint in counterpoint with the full community of the redeemed. Doubtless she, like many poets before her, took delight in the vision of the City as a work of art. One might recall the tenth-century hymn "Urbs beata Hierusalem," sung at the consecration of churches,[94] or the later *rhythmus* by Hildebert of Lavardin:

Me receptet Syon illa,	May noble Zion harbor me,
Syon David urbs tranquilla;	Zion, David's tranquil city;
cuius faber auctor lucis,	her founder is the fount of light,
cuius porte lignum crucis;	her gates the wood of Calvary,
cuius claves lingua Petri,	her keys the tongue of Peter;
cuius cives semper leti;	her citizens are ever joyful,
cuius muri lapis vivus,	her walls are made of living stone,
cuius custos rex festivus.	her keeper is the festal king.
In hac urbe lux solennis,	In this city solemn light,
ver eternum, pax perennis;	spring eternal, lasting peace.
in hac odor implens celos,	In her, fragrance filling heaven;
in hac semper festum melos.[95]	in her, music ever festive.

What is unusual in the *Symphonia,* however, is Hildegard's interest in the process of building the City, a theme to which she also devoted the third book of the *Scivias*. She cared not only for the *edificium* but also for the *edificatio,* the relation between the saint's life of spiritual effort on earth and his or her glory in heaven. In this context, the image of building is but one of several Hildegard used to evoke the Godward striving of the earthborn. Saint Maximin longs for the eagle's wings and rises "like the smoke of incense / to the pillar of praise" (no. 54). Ursula races through the skies like a sapphire cloud (no. 64), and the voice of her blood mounts up to the throne of God (no. 65). Music itself is

[94]Printed in Dreves and Blume, eds., *Analecta hymnica* 2: 73 (no. 93).

[95]Hildebert of Lavardin, "De sancta Trinitate," in *Carmina minora,* ed. A. Brian Scott (Leipzig, 1969): 52–53.

an ascending motion, and so is prayer. The whole life of the Church on earth continually aspires heavenward, infusing a powerful dynamism into a vision that, in its meticulously well-ordered detail, might otherwise have the appearance of stasis. The glorified saints, in turn, look down on the earth in compassionate solicitude for those who invoke them.

In a well-known icon of the Trinity, God's dealings with the human race are summed up in three succinct images—a tree, a building, and a mountain.[96] These emblems, in their several permutations, can also be seen as master themes of the *Symphonia.* The tree and the building are metonymic for the two images of supreme fulfillment—the Garden at the beginning of time, the City at its end. Banished from the Garden, the human race makes its slow and tortuous pilgrimage toward the City by way of the Mountain, which stands for so many theophanies in Scripture: Sinai of the Law, Tabor of the Transfiguration, Calvary of the Passion, Olivet of the Ascension. In the *Symphonia,* as we have seen, the Garden evokes the lost virginal Eden that Mary reentered. It is a purely natural image, but it is also purely miraculous, for Hildegard says nothing of cultivation. Only the warmth of the sun and the dew of heaven bring forth the marvelous flower. When the same image is used of a saint, it has the connotation of pure grace blossoming in the soul without need of effort. Thus the virgin apostle John is praised as a "wondrous flower" that never withered or faded, because the gardener of Eden planted him (no. 35). The building of the City, on the other hand, is a collaborative effort; in the *Scivias* it is a universal image for the moral life, representing the constant interaction of divine grace with human struggle. Typical here is Saint Maximin, portrayed in a single strophe as both "architect" and "wall of the temple" (no. 54, 3b). The active and the passive image present the same reality, sanctification, from man's side and from God's.

Finally there is the mountain, a complex image that can be

[96] I have in mind the widely reproduced fourteenth-century icon by Andrei Rublev, now in the Tretyakov Gallery, Moscow. The icon symbolically depicts the hospitality of Abraham (Gen. 18:1–15): three angels signifying the divine Persons are seated around a table, and the landscape in the background is reduced to the three symbolic objects.

nuanced in several ways. As a time-honored symbol of contemplation, it represents supreme human effort drawing near to God; thus Saint Disibod's life as a hermit is signified by the "mountain of a cloistered mind" (no. 45) which shall never be leveled in God's judgment (no. 42). Because Hildegard's monasteries, first St. Disibod and then the Rupertsberg, were themselves built on mountains, she arrived naturally at an equation between the mountain and the exalted saint, or the monastic life as such. On the other hand a mountain, as a natural image of the sublime, can evoke the vast distance between God and man. A monastery at the summit of a cliff is meant to be, like the divine majesty, inaccessible and awesome; it suggests alienation from the things of this world. In "O Ecclesia" (no. 64), Hildegard says that the martyr's "scorn for the world is / like Mount Bethel." This image seems to be the prerogative of a spiritual elite. If the City is the ultimate symbol of community, the Mountain stands for its complement, the ascetic spirit that renounces secular community in order to meet God in the heroic encounter of contemplation or martyrdom.

For the sake of analysis, I have isolated these three images in order to study the thematic connotations of each. But in actuality they occur side by side, along with many others (fire and water, dawn and daylight, weddings, armies) which cannot be examined here. I believe the attentive reader will discover that, although Hildegard's images may at first seem to proliferate madly and mingle promiscuously, her songs in fact develop a limited range of themes that "chime together," as she liked to say, to create the symphonic harmony advertised in her title. And her images, though they may strike the uninitiated as verging on surrealism, carry precise conceptual values that stabilize, but never freeze, the mercurial flow of her imagination.

The Manuscripts and the Order of Songs

The *Symphonia* as an ordered cycle, including both texts and music, comes down to us in two late-twelfth-century manuscripts, one complete and one fragmentary. The older, defective manuscript is codex 9 at the library of St.-Pieters-&-Paulusabdij, Den-

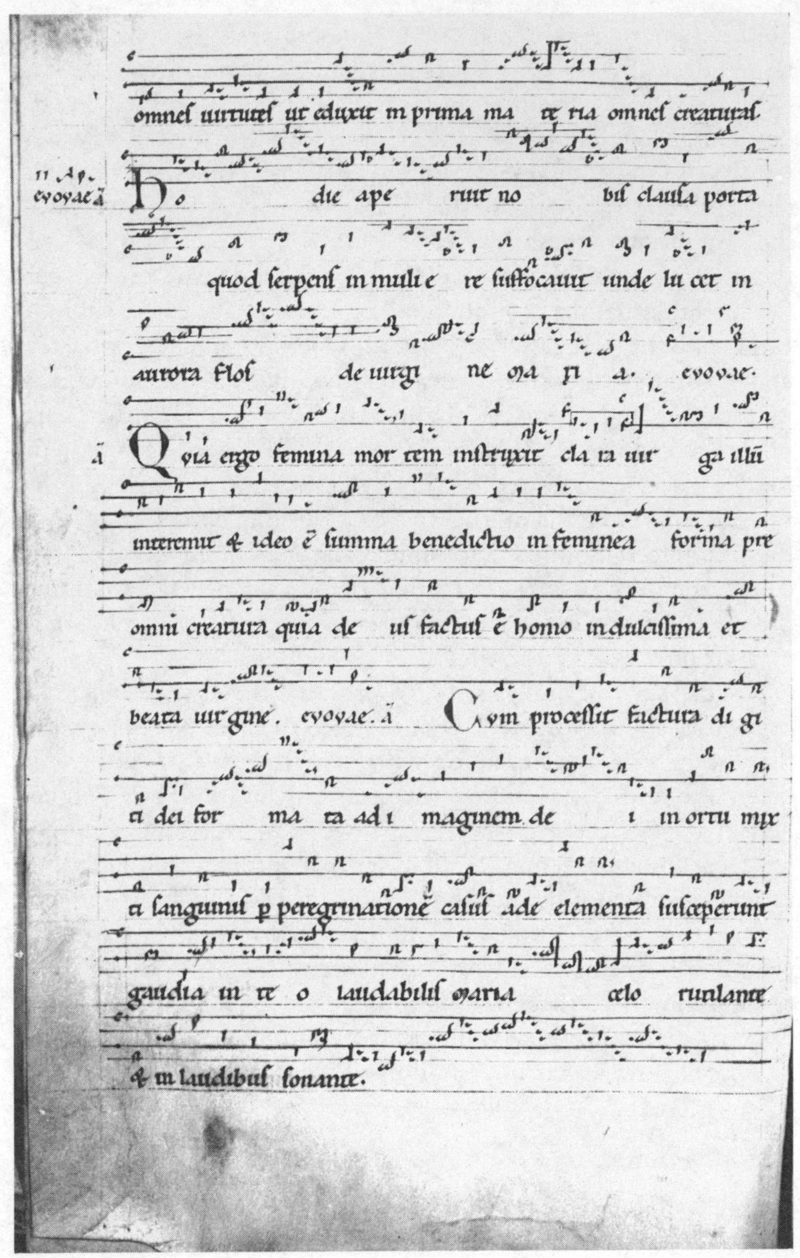

Dendermonde, St.-Pieters-&-Paulusabdij, Cod. 9, fol. 154v, containing the songs "Hodie aperuit," "Quia ergo femina," and "Cum processit factura" (nos. 11–13).

Wiesbaden, Landesbibliothek, Hs. 2 ("Riesenkodex"), fol. 467r.

dermonde, Belgium (hereafter D). It is this codex which Hildegard sent to the monks of Villers; it was produced in the Rupertsberg scriptorium around 1175, probably under her direct supervision. The second manuscript is the so-called Riesenkodex or "giant codex" containing Hildegard's collected works (Wiesbaden, Hessische Landesbibliothek, Hs. 2; hereafter R). Prepared at the same scriptorium in the decade after the abbess's death (c. 1180–1190), the Riesenkodex was apparently compiled with a view to her canonization, for it contains all her "inspired" writings and excludes only the scientific works that she wrote on her own initiative, so to speak.[97] This is the celebrated volume that the humanist Trithemius of Sponheim and later Goethe saw and admired. Today it remains an impressive object, bound with a heavy sixteenth-century leather binding, metal studs, and a chain; it measures twelve by eighteen inches and weighs no less than thirty-three pounds. Of its 481 parchment leaves, written in double columns, the last sixteen (fols. 466ra–481vb) contain the *Symphonia* and the *Ordo virtutum.*

R also includes lyrics without neumes at two points: fourteen occur in the final *Scivias* vision (fols. 132va–133rb) and twenty-six in the miscellany (fols. 404rb–407va). These doublets have independent textual authority, for the *Scivias,* the *Symphonia,* and the miscellany were copied into the manuscript by three different hands and represent separate exemplars.[98]

Unlike the Riesenkodex, the much smaller Dendermonde manuscript (approximately eight by eleven inches) is in a poor state of preservation and has lost several leaves, although the ones that remain are quite legible. It originally consisted of 173 folios containing the *Book of Life's Merits,* the *Liber viarum Domini (Book of the Ways of the Lord)* by Hildegard's friend Elisabeth of Schönau, and the *Symphonia.* After its sojourn at Villers, the manuscript subsequently found its way to Gembloux, thence to

[97]For a detailed discussion of this MS. see Schrader and Führkötter, *Echtheit* 154–79. A photographic facsimile of folios 466–481, containing the music, has been published by Joseph Gmelch, *Die Kompositionen der heiligen Hildegard* (Düsseldorf, 1913).

[98]Schrader and Führkötter, *Echtheit* 157.

Afflighem, and finally to Dendermonde.[99] The text that concerns us is found in folios 153^{r}–170^{v}, which today have become detached from the rest of the manuscript. The songs are neatly written in single columns with twelve lines of text and music to a page. One sheet is missing after folio 155^{v} and another after folio 164^{v}; thus the hymn "Ave generosa" (no. 17) and the sequence "O Ierusalem" (no. 49) are fragmentary. The first of these gaps is also responsible for the loss of a few Marian songs, as it occurs in the part of the *Symphonia* devoted to the Virgin. In addition, at least one page and possibly an entire gathering has been lost at the beginning of the *Symphonia,* for there is no title in the manuscript, and the first song that does appear, "O magne Pater" (no. 6), is accompanied by a *differentia* or psalm cadence that must belong to an antiphon from the preceding page. It is most likely that the missing page contained the responsory "O vis eternitatis" (no. 1) and various antiphons addressed to God the Father and Christ (nos. 2–5). If Peter Dronke is right in positing the loss of a full eight-leaved gathering at this point, it may have contained the *Ordo virtutum,* as he surmises.[100]

In its present fragmentary state, D contains fifty-seven songs, as opposed to seventy-five in R. But the loss of pages from D and the addition of late compositions to R do not fully account for the differences between the two manuscripts. Most significantly, the cycle has been completely rearranged in R: the order of songs within each section is different, the sections themselves have been reshuffled, and the longer pieces have been separated from the shorter ones and placed together at the end of the work, thus creating two cycles instead of one. In brief, the arrangement of the *Symphonia* in the two manuscripts is as follows:

D	**R**
[initial gap in MS.]	*(shorter songs)*
God the Father—2 songs	God the Father, Christ, Sapientia—7 songs

[99]Information graciously supplied by Dom E. Van de Vyver, OSB, librarian at St.-Pieters-&-Paulusabdij, Dendermonde.

[100]Dronke, "Composition" 391.

	Holy Spirit, Karitas—2 songs
Virgin Mary—12 songs [with gap in MS.]	Virgin Mary—11 songs
Holy Spirit, Karitas, Trinity—5 songs	
Angels—2 songs	Angels—2 songs
Patriarchs and prophets—2 songs	Patriarchs and prophets—2 songs
Apostles—2 songs	Apostles—2 songs
Saint John—2 songs	Saint John—2 songs
Saint Disibod—3 songs	
Martyrs—2 songs	Martyrs—2 songs
Confessors—2 songs	Confessors—2 songs
	Saint Disibod—4 songs
Saint Rupert—3 songs	Saint Rupert—3 songs
Virgins—3 songs	Virgins—2 songs
	Saint Ursula—11 songs
Widows—1 song	
Innocents—1 song	Innocents—1 song
Saint Ursula—13 songs	
Ecclesia—2 songs	Ecclesia—4 songs
	Kyrie
	(longer songs)
	Holy Spirit—2 songs
	Virgin Mary—4 songs
	Saints:
	Matthias—1 song
	Boniface—1 song
	Disibod—1 song
	Eucharius—2 songs
	Maximin—1 song
	Rupert—1 song
	Ursula—2 songs
	"Symphony of virgins"
	"Symphony of widows"

In both versions, the *Symphonia* is clearly arranged along hierarchical lines. God is honored first, then the Virgin Mary, highest of created beings; after her come the angels and the various ranks of saints—patriarchs and prophets, apostles, martyrs, confessors (bishops and other saints not martyred), virgins, widows, and innocents. Finally come the antiphons to be used at the dedication of a church, in which the "saint" to be honored is Ecclesia herself, the personified bride of God and community of the faithful. Individual saints are celebrated under the general category to which they belong: John among the apostles, Rupert among the confessors, and so forth.

The cyclical principle itself was not new. In the ninth century Notker of St. Gall arranged the songs in his *Liber ymnorum* according to the liturgical year, beginning with Christmas. The second book of Abelard's *Hymnarius Paraclitensis* follows the same principle, but the third, devoted to the saints, is organized like the *Symphonia*. After the Marian hymns come those honoring the angels, apostles, evangelists, martyrs, confessors, virgins, and holy women, with individual saints under their proper categories. The book ends with All Saints (Hildegard's Ecclesia).[101] Since this principle governs D, it probably derives from Hildegard herself, so it is this order which I have followed in arranging this edition. In order to remain faithful to Hildegard's structural principles, I have inserted the additional material from R where it fits naturally into the D arrangement, rather than following the pattern of duplication created by the R redactor. Within subsections I have followed the order of songs in D, filling the gaps with material from R which we can reasonably suppose was contained on the missing leaves.

The scribe who copied the *Symphonia* for the Riesenkodex cannot have used D as an exemplar, since that manuscript had already been given to the monks of Villers. Either both extant manuscripts were created from a single exemplar, now lost, or, as I have suggested, the nuns had retained the music in loose leaves or gatherings. The second possibility would account for the loss of two songs and the rearrangement of pieces within sections. But in either case, the R scribe introduced new principles of order and, in effect, regularized what he or she may have perceived as eccentricities in the earlier arrangement. In addition to separating

[101] Joseph Szövérffy, ed., *Peter Abelard's Hymnarius Paraclitensis*, 2 vols. (Albany, 1975).

the longer songs from the shorter antiphons and responsories, the redactor of R made the following revisions in the D order:

(a) In D, twelve songs to the Virgin Mary fall *between* two addressed to God the Father and five to the Holy Spirit or the Trinity. In R, all nine songs addressed to God precede those which honor Mary.
(b) D places Saint Disibod among the apostles; R more plausibly ranks him as a confessor.
(c) In D, Saint Ursula and her companions follow the Holy Innocents; in R they appear with the virgins.

All these changes serve to normalize oddities in the original order; but the oddities themselves can tell us something about Hildegard's perceptions. To begin with the second, Saint Disibod was a seventh-century Irish missionary to the Rhineland, who is said to have founded a monastery and been appointed bishop.[102] As the first evangelist in the region, he would merit the title of *apostolicus vir* or, by extension, apostle. By placing her patron in the same league with Saint John the Evangelist, Hildegard was undeniably exalting his status, and thereby the prestige of the monastery which bore his name.[103] As for Saint Ursula and her companions, these legendary maidens could have been revered among either the virgins or the martyrs. But Hildegard surprisingly chose to set them among the Holy Innocents. In so doing she emphasized the similarity between the eleven thousand girl-martyrs and the young boys slain by King Herod; and it is also the innocence of Ursula which she highlights in "O Ecclesia" (no. 64). In the same composition, the martyred girl becomes a prototype of the virgin Church, which occupies the next and final place in the cycle. Thus Hildegard used the figure of Ursula to achieve a smooth and convincing transition, giving the impression that she

[102]Hildegard of Bingen, *Vita Sancti Disibodi,* PL 197: 1095–1116.

[103]Cf. Richard Landes, "The Making of a Medieval Historian: Ademar of Chabannes and Aquitaine at the Turn of the Millennium" (Ph.D. diss. Princeton, 1984), a study of an eleventh-century monk who devoted his entire life to advancing the cult of his patron, Saint Martial of Limoges, to the status of apostle.

ultimately meant the *Symphonia* as a *Gesamtwerk* rather than a miscellany.

The most interesting of the oddities is the place of the Virgin, who has the most prominent role in the entire work. By setting Mary midway between God the Father and the Holy Spirit, in the place where one would expect to find Christ, Hildegard was making a pointed theological statement. The Virgin, for her, was not one saint among others but the unique Mother of God, "the fixed end of the eternal counsel," as Dante has Saint Bernard say in the *Paradiso.* As the chosen vessel of the Incarnation, Mary belongs not with the other saints, a little lower than the angels, but in the very heart of God, the place of her Son. Every one of the sixteen lyrics addressed to her celebrates her divine childbearing, which God had ordained from before the foundation of the world. The songs, then, are so many verbal and musical icons of the Madonna and Child. For this reason I have preserved the eccentricity in the construction of D, even though the R redactor apparently felt it to be a sin against theological propriety. Thus the section on "Father and Son" is followed by that on "Mother and Son."

Readers familiar with the German edition of the *Symphonia* will notice this restoration of its original structure as one of the chief differences in the present text. The German editors, Barth, Ritscher, and Schmidt-Görg, first printed the fifty-seven songs from D and then picked up the remaining pieces in the order that they appear in R, thus trebling the hierarchical pattern and reducing the overall structure of the cycle to incoherence.

Aside from D and R, two other manuscripts contain fragments of Hildegard's music. A thirteenth-century codex in Vienna (Nationalbibliothek, Cod. 1016) includes neumes for the two short pieces she composed for Mass, the Kyrie and the alleluia-verse (no. 18), on folios 118^{v}–119^{r}. Her responsory "O vos imitatores" (no. 39) appears with its music on folio 40^{v} of an important early manuscript, written c. 1154–1170 at the Rupertsberg and the monasteries of Zwiefalten and St. Disibod. This manuscript, now in Stuttgart (Landesbibliothek, Cod. Theol. Phil. 253), also includes texts without neumes for no. 6, "O magne Pater," and no. 68, "O orzchis Ecclesia," both on folio 28^{r}. In addition, the Stuttgart manuscript contains one segment of the miscellany, including nine Marian songs, on folio 54^{r-v}. A second Vienna manuscript (Cod. 881) incorporates texts of three songs to Saint Disibod (nos. 41, 42, 45) in a letter to Abbot Kuno, folios 42^{v}–43^{v}. Finally, the Vienna codex 963 contains a complete text of the miscellany on folios 155^{r}–159^{v}.

The Text and Translations

In establishing the text for this edition I have relied primarily on D and R, although I have also collated the lyrics that appear in the Stuttgart codex 253 and the three Vienna codices, 881, 963, and 1016. Readings from the *Symphonia* proper are preferred, but I have adopted a few superior variants from the *Scivias* and miscellany versions of the text. Most of the variants are due to simple scribal errors or commonplace spelling variants. I have followed the orthography of the manuscripts; in the case of variants I have chosen the spelling more widely attested or, if neither is preferred, the more standard usage. Punctuation is my own.

Both D and R indicate the beginnings of stanzas, strophes, and responsorial verses with capital letters. In this edition, I have used Arabic numerals to number the stanzas of hymns and long free-form compositions; numerals followed by letters (1a, 1b) designate the strophic pairs in sequences. Antiphons and responsories have only line numbers for convenient reference. Line breaks are not indicated in the manuscripts at all, for text and music are written continuously. In most cases I have based my divisions of the text on the melodic divisions marked in the editions of Barth, Ritscher, and Schmidt-Görg, and of Christopher Page.[104] The musical phrasing itself, however, is often conjectural. To avoid an unduly jagged appearance, I have diverged from it in pieces that are so melismatic that almost every word constitutes a separate

[104]Page's *Sequences and Hymns* (Antico Church Music, 1983) includes nos. 17, 19, 20, 28, 45, 49, 53, 54, and 64 in the present edition. For the other pieces I have used the music as edited by Barth, Ritscher, and Schmidt-Görg. In the case of the five antiphons discussed by Marianne Richert Pfau (nos. 3, 11, 14, 25, and 40) I have followed her suggestions about phrasing.

melodic phrase. The lines in this edition are generally shorter than those in the Barth-Ritscher text and tend to highlight rhymes and other rhythmic features of the language.

For the responsories, the manuscripts normally give only the initial words of the repetenda and the doxology. I have silently expanded these, noting only the cases where they are missing altogether. In the prose translations, however, I have omitted the doxology to save space.

Translating the *Symphonia* has been a challenge. Poetry is defined all too well as that which gets lost in translation, but in the case of songs, half is already lost when the music is sacrificed. In a spirit of desperation, I have resorted to the compromise of providing *two* sets of translations, one for students and one for readers of poetry. The prose translations, printed in small type at the bottom of the right-hand page, attempt to reproduce Hildegard's texts as literally as good English style will permit. With their help, a reader with even rudimentary Latin should be able to make sense of the originals. I have left all their idiosyncrasies intact. Line divisions in the prose correspond as closely to the Latin line breaks as possible.

My verse translations, on the other hand, are frankly and blithely interpretive. Petrarch once advised Boccaccio that "the similarity [between text and translation] should not be like that of a painting or a statue to the person represented, but rather like that of a son to a father"—or daughter to mother, as the case may be.[105] In what I hope is a filial spirit, I have tried to convey the freshness and emotional vitality of Hildegard's songs in an idiom that is still fresh and vital to the modern reader, without deviating from their express content. In a more literal version, it is all but impossible to evoke the genuine excitement of her poetry without regressing into a style that sounds either generically medieval or aesthetically preposterous. For instance, Hildegard's sprawling syntax, with its dependence on participles and relative clauses,

[105]Petrarch, *Epistolae Familiares* 23.19, trans. Nicholas Kilmer, in *Francis Petrarch: Songs and Sonnets from Laura's Lifetime* (San Francisco, 1981): xv–xvi. I would like to thank David Myers for this quotation and for his benignly scathing criticism.

creates a space for ample and leisured meditation, contrasting with the elegant tightness of the Victorine sequence. In English, however, periodic sentences have a faded, pseudo-Miltonic resonance that is totally alien to Hildegard's spirit. To take another example, our poet overuses superlatives. But in Latin the threat of an overwrought, hysterical tone is countered by the ringing magniloquence of lines such as "O dulcissima / atque amantissima mater, salve" (no. 8). The nearest equivalent in English—"Hail, O sweetest and most loving mother"—is saccharine injurious to any reader's poetic health. Medieval poetry in general favored hyperbole, and Hildegard in particular was no advocate of the *via negativa*. Her way of approaching the ineffable was to make the strongest positive statement her tongue could express. Modern English, on the other hand, is a language of understatement, and in free verse it is almost a truism that less is more. So, in order to convey the rapt intensity of Hildegard's praise, I have actually had to tone down some of her expressions.

Traditional metaphors pose another challenge. The symbolism of the medieval Church provided poets with an inexhaustible fund of material for devotion and imaginative play. When sensitively handled, this symbolism could be an aid rather than a barrier to fresh vision. But the risk of staleness is ever present, especially with the most ubiquitous images: the Holy Spirit is a dove, Mary a flowering branch, and so forth. I have tried to revivify some of these metaphors by expanding images that Hildegard presents but then fails to develop:

> Hodie aperuit nobis
> clausa porta
> quod serpens in muliere suffocavit.
> (no. 11)

The closed gate of the temple (Ezek. 44:2) signifies Mary's virginity, open to Christ alone and thereby opening—what? "That which the serpent choked in the woman." Although the general drift is clear, the exact sense defies explanation; how can the same unspecified entity be first "choked" and then "opened"? A slight expansion will clarify the image:

Today a closed portal
has opened to us the door
the serpent slammed on a woman.

On the other hand, I have tried to avoid excessive clarity when the original is enhanced by its phantasmagoria of mixed metaphors, as in "O cohors milicie floris" (no. 33) and "O spectabiles viri" (no. 31).

Readers of the *Symphonia* will find passages of great simplicity as well as some that appear strained and mannered. I have attempted to recreate each piece in an appropriate tonality, even at the price of a few obvious transpositions. As Diehl observes, medieval religious poets were themselves engaged in a kind of "translation"—"a concentration on finding a way to render something already said into words that a new audience will understand, an overall function of representing the original to the audience."[106] One technical term for this process was, fittingly enough, *conversio*. For the rest, the reader should bear in mind that mere words, even in their original tongue, cannot faintly approximate the experience of music and prayer which is the Divine Office. So the English poems in this volume should be read less as translations in the normal sense than as adaptations for a wholly new medium. Whether they cast a fleeting shadow of the seer's living light or whether they send the reader back in indignant love to the originals, they will have accomplished their task.

[106]Diehl, *Religious Lyric* 13.

List of Manuscripts

D Dendermonde, Belgium, St.-Pieters-&-Paulusabdij Cod. 9 (Rupertsberg, c. 1175)

R Wiesbaden, Landesbibliothek Hs. 2, “Riesenkodex” (Rupertsberg, 1180–1190)
- R^a *Scivias,* fols. 132va–133rb
- R^b Miscellany, fols. 404rb–407va
- R^c *Symphonia,* fols. 466ra–478va

S Stuttgart, Landesbibliothek Cod. Theol. Phil. 253 (Rupertsberg, St. Disibod and Zwiefalten, 1154–1170)

V^1 Vienna, Nationalbibliothek Cod. 881 (Rupertsberg, 1164–1170)

V^2 Vienna, Nationalbibliothek Cod. 963 (St. Maria in Rommersdorf, 13th century)

V^3 Vienna, Nationalbibliothek Cod. 1016 (13th century)

Order of Songs in the Manuscripts

D = Dendermonde, Belgium, St.-Pieters-&-Paulusabdij Cod. 9 (Rupertsberg, c. 1175). R = Wiesbaden, Landesbibliothek Hs. 2, "Riesenkodex" (Rupertsberg, 1180–1190). The column marked "R" refers to the *Symphonia* as it appears in R, fols. 466ra–478va. The *Scivias* (col. 1) appears in R, fols. 132va–133rb, and the miscellany (col. 4) in R, fols. 404rb–407va.

Incipit	*Scivias*	D	R	Miscellany
1. O vis eternitatis			1	10
2. O virtus Sapientie			4	
3. O quam mirabilis			5	
4. O pastor animarum			6	12
5. O cruor sanguinis			7	11
6. O magne Pater		1	2	6
7. O eterne Deus		2	3	
8. Ave Maria		3	17	22
9. O clarissima mater		4	18	23
10. O splendidissima gemma	1	5	10	
11. Hodie aperuit		6	12	24
12. Quia ergo femina		7	13	25
13. Cum processit factura		8	14	
14. Cum erubuerint		9	15	
15. O frondens virga		10		13
16. O quam magnum miraculum		11	16	20

Incipit	*Scivias*	D	R	Miscellany
17. Ave generosa		12	56	14
18. O virga mediatrix			53	19
19. O viridissima virga			55	18
20. O virga ac diadema		13	54	15
21. O tu suavissima virga	2	14	19	
22. O quam preciosa			20	26
23. O tu illustrata			11	21
24. Spiritus sanctus vivificans		15	8	
25. Karitas habundat		16	9	
26. Laus Trinitati		17		
27. O ignee Spiritus		18	52	17
28. O ignis Spiritus Paracliti		19	51	16
29. O gloriosissimi lux vivens	3	20	21	
30. O vos angeli	4	21	22	
31. O spectabiles viri	5	22	23	
32. O vos felices radices	6	23	24	
33. O cohors milicie floris	7	24	25	
34. O lucidissima apostolorum	8	25	26	
35. O speculum columbe		26	27	
36. O dulcis electe		27	28	
37. O victoriosissimi	9	31	29	
38. Vos flores rosarum	10	32	30	
39. O vos imitatores	12	33	31	
40. O successores	11	34	32	
41. O mirum admirandum		28	33	
42. O viriditas digiti Dei		29	34	
43. O felix anima			35	
44. O beata infantia			36	
45. O presul vere civitatis		30	59	
46. O felix apparicio		35	37	2
47. O beatissime Ruperte		36	38	3
48. Quia felix puericia			39	
49. O Ierusalem		37	63	1
50. Mathias sanctus			57	
51. O Bonifaci			58	
52. O Euchari columba			60	
53. O Euchari in leta via			61	
54. Columba aspexit			62	
55. O pulcre facies	13	38	40	
56. O nobilissima viriditas	14	39	41	
57. O dulcissime amator		40	66	4
58. O Pater omnium		41	67	5

Incipit	*Scivias*	D	R	Miscellany
59. Rex noster promptus		42	46	
60. Spiritui sancto		43	43	
61. O rubor sanguinis		44	44	
62. Favus distillans		45	42	
63. In matutinis laudibus		46	45	
64. O Ecclesia		47	64	
65. Cum vox sanguinis		48	65	
66. O virgo Ecclesia		49	47	7
67. Nunc gaudeant		50	48	8
68. O orzchis Ecclesia			49	9
69. O choruscans lux stellarum			50	

Appendix

The *Symphonia* and the "Epilogue to the Life of Saint Rupert"

The text printed in Cardinal J.-B. Pitra's *Analecta sacra* under the title of "Epilogus ad Vitam S. Ruperti" (pp. 358–68) is in fact a miscellany of songs, homilies, letters, and dramatic materials, some of which appear independently in other manuscripts. Only the first three of its twenty-six lyrics have anything to do with Saint Rupert, so the title is evidently a misnomer. However, in the Riesenkodex the text follows Hildegard's *Vita S. Ruperti* without a break (fols. 404ʳ–407ᵛ), giving the impression that it is part of the same composition. The songs are written continuously and are in no way distinguished from the surrounding prose.

The existence of this baffling text raises several questions of interest to students of Hildegard's poetry. For instance, when was the miscellany compiled, by whom, and for what purpose? What were its original components, and in what contexts were they composed? Most important, are the song-texts in the miscellany prior or posterior to those in the *Symphonia*? And how are the significant differences to be explained? Not all these questions can be answered conclusively at the present stage of research. As a necessary first step, however, we can begin by dividing the miscellany into its component parts. The text as it appears in the Riesenkodex and in Pitra's edition seems to comprise at least ten independent segments:

(a) three songs that may form a genuine "epilogue to the life of Saint Rupert" (nos. 49, 46, 47);
(b) a prose text on creation, fall, and redemption with incipit "Primus sonus ita permansit," including the lyrical piece "O Verbum Patris" (Pitra, section I);
(c) a group of three lyrics dealing with nuns as brides of Christ: "O Fili dilectissime" (a prayer of Mary) followed by the "Symphonia virginum" and "Symphonia viduarum" (nos. 57, 58), along with "O magne Pater" (no. 6) and "O factura Dei" (Pitra, section II);
(d) a short dramatic exchange concerning schism, followed by three antiphons on the Church (nos. 66, 67, 68; Pitra, section III);
(e) three prayers to Christ and the Father (nos. 1, 5, 4) and three songs to the Virgin (nos. 15, 17, 20), connected by a short prose text (Pitra, section IV);
(f) a prose text on salvation history, followed by a sequence and hymn to the Holy Spirit (nos. 28, 27; Pitra, section V);
(g) a collection of political prophecies addressed to the Rupertsberg nuns (Pitra, section VI, p. 363);
(h) a text in praise of Mary with incipit "Spiritus sanctus," including the lyrical piece "O magna res" and nine Marian songs (nos. 19, 18, 16, 23, 8, 9, 11, 12, and 22; Pitra, section VI, p. 364);
(i) a general homily directed to the nuns (Pitra, section VII);
(j) a more specific homily in which Hildegard chastises the nuns for poor discipline and exhorts them to stricter observation of the Rule (Pitra, sections VIII–IX).

The segments are linked together with formulas such as "Iterumque vox de celo sonabat," which may be editorial. I have discovered two of these segments to date in other manuscripts, where they appear among Hildegard's correspondence. "Primus sonus" (b) appears in the early manuscript S, folio 28^{v}, and in V^{3}, folio 116^{r}, as an epistle ending with the prayer formula "Tu autem rex" in place of the lyrical "O Verbum Patris." The same manuscripts contain a letter with the incipit "Dominus dicit filiabus suis: In antiquo tempore Spiritus sanctus," continuing with the rest of (h) through "O magna res" (V^{3}, fol. 121^{r-v}); S, folios 53^{v}–54^{v}, continues with the nine Marian songs. Lieven Van Acker's forthcoming edition of Hildegard's correspondence for the *Corpus Christianorum: continuatio mediaevalis* may reveal additional sources for these so-called letters. Once the miscellany can be confidently broken down into its components, it may be easier to assess the place of the *Symphonia* lyrics in the liturgical life of the Rupertsberg.

As for dating, the internal evidence is not conclusive but points to the late 1150s. The three songs for Saint Rupert (a) form a fitting appendix to his *vita,* which Hildegard wrote with the double purpose of reviving the saint's cult and establishing her monastery's right to the lands that she claimed as his patrimony. The saint's life is linked with the songs by a passage recounting the decay and abandonment of Rupert's original monastery and the dispersion of its lands. Hildegard then refers to "a few vineyards belonging to the [former] church" of St. Rupert, which she and her nuns had bought from Bishop Hermann of Hildesheim and his brother Bernard (PL 197, 1092a). Hermann did not become bishop until 1162, but the sale evidently took place in 1155, a plausible date for the *vita.*[1] The episcopal title would have been added by a later scribe.

The antiphons and prose text in (d) refer to a schism that could have been the one precipitated by Arnold of Brescia in 1155 (see Commentary, no. 66). In homily (j), Hildegard again mentions schism, lamenting "the spiritual people who have torn [Christ's] robe and divided [his] garment," but she adds that "the time of ultimate schism (*plenitudinis schismatum*) has not yet come." Both allusions could refer to the papal schism provoked by Frederick Barbarossa in 1159, except that "Nunc gaudeant" (no. 67) celebrates the restoration of unity, which did not occur until Hildegard was 79. So here we have either a firm date of 1155 or a perplexing terminus a quo of 1159.

In the same segment (j), Hildegard complains about the worldliness of her nuns, which she says God "suffered for eight years, but for five years kept silent; for three years, however, [he] chastised them inwardly and outwardly." The chastisements pre-

[1]*Mainzer Urkundenbuch,* ed. Peter Acht (Darmstadt, 1968), vol. 2, pt. 1, p. 415 (no. 230). A charter from Archbishop Arnold of Mainz, dated May 1158, confirms the purchase. Hildegard's note in the *Vita S. Ruperti* identifies Hermann and Bernard as the sellers, but Bernard died in 1155 and the charter indicates a payment made to his sons.

sumably included their strife with the monks of St. Disibod as well as Hildegard's severe illness in the mid-1150s, during which she both saw and tasted the purgatorial sufferings described in her *Book of Life's Merits* (Pitra 367–68). Homily (j) therefore dovetails with the preface to that book and with the memoirs recorded in Hildegard's *Vita.* If the "eight years" began with the nuns' migration in 1150, the text could have been written no earlier than 1158, when Hildegard began writing the *Book of Life's Merits.* The various parts of the miscellany, then, appear to have been composed in the late 1150s.

We must next consider when the miscellany itself was compiled. The earliest manuscript of the complete text appears to be the Riesenkodex (1180s); but the other manuscript copy (V^2), while later, may be based on an older archetype.[2] In both sources the text is untitled, although in V^2 it begins with a new initial (fol. 155^r) after the three songs to Saint Rupert. Since the compilation of these diverse materials serves no apparent purpose, one can only assume that it was made by an editor of Hildegard's *Gesamtwerk* who wished to lose no scrap of inspired writing but knew nothing about the original context or purpose of these texts. In *Die Echtheit des Schrifttums der hl. Hildegard* (1956), Schrader and Führkötter proposed the abbess's nephew Wezelinus, provost of St. Andreas in Cologne, as principal editor of the Riesenkodex. More recently Van Acker has suggested that the earliest recension of Hildegard's letters, the archetype of V^2, dates back to Volmar's lifetime. Any one of her secretaries may have found a number of lyrical and homiletic fragments among Hildegard's "unpublished" papers, sensed a general affinity among them, and decided to copy the collection *faute de mieux* among the abbess's letters.[3] The frequent address, "o filiae meae," may have inspired

[2]This manuscript (Vienna, Nationalbibliothek, Cod. 963) dates from the thirteenth century. It contains many errors not found in R, and on folio 159^r there is an interpolation from the *Ordo virtutum* which R lacks. See Lieven Van Acker, "Der Briefwechsel der hl. Hildegard von Bingen," *Revue bénédictine* 98 (1988): 141–68. There are two fifteenth-century copies of the R letter collection: British Library, Cod. Add. 15102 and Harley 1725. There is a copy of the letters from V^2 in Trier, Stadtsbibliothek 722.

[3]The original compiler may even have been Guibert of Gembloux, who became Hildegard's secretary in 1177 and remained at the Rupertsberg until 1180. It is

the hypothesis that the documents were epistles to Hildegard's congregation, although some are patently homilies. The placement of the miscellany in the epistolary section of the Riesenkodex should not be taken too seriously, however, for several short works such as the *Vita S. Ruperti* and an exposition of the Athanasian Creed are placed there as well. So in fact are Hildegard's public sermons.

I have suggested above that the component texts were originally liturgical transcripts recording the lyrics that Hildegard composed for particular celebrations, the homilies she preached, and, in some cases, dramatic scenarios that the nuns performed. This hypothesis, based on an old speculation of Cardinal Pitra, seems to account best for the fragmentary nature of the collection and the alternation of lyrics with didactic and homiletic prose. If such was the case, however, the celebrations probably occurred during the 1150s. A compiler reviewing the texts two or three decades later, and one who was not a member of the community, may well have failed to recognize the origin of the material and may not even have realized that it included song-texts. Since the *Symphonia* itself was copied for the Riesenkodex by a different hand, the two scribes collaborating on the same grand project might not have known that they were duplicating material.

The question of priority must rest on a close comparison of the song-texts as they occur in the *Symphonia* and the miscellany. Perhaps the greatest difference, apart from the absence of music, lies in the omission of liturgical cues from the miscellany. Responsories are copied without their repetenda or doxologies, hymns without the amen, and other pieces without the alleluia. The liturgical *hodie* in no. 11 is replaced by *nunc,* and in five pieces the first person plural, appropriate to a praying community, is replaced by a more neutral third person (nos. 4, 5, 11, 15, 27). In two pieces, nos. 57 and 67, the miscellany text includes "prosy" connectives (*ideo, enim, autem*) which are less appropriate to liturgical chant and do not appear in the *Symphonia.* Finally, the

---

noteworthy that in the R miscellany Saint Rupert's name is consistently spelled *robertus,* the form current in Guibert's diocese of Liège, as opposed to the German forms *rupertus* in the *Symphonia* MSS. and *Ruoppertus* in V^2.

sequence "O Ierusalem" (no. 49) in the miscellany includes an entire strophe that does not appear in the *Symphonia*. The strophe is of purely local and historical interest to the nuns (it describes their migration from the monastery of St. Disibod to the Rupertsberg) and obviously does not belong in a sequence intended for widespread liturgical use. These differences suggest that the miscellany consists of rough, "in-house" transcriptions that Hildegard later revised to make them more suitable for liturgical celebrations outside the Rupertsberg. In her revisions she formalized the liturgical genre of each piece, substituted the more prayerful *nos* for the impersonal *mundus* or *homines*, polished the texts, and excised one obscure topical reference. It is also possible that the text-forms that survive in the miscellany predate the composition of the music, for it seems unlikely that Hildegard would delete several words and a whole strophe from the text if she had already created the melodies. Admittedly, however, the evidence is too thin to render these conclusions anything more than tentative speculations.

Whether or not the miscellany is prior to the *Symphonia*, it is clear that we are dealing with two independent recensions of the song-texts. Aside from the differences discussed above, I have counted nine "neutral," non-trivial variants where the miscellany texts in R^b and V^2 agree against the *Symphonia* texts in D and R^c. In addition, the two recensions were evidently corrected by different hands, for the *Symphonia* text contains five grammatical errors that are corrected in the miscellany, and the latter has three obvious errors that are corrected in the *Symphonia*. All these mistakes, unlike the purely scribal blunders, may be "authentic" in the sense that Hildegard's own grammar was notoriously shaky, and she often acknowledged her dependence on copy editors.

I have attempted to draw some broader conclusions from this analysis in the Introduction, pp. 9–11 above. My hope is that this preliminary investigation will spur other scholars to greater interest in this fascinating and neglected text.

Music and Text in Hildegard's Antiphons

BY

MARIANNE RICHERT PFAU

In her collection known as *Symphonia armonie celestium revelationum,* Saint Hildegard provides us not only with a wealth of poetic material, wide-ranging in scope and subject matter, but also with an extraordinary profusion of ecclesiastical song. These "novel songs," for which she was recognized as early as 1148,[1] present a musical repertory just as unique and in many ways just as challenging to the modern sensibility as the poetry of the *Symphonia.*

Although it is vital to apply specialized knowledge to each facet of Hildegard's artistic creation—that is, to treat the poetic texts from linguistic and literary points of view, and the music from an informed musical perspective—such separation of text and music should not be allowed to obscure the fundamental unity of the artwork. Ideally, literary and musical analysis should merge in a final interpretation of any individual song as well as of the repertory as a whole.

Analyses of Hildegard's compositions have tended to concentrate either on text or on music, focusing on one to the exclusion of the other. But the interaction between the two elements and

[1]Peter Dronke, *Poetic Individuality in the Middle Ages* (Oxford, 1970): 153, n. 11.

their mutual enrichment has hardly been addressed.[2] To fully appreciate the beauty of this work it is essential to experience text and music as an aesthetic whole, as the unity it was for Hildegard.

The general issue of text-music relations in medieval composition demands careful scrutiny. As a result of the probing work of Ritva Jonsson and Leo Treitler, it is now impossible to uphold the old view that the medieval composers were supposedly indifferent to the texts they were setting.[3] These authors have argued to the contrary, positing a most intimate relationship of text and music in *cantus* that rests primarily on syntactic parallels rather than on affect.

An integrated approach to music and text is particularly appropriate for Hildegard's compositions because of her claim to have received these pieces in her visions. Although the fact that many of the texts survive in a prose context without music as well as in the musical context of the *Symphonia* makes this claim difficult to interpret,[4] I will proceed on the assumption that Hildegard actually heard her pieces as text-music compounds, as unified expressions of the divine inspiration that sustained her. Such a view of Hildegard's songs also accords with the medieval conception of melody as a movement of the voice, as *cantus* declaiming language through melodic inflections, which is the basis of all medieval Western notational systems.[5]

Any attempt to bring the intimate connection of text and music

[2]A notable exception is the discussion by Barbara Thornton (*Ordo virtutum*, Sequentia Ensemble [Deutsche Harmonia mundi, 1982], jacket notes). As a performer of this repertory, Thornton expresses the perspective of one who must of necessity confront the problems pertaining to both words and music. The interaction of words and music has not, however, been discussed from a theoretical perspective. Even John Stevens, in *Words and Music in the Middle Ages: Song, Narrative, Dance, and Drama, 1050–1350* (Cambridge, 1986): 397–99, is silent on this issue as it relates to Hildegard's songs.

[3]Ritva Jonsson and Leo Treitler, "Medieval Music and Language: A Reconsideration of the Relationship," in *Studies in the History of Music*, vol. 1, *Music and Language* (New York, 1983): 1–23.

[4]Peter Dronke, "Problemata Hildegardiana," *Mittellateinisches Jahrbuch* 16 (1981): 99–100.

[5]Leo Treitler, "Reading and Singing: On the Genesis of Occidental Music-Writing," in *Early Music History* (New York, 1984), 4: 145–46.

in Hildegard's *Symphonia* into focus, however, must be rooted in a familiarity with her compositional style. When first approaching one of Hildegard's compositions, a modern audience might ask what it is that gives shape to the piece; how the composer projects a sense of form, syntax, balance; how she achieves variety or unity, contrast or resemblance, dynamic tension or repose. Further, one might wish to understand how these diverse elements cohere and how they unite to set the characteristic tone and expressive quality of a composition.

The song "O successores" (no. 40) is in many ways a model of structural control. A listener who might initially be taken with the shifting expressive quality within the piece will soon become aware of the high degree of order that governs the melodic unfolding. The opening phrase fulfills the function of an intonation in that it sets up one central pitch—the final D—as a reference point for the piece as a whole.[6] In phrase 1 this D is repeatedly circumscribed from above (F–E–D) and below (C–D). It thus constitutes the tonal fulcrum of each small melodic motion. While at first the intervallic span around this D-axis comprises no more than a third above and a tone below, the sound space widens over the course of phrases 2 and 3 to include a fifth above (D/a) and a fourth below (D/A). Phrase 4 gravitates toward the lower spectrum of this space in its slightly extended approach to the final. Thus, throughout the first four phrases, Hildegard explores and defines an overall sound space of an octave (A–a), placing the pitch on which all melodic motion comes to rest (D) in the center of this space.

Soon, however, the upper registral boundary (a) seems too narrow a ceiling. Without any preparation, phrase 5 dramatically

[6]The transcriptions of the compositions provide the reading of the source indicated. Variants are given in M.-I. Ritscher, OSB, *Kritischer Bericht* (Salzburg: Otto Müller Verlag, 1969). The layout offered here is determined by my analysis of the musical phrasing. Staves without clefs continue the previous phrase. Small note heads represent individual *puncti*. Following common practice, slurs reflect compound neumes, liquescent neumes are indicated by a slash, and b-flats over the staves are editorial. All analytical annotations appear in parentheses. Pitches are labeled according to the medieval gamut: Gamma A B C D E F G a b/b-flat c d e f g a' b' c' d'.

expands as it departs from this former upper extreme into a new and higher register. For a while, this greatly enlarged vertical dimension (A–d) serves the new affective quality of the setting well. Phrase 6, which emphasizes the high range of this new sound spectrum, is somewhat balanced by the low phrases 7 and 8. But the last and longest phrase (9) breaks open even this extended space, catapulting up from the rising fifths of phrases 6, 7, and 8 to a new height (f). The definitive ascent of phrase 9 stands in notable contrast to the provisional one of phrase 6, and the high vocal extreme is immensely effective. Coming near the end of the piece, this final expansion creates a strong sense of climax for the setting as a whole.

Thus the sense of an overall formal dynamic in "O successores" derives in part from expanding sound spaces. But how the melodies move within each of these spaces is also significant and equally compositionally controlled. In the present antiphon setting those phrases which keep to the initial limited spectrum characteristically display stepwise melodic motion, enlivened by some skips of a third, while those moving within the ensuing extended sound spaces exhibit large upward skips spanning the important fifths D–a and fourths a–(c)–d. The coordination of these two principles—narrow sound space with prevailing conjunct melodic motion (phrases 1 through 4), expanded space with disjunct motion (phrases 5 through 9)—in this antiphon setting not only signals a twofold overall formal scheme but is responsible to a large degree for investing this scheme with its sense of climax.

From a closer perspective, too, the notion of sound space allows a clear perception of Hildegard's principles of internal ordering. Phrase 2 sets up a sequence of melodic events which becomes normative for the piece as a whole. The first melodic event [a] explores the space from the final to the fifth above (D–a), traversing it in terms of a simple and balanced melodic curve. The second event [x] constitutes a brief "dipping down" to A, placed near the middle of the phrase. A cadential event [y] concludes the overall melodic motion, approaching the final both from above (F) and from below (C).

Throughout the piece as a whole the medial and the cadential units [x and y] occur together and are generally stable. The characteristic skips from C to A and back to C, because they are variably placed, serve to blur the boundaries between them. These events are structural insofar as they segment the setting into clearly distinguished musical phrases. Within each of the two major sections (phrases 1 through 4 and phrases 5 through 9) the large-scale form relies heavily upon motivic resemblances. The layout of the musical example clarifies these structural similarities, especially where surface details tend to hide the common underlying order.

Despite the repetitive formal scheme, Hildegard's work produces an impression of melodic flexibility. This effect can be attributed to her skillful introduction of changes in surface detail. By adding or omitting individual pitches or pitch groups in the melodic patterns, Hildegard constantly stretches or contracts the melodic fabric. Elements c and d of phrase 5 form the basis for the soaring arch [c+, d] of phrase 9. In contrast, the three internal elements of phrase 6—b, c, and d—are compressed and fused together in phrases 7 and 8. Finally, the cadential element [y] undergoes both pronounced expansions and contractions. The extremes appear in close succession at the ends of phrases 8 and 9 [y and y+]. As a whole, the setting provides a most lucid example of Hildegard's typically asymmetric melodic parallelisms, illustrating the composer's ability to enliven her motivic resonances through graceful melodic decoration.

These examples of asymmetry in "O successores" show that such intriguing irregularities affect not simply melodic detail but, more important, the pacing of melodic events within the context of the musical process at large.[7] They give a characteristic proselike quality to this setting which unfolds against the highly structured formal background. But this proselike quality is not simply a hallmark of Hildegard's compositional style; rather, it seems directly linked to the nature of the text she sets. The "irregular prose quality" sensed in the music is, in fact, a characteristic of the text, so the flexibility of melodic line is best understood as a response to textual idiosyncrasies.

Similarly, the overall formal plan of the musical setting must be

[7]Previous analysis has tended to "reduce" Hildegard's compositional style to a patchwork of melodic stock motives, disregarding the dynamic aspects of an integrated musical process. See Ludwig Bronarski, *Die Lieder der hl. Hildegard: Ein Beitrag zur Geschichte der geistlichen Musik des Mittelalters* (Leipzig, 1922); Joseph Schmidt-Görg, "Die Gesänge der heiligen Hildegard," in Pudentiana Barth, M.-I. Ritscher, and Joseph Schmidt-Görg, eds., *Hildegard von Bingen: Lieder* (Salzburg, 1969): 9–16.

seen as a reflection of the text, for it accords with a specific parsing of the poetry. A clear illustration of this text-music coordination can be seen at the juncture of phrases 4 and 5, that is, between the two major sections of the piece. Not only does Hildegard introduce a new melodic element [c] to mark the beginning of the new section, but phrase 5 is the only one in this setting which takes off from a new, unmediated tonal plane (the fifth a). In the context this subtlety suffices to create the comparatively strongest musical articulation. It is carefully coordinated with the strongest articulation in the text, signaled by the word *sicut;* thus the musical syntax can be said to parallel the inner structure of the text itself. The consistency of this parallel is evident in the musical layout, in the transcription that provides a parsing equally plausible for the poetic lines and for the musical composition.

Another vital indication of text-music interaction is in the differentiation between neumatic and melismatic passages. The present antiphon setting departs only once from the prevailing declamatory texture. Clearly, the singular melisma on *agni* in the final phrase (9) serves as much to provide a musically convincing and compositionally satisfying aesthetic closure as to reflect the textual climax with which the poem concludes.

"O successores" makes it plain that an appreciation of Hildegard's musical decisions often relies upon considerations of textual aspects. In the antiphon setting "O quam mirabilis" (no. 3), we can see that Hildegard's musical response is similarly governed by textual characteristics, but the markedly different formal structure of this poem results in a rather different musical setting.

The tripartite syntactic structure of this poem, which projects an image of divine foreknowledge, is delineated by two outer statements of praise (phrases 1–3 and 6–7) flanking a central expository truth (phrases 4–5). A number of subordinate units appear within this frame, all introduced by relative pronouns (*que, quem, que*). The smallest syntactic groups generally consist of two or three words. With its various hierarchical levels of syntax, "O quam mirabilis" is one of Hildegard's more complex antiphon texts.

The music matches the textual structure in a way that reminds us even more strongly than does "O successores" of the pervasive medieval tradition in which the "composition and analysis of melodies follows the segmentation of language, establishing a phrase hierarchy articulated by the counterparts of the commas, colons, and periods."[8] Perhaps the best-known exponent of this

[8]Jonsson and Treitler, "Medieval Music and Language" 7.

theoretical tradition, a certain John, writes in his *De musica* of about 1100:

> Just as in prose three kinds of *distinctiones* are recognized, which can also be called "pauses"—namely, the colon, that is, "member"; the comma or *incisio;* and the period, *clausula* or *circuitus*—so also it is in chant. In prose, where one makes a pause in reading aloud, this is called a colon; when the sentence is divided by an appropriate punctuation mark, it is called a comma; when the sentence is brought to an end, it is a period. . . . Likewise, when a chant makes a pause by dwelling on the fourth or fifth note above the final, there is a colon; when in mid-course it returns to the final, there is a comma; when it arrives at the final at the end, there is a period.[9]

In this passage the interrelation of words and music is expounded through concrete analogies between syntax in language and melodic structure in chant. As might be expected, Hildegard's music does not exactly reflect John's precepts, but her musical shaping can be discerned well enough against such a theoretical background. Whether or not Hildegard knew this particular passage from John, it is conceivable that she was aware of such parallels between structures of language and music drawn by contemporary theorists, for these parallels not only informed the understanding of the vast repertory of chant sung by ecclesiastics in the daily celebration of the liturgy, they had also become a normative principle for composing new song.

Although John apparently had in mind texts that defined the hierarchical structure of larger sense units through a system of visual clues—actual punctuation marks—such clues are missing from Hildegard's texts. Neither musical manuscript of the *Symphonia* bears any indication of internal punctuation. Yet, when the same texts are transmitted without neumes in other contexts, the scribes often provide punctuation.[10] This fact suggests that the musical phrasing itself furnishes the essential clues for internal

[9]Claude Palisca, ed., *Hucbald, Guido, and John on Music: Three Medieval Treatises,* trans. Warren Babb (New Haven, 1978): 116.

[10]An inventory of internal punctuation marks is provided in my dissertation: "Hildegard von Bingen's *Symphonia:* A Musical Analysis and Contextual Study" (Ph.D. diss., SUNY at Stony Brook, 1988).

segmentation of the texts. It provides clear evidence that, like the earliest musical notations, Hildegard's comparatively late neumatic notation replaces other visual clues about the parsing of these texts, making commas and periods redundant.[11] The way in which syntactic correlations between text and music manifest themselves in her songs varies in each individual case. There can be no simple linear parallelisms, but in any event the phenomenon of the differing transmission of Hildegard's songs in prose and lyrical contexts points to a conception of this repertory as performed reality of sound, either as poetry to be read aloud or as song to be sung.

In "O quam mirabilis" each of the largest sense units is marked by an arrival on the final c. Every internal articulation signaled by a pronoun in the text is reflected by a melodic return to the same pitch. Furthermore, most smaller syntactic textual units coincide with an internal melodic arrival on the fifth g. And, finally, the phrase with the greatest number of syllables (5) has a minor musical articulation after *sua* on the third e. Thus the final c functions as primary tonal goal, while g forms a secondary tonal focus, and e provides a subordinate internal articulation.

Although in "O quam mirabilis" this kind of musical hierarchization does not completely correspond to textual parsing, the two structural principles do run parallel through most of the setting. With the exception of the primary cadential arrival (on the final c) on the word *forma* in phrase 5, which is puzzling because it suggests a musical division where none exists in the text, musical and textual syntax mirror each other consistently enough to allow the musically and textually plausible grouping of phrases shown in the transcription.

In this composition, as in "O successores," sound spaces that hinge on the three focal pitches are carefully delineated. The course the voice takes through each of these spaces is meticulously controlled, and the tonal context coloring each individual pitch is precisely calculated.[12] In this piece, however, the final is

[11]Treitler, "Reading and Singing" 147.

[12]Guido of Arezzo and Hermannus Contractus both define the individual tone in terms of the intervallic patterns that surround it. Guido calls this quality—for him an essential aspect of any individual tone—its *modus vocum*. In many of

located at the bottom of the overall sound space (c–g–c′), not in the middle, as in the previous setting.

Again as in "O successores" the spaces of a fifth and a fourth are exceptionally well defined, and from *prescientia divini pectoris* on (phrase 2), are used with great consistency. In its clear tripartite structure this second phrase is paradigmatic for the piece as a whole. The first melodic gesture [a] begins its ascent with a characteristic skip of a third, surpasses the goal pitch by a tone, and pauses on g. The medial element [b] departs from this g, ascends to c′ (in subsequent phrases this ascent is often marked by another rising third), and returns to g. The third period [c], with its bold profile marked by a big downward leap (g–c), confirms the final by traversing an ancillary f/b-flat space, before coming to rest on its starting point, c. The process of phrase 2 as a whole results in a balanced gestalt of an arch that, in its internal tripartite shaping, parallels the large-scale three-part form of the piece. This rather unusual integration of formal levels—not generally found in chant—reflects Hildegard's concern with formal and conceptual unity so amply evidenced in her work at large.

The structural parallelisms are even more strict in "O quam mirabilis" than in "O successores," for here all subsequent phrases repeat the three paradigmatic melodic events of phrase 2. Although details within these repetitions change, the composition comes to life primarily through the remarkable extensions of both horizontal and vertical dimensions at the culmination of each of the three major sections. The first of these extensions occurs on *faciem hominis quem formavit* in phrase 4, where the c no longer appears as base for the two sound spaces of fifth and fourth but is enveloped for the first time within an overall G–g context. The descent (c–a–G) on *quem,* which introduces a low register not heard before in the setting, is itself a rather striking motivic ges-

Hildegard's compositions, the degree to which these tonal qualities are defined itself functions as an aesthetic force. See Palisca, ed., *Hucbald, Guido, and John on Music* 63–65, 110–12; Leonard Ellinwood, ed., "Musica Hermanni Contracti," *Eastman School of Music Studies* 2 (1952): 57. See also Matthias Bielitz, "Einzelton, Intervall und melodische Bewegung," in *Musik und Grammatik: Studien zur mittelalterlichen Musiktheorie* (Munich, 1977): 124–30.

ture that finds reverberations in the concluding phrase on *(susci) - ta (-vit)*.

An intriguing manipulation of dimensions occurs in the middle of the work (phrase 5), again at a place in the text which emphasizes the human element of creation, *opera sua / in eadem forma hominis / integra aspexit*. Here the balance among the three melodic events a, b, and c seems reversed. Elements a and b are fused together, making a rapid ascent to the high c′ which greatly concentrates the melodic energy. As though to offset this extreme compression, element c is drawn out, dwelling for the first time on the low spectrum of the antiphon's sound space. This downward orientation brings with it an insistence on the f/b-flat descent which solidifies the darkened tonal quality of the final already evident in the opening section of the piece.

The last extension of element c on *suscitavit* illustrates Hildegard's exceptional sensitivity to nuance. Not only is its placing appropriate to the text—the object of phrase 7 as a whole is *hominem*—but the many melodic skips on *suscitavit* resonate with the animated quality of the poetic imagery. Furthermore, by enlarging the profile of the previous f/b-flat descent by a tone (g/b-flat) in the very last neumatic group of the setting, Hildegard strengthens the degree of closure, at the same time recalling with this closing of the whole the closing of the first part. Such musical references create associations among the three sense units and the ideas they project. Here, they draw together images of the human who for Hildegard occupies the most prominent place in all creation.

Having observed correspondences in text and music, we should consider some of the "nonparallels" as well—a far more difficult and often perplexing endeavor. The musical cadential inflection at *forma*—in the middle of phrase 5—for example, does not, however, seem quite as inconsistent with the text when we consider the setting as a whole. Through the growing insistence on melodic elements c and c′ in phrases 4 and 5, Hildegard seems to lend special emphasis to the striking density of phonetic sounds at *faciem hominis, formavit,* and *forma hominis* which produces the concentration of imagery in the poem.

Similarly, the obvious independence of textual and musical designs in the repeated exclamation *o quam mirabilis est* may be understood in terms of the overall dynamic of the unfolding composition. If we look at the text as a purely static structure, the recurrence of the exclamation marking the third section of the poem will appear as just that, a recurrence. But Hildegard avoids both a musical repetition of the opening melodic phrase—a wise choice for purely compositional reasons alone—and a parallel musical syntax that might have resulted in a new phrase on *inspiratio*. Rather than simply referring back to the initial musical "intonation," which, as it turns out, is close in character to the cadential element c, she chooses instead to continue the melodic process that leads to a fusion of segments a and b, with the result that *o quam mirabilis est* of phrase 6 receives new direction and energy. This choice of a new melodic phrase seems appropriate, for as the text evolves, the exclamation acquires a rather specific context of meaning and accumulates definite semantic overtones. Thus when it is heard the second time it bears a very different sense from the general and universal expression of awe in phrase 1. While we cannot know what considerations might have guided Hildegard's compositional choices, the sense of the unfolding image in the text may have influenced her decision not to select a kind of A–B–A form but instead to seek a continuously evolving musical idiom for her antiphon text. In this case, such an idiom undoubtedly serves both the purely musical requirements and the textual dynamic.

The antiphon in praise of the feminine quality of Love, "Karitas habundat" (no. 25),[13] while also relying very much on melodic resemblance, seems to gain its propelling force from the *homoioteleuton* in the text rather than from the dynamic unfolding of a complex topos, as occurs in "O quam mirabilis." In this piece the striking density of "i" and "a" sounds in the text elicits a musical response that effects a more definite shape of the poem than is suggested by textual parsing alone. Through the recurring caden-

[13]Christoph Hohlfeld, *Geistliche Musik des Mittelalters und der Renaissance: Hildegard von Bingen*, Instrumentalkreis Helga Weber (TELDEC Hamburg, 1980), jacket notes; facsimile in jacket.

tial figures in the music, descending in a similar fashion to the final D, the recurring vowel sounds in the text attain their status as shaping agents of the poetic lines. Thus, while the single-minded phonetic quality of the text inspires similar musical responses, the music—by emphasizing this particular textual aspect—in turn clarifies the poetic parsing. Furthermore, the musical rhymes seem to deepen the "meditation" on the image of Divine Love which is central to the poem, for the aural associations of *i* and *a* they help bring into relief are probably inspired by the phonetic property of the word *karitas* itself.

But text and music are integrated at a yet deeper level than that of phonetic parallelism. The musical process allows Hildegard to express more forcefully the inner dynamic of her poem. A comparison of the opening melodic figure on *Karitas* (phrase 1) with that on the final word *dedit* (phrase 5) shows that the two are so closely related that some observers would probably consider them a single recurring "motive." The opening figure, however, is confined to the rather common skip of a fifth plus third (D–a–c), which results in an overall traverse of a seventh. But on *dedit* the figure is stretched vertically to span a full octave (D–a–d). By reason of this vertical expansion alone, *dedit* becomes a special moment in the piece.

Other factors intensify the climactic moment of this last phrase. Most notably, the placement throughout the setting of the high d seems responsible for the increasing musical energy. In phrase 2 the high boundary pitch is reached by the short approach of a–c–d (note the resonance of the syllable *de*). In phrase 4 the same approach is prefaced by a lower lead-in (D–A/a–c–d), preparing the placement of d on the word *summo*. On *dedit,* however, the entire octave span of D–d is embraced in one bold gesture, a move that produces a concentration of musical energy which carries through the extended final melisma. Phrase 4 nicely prepares this new level of melodic energy, for it is the only one that does not return to the final but remains high at the end. Thus the extended closing section (phrases 4 and 5) is not at all built on a mere routine recurrence of a typical melodic motive, but, through the interplay of the various factors discussed here, evolves as the most expressive moment of the setting as a whole.

It might be added that the melodic reminiscence of the opening gesture contained in the final stretched-out figure on *dedit* allows Hildegard to refer again to *Karitas,* the subject of the terminal verb. Significantly, too, this melodic association comes just at the point where the text departs from the pattern of *homoioteleuton*. Through this melodic reference the music further intensifies the single-mindedness of the text, in effect centering the setting as a whole on its principal image of *Karitas*.

In the pieces we have examined up to this point, Hildegard relies heavily on various structural parallels and resemblances. The sixteen Marian songs, however, which form a distinct group

within her *Symphonia,* are built essentially on contrast. In one way or another, all the poems are based on the opposing roles of woman in salvation history, embodied in the figures of Eve and Mary. Two antiphon settings from this group illustrate how the composer responds to this contrast.

In "Cum erubuerint" (no. 14), Hildegard expresses the opposition in a remembrance of the fall set against the sound of Mary's redeeming voice, which she credits with the power to transform human fate. Three major syntactic units mark the text: *Cum erubuerint . . . casus, tunc . . . voce,* and *hoc . . . casu.* The echo of *casus/casu* links the two outer units both semantically and phonetically. The contrasting medial unit, *tunc tu clamas clara voce,* functions in its syntactic position as a center around which the two outer segments are balanced. The longer and syntactically more complex outer statements set this principal clause in relief.

Melodically, this tripartite structure of the text is articulated by the initial, medial, and final melismas of phrases 1, 3, and 5—on *Cum,* on *cla-(ra voce),* and on *casu*—which stand out from the prevailing syllabic texture of the setting. The brief piece derives much of its compelling force from a process of expansion in which these melismas grow from fourteen notes to sixteen to forty-eight (!) and concurrently expand from the range of a fourth, to an octave, to a fourth plus octave. These vertical expansions are strategically placed near the beginning of each melisma.

The first of the three melismas (*Cum*) establishes the tonal reference system for the piece, grounding it on E. Its three internal units circumscribe the final, barely moving away from it as they define it within a D/G melodic context. The melisma on the words *cla(-ra voce),* in contrast, moves within a higher and at the same time much larger sound space than does the initial melisma on *Cum.* After setting up the fifth (b) within a context of G, the melody elevates itself via the third d to the climactic pitch g. The word boundary is marked by a brief return to the modal fourth e first introduced on *cla(-mas)* near the opening of phrase 3. From here on, the melody descends over the last text syllable to come to rest on its beginning pitch. The high boundary tone g, which functions as pivot of the melodic curve, is situated almost perfectly at the mid-point of the phrase.[14] Furthermore, the singular d–g′ skip on *cla(-ra)* resonates with the first pronounced skip (D–g) of the initial melisma on *Cum,* pointing again to Hildegard's sense of large-scale integration.

The last and longest melisma, over the culminating word *casu,* not only presents a climactic continuation of the musical process by reason of its sheer length, but it traverses such an extensive range that the effect is stunning, immensely heightening the intensity of the setting as a whole. Beginning on an extremely low pitch not heard before, the B below the final, the melody soars up

[14]Pozzi Escot, "The Gothic Cathedral and Hidden Geometry of St. Hildegard," *Sonus* 5 (1984): 14–31.

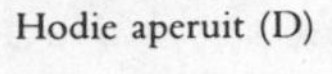

(1) Ho- di- e

(2) a- pe- ru- it

(3) no- bis

(4) clau- sa por- ta

(5) quod ser- pens in mu- li- e- re suf- fo- ca- vit

(6) un- de lu- cet in au- ro- ra

(7) flos de Vir- gi- ne

(7)* (R) flos de Vir- gi- ne

(0) Ma- ri- a. e v o v a e

through the entire modal octave over F to high c. The subsequent long descent, which eventually brings the melody to rest on the final, only partially resolves this thrust. On the whole, the choice of a continually evolving mode of expression for "Cum erubuerint," leading up to this climax, seems to lend special emphasis to the redeeming power of Mary, signified by her clear voice, and to call humanity to celebrate its new freedom from the consequences of the fall.

In the short antiphon "Hodie aperuit" (no. 11), another setting within the group of Marian songs, the opposing manifestations in salvation history of "woman fallen" and "woman redeeming" are projected through the contrasting images of serpent and flower. The stress is clearly on the *flos de Virgine Maria* that glistens in the dawn as sign of mankind's freedom from the suffocating power of the serpent. Musically, the setting is characterized throughout by ornate melismatic phrases of varying lengths. Significantly, the one exception coincides with the remembrance of the serpent's destructive power. While the melismatic lines of phrases 1 through 4 describe flexible, animated contours, the more declamatory serpent passage interrupts this fluidity. The passage in effect divides the two major sections of the setting. In the first part the melody generally gravitates downward, while from *unde lucet* on, it soars, reaching an extraordinary culmination on the word *flos*.

The differences of melodic direction and range which seem to be motivated by the contrasting images in the text also coincide with an opposition involving the tonal reference system for the final c. In the first long melisma on *Hodie,* c emerges very clearly as the central pitch within the overall sound space of the octave G–g. Beginning with phrase 2, however, c appears in a new context, within the space of the octave F–f. This overall downward shift by a tone effects an exchange of the fourth and fifth spaces around the central c. Even more important, it effects a transformation of the quality of the tone c itself. Under the new reference system, the stepwise descents from b-flat to F, and correspondingly from high f down to b-flat, take on more than a motivic character.

The two reference systems are a generating force in the unfolding piece. While the phrase on *clausa porta* (4) clearly shifts back to the initial G context, a gradual transformation from the G to the F context occurs within the following phrase, *quod serpens in muliere suffocavit* (5). From here on, the phrases alternate between the two systems, so that their interplay becomes an integral part of the general process of the piece.

In the second part, the F-context provides a tonal anchor for the fantastic upward surge toward the climax on *flos*. More astonishing yet, it also provides the tonal context at the conclusion of the piece. Thus the setting begins in one tonal reference system but ends in another. Such large-scale transformation is remarkably bold. It is neither frequent in Hildegard's own musical composition nor common in the liturgical chant repertory of her day. Contemporary music theory provides for such mixtures only in terms of exceptions. Clearly, then, the setting is in many ways extraordinary, even eccentric.

This eccentricity may in fact have seemed too bold to those transmitting the work, for "Hodie aperuit" survives in two rather different versions. Generally, musical variants in the two main neumated sources for Hildegard's *Symphonia* involve minor changes as well as some obvious copying errors. In the case of "Hodie aperuit," however, the changes involve substantive conceptual matters. The most decisive disparity concerns the passage in phrase 7 from the middle of *flos* to *de Virgine*. The entire section is written a fifth lower in R than it is in the earlier source D, whose transcription is offered here. In this case, the registral shift does not seem to be a mere mistake, for the scribe has added a few notes as well as b-flat signs that alter the tonal plan of the section. These changes suggest deliberate redaction. This observation would seem to support the generally accepted view of R as a purposefully edited source. But whether the "editing" here reflects Hildegard's wishes and constitutes a reworking of her piece or whether it is a "correction" by another hand motivated by different aesthetic principles—or more prosaically by practical reasons related to performance—is an open question. Although neither reading can be judged as "wrong," the version in D may be the more "authentic," as it is in keeping both with Hildegard's preference for registral extremes and her power to integrate such extremes within the overall dynamic conception of her work.

The kinds of continuities between language and music I have focused on here represent too complex an issue to be exhausted in a brief investigation of a small number of songs. As I hope I have shown, however, it is this approach that will yield important evidence of how Hildegard herself, through her music, projects the inner dynamics of her poetic texts, an aspect of her composition too easily overlooked.

Having grown accustomed to measuring text-music relationship almost exclusively in terms of affective expressiveness—a procedure well suited to eighteenth- and nineteenth-century repertories but not necessarily to medieval composition—we have tended to underestimate parallels between musical and textual syntax. Such parallels, however, often provide the most valuable clues about the "performance" of Hildegard's poetic texts—not simply about their actual delivery but, more important, about the process of the unfolding images, realized in the unfolding musical sound that makes immediate, "present," the visionary truth whose vivid expression must be regarded as Hildegard's ultimate goal.

As has been suggested in the preceding analyses, the words and music in Hildegard's compositions are mutually influential. The text determines many musical choices; the music may clarify textual syntax and large-scale form that in turn contribute to the meaning. While each of the antiphons we have analyzed here has a different musical shape, reflecting textual idiosyncrasies, it is striking to see that all but one of the five settings follow a musical process that concludes in climax. This pattern makes us wonder whether Hildegard deliberately plants important words at the end of these poems in order to allow for a final musical high point, or whether her apparent preference for dynamic musical forms invigorates the poems with a more pronounced sense of growth and climax than might be projected by the words alone. However this may be in the individual song and in the repertory as a whole, this ascending quality of her music certainly reveals something of the joy in celebrating the celestial harmony to which Hildegard's *Symphonia* invites her audience.

Symphonia armonie celestium revelationum

TEXT AND TRANSLATIONS

I
Father and Son

1. O vis eternitatis

O vis eternitatis
que omnia ordinasti in corde tuo,
per Verbum tuum omnia creata sunt
sicut voluisti,
et ipsum Verbum tuum
induit carnem
in formatione illa
que educta est de Adam.

Et sic indumenta ipsius
a maximo dolore
abstersa sunt.

O quam magna est benignitas Salvatoris
qui omnia liberavit
per incarnationem suam,
quam divinitas exspiravit
sine vinculo peccati.

Et sic indumenta ipsius
a maximo dolore
abstersa sunt.

Gloria Patri et Filio
et Spiritui sancto.

Et sic indumenta ipsius
a maximo dolore
abstersa sunt.

17–24 *om.* R^b, V^2

1. Responsory for the Creator

Strength of the everlasting!
In your heart you invented
order.
Then you spoke the word and
all that you ordered
was,
just as you wished.

And your word put on vestments
woven of flesh
cut from a woman
born of Adam
to bleach the agony out of his clothes.

The Savior is grand and kind!
from the breath of God he took flesh
unfettered
(for sin was not in it)
to set everything free
and bleach the agony out of his clothes.

Glorify the Father,
the Spirit and the Son.

He bleached the agony out of his clothes.

O strength of eternity, / you ordained all things in your heart. / By your Word all things were created / as you willed, / and your own Word / put on flesh / in that form / that was taken from Adam. // And thus his garments / were cleansed / from the greatest suffering. // O how great is the Savior's kindness! / He delivered all things / by his incarnation, / which the Godhead breathed forth / with no chain of sin. // And thus his garments / were cleansed / from the greatest suffering.

2. O virtus Sapientie

O virtus Sapientie,
que circuiens circuisti,
comprehendendo omnia
in una via que habet vitam,
tres alas habens,
quarum una in altum volat
et altera de terra sudat
et tercia undique volat.
Laus tibi sit, sicut te decet,
o Sapientia.

3. O quam mirabilis

O quam mirabilis est
prescientia divini pectoris
que prescivit omnem creaturam.
Nam cum Deus inspexit
faciem hominis quem formavit,
omnia opera sua
in eadem forma hominis
integra aspexit.
O quam mirabilis est inspiratio
que hominem sic suscitavit.

2. Antiphon for Divine Wisdom

Sophia!
you of the whirling wings,
circling encompassing
energy of God:

you quicken the world in your clasp.

One wing soars in heaven
one wing sweeps the earth
and the third flies all around us.

Praise to Sophia!
Let all the earth praise her!

O energy of Wisdom! / you circled, circling, / encompassing all things / in one path possessed of life. / Three wings you have: / one of them soars on high, / the second exudes from the earth, / and the third flutters everywhere. / Praise to you, as befits you, / O Wisdom!

3. Antiphon for the Creator

Marvel at the heart
divining, at the hand
designing.

He modeled the head
of a single man -
and saw, in that globe of clay,
the world in sum.

O marvel!
God was inspired and Adam
breathed, looked
about him, lived.

O how marvelous is / the foreknowledge of the heart of God, / that foreknew all creation. / For when God looked / on the face of the man he had formed, / he saw all his works whole / in the form of that man. / O how marvelous is the breath of the Spirit / that roused man to life!

4. O pastor animarum

O pastor animarum
et o prima vox
per quam omnes creati sumus,
nunc tibi, tibi placeat
ut digneris
nos liberare de miseriis
et languoribus nostris.

---

3 creati sumus] creature create sunt R^b, V^2 4 nunc tibi] nunc pater R^b, V^2 6 nos] tuos R^b, V^2 7 nostris] suis R^b, V^2

5. O cruor sanguinis

O cruor sanguinis
qui in alto sonuisti,
cum omnia elementa
se implicuerunt
in lamentabilem vocem
cum tremore,
quia sanguis Creatoris sui
illa tetigit,
ungue nos
de languoribus nostris.

---

4 inplicuerunt R^c 9 unge V^2; nos] tuos R^b, V^2 10 de vulneribus suis R^b, V^2

4. Antiphon for the Redeemer

Pastor of our hearts and voice
primordial:
you spoke before the world was,
we sprang to hear.
Now we languish,
we are wretched, ill.
Set us free! we beseech,
make us well.

O shepherd of souls, / O primal voice / by which we all were created: / now let it be / your good pleasure / to set us free from our miseries / and our diseases.

5. Antiphon for the Redeemer

Blood that bled into a cry!
The elements
felt its touch and trembled,
heaven heard their woe.
O life-blood of the maker,
scarlet music, salve our wounds.

O outpoured blood / that resounded on high, / when all the elements / folded themselves / into a voice of lament / with trembling: / for the blood of their Creator / touched them! / Anoint us, / heal our diseases.

6. O magne Pater

O magne Pater,
in magna necessitate sumus.
Nunc igitur obsecramus,
obsecramus te
per Verbum tuum,
per quod nos constituisti plenos
quibus indigemus.
Nunc placeat tibi, Pater,
quia te decet,
ut aspicias in nos
per adiutorium tuum,
ut non deficiamus,
et ne nomen tuum in nobis obscuretur,
et per ipsum nomen tuum
dignare nos adiuvare.

3 obsecramus *om.* V[2] 8 Nunc] quod R[b], V[2] 15 adiuvarere R[c]

6. Antiphon for God the Father

Father.
Great is our need and we beg,
we beg with a word that was
fullness within us:
look again.
It is fitting—let your word
look again that we fail not,
that your name be not
darkened within us.
Tell us your name again
lest we forget.

Great Father, / we are in great need! / Now then we beseech, / we beseech you / by your Word, / through which you created us full / of the things we lack. / Now, Father, may it please you, / for it befits you, / to look upon us / and help us, / that we may not perish, / that your name be not darkened within us: / and by your own name, / graciously help us.

7. O eterne Deus

O eterne Deus,
nunc tibi placeat
ut in amore illo ardeas
ut membra illa simus
que fecisti in eodem amore,
cum Filium tuum genuisti
in prima aurora
ante omnem creaturam,
et inspice necessitatem hanc
que super nos cadit,
et abstrahe eam a nobis
propter Filium tuum,
et perduc nos in leticiam salutis.

7. Antiphon for God the Father

Burn everlasting one in love
as you loved when you first were
father in the burning
dawn before the world's day!

Loving your son you loved
us all into being; let us
all be his limbs.

See the need that befalls us!
Lift it away from us
and for your child's sake lead us
into safety, into bliss.

O eternal God, / may it please you now / so to burn in love / that we may become the limbs / you made in the same love / when you begot your Son / in the primal dawn / before all creation. / Look upon this need / that befalls us, / and lift it from us / for the sake of your Son, / and lead us into the bliss of salvation.

II

Mother and Son

8. Ave Maria

Ave Maria,
o auctrix vite,
reedificando salutem,
que mortem conturbasti
et serpentem contrivisti,
ad quem se Eva erexit
erecta cervice
cum sufflatu superbie.
Hunc conculcasti
dum de celo Filium Dei genuisti:

Quem inspiravit
Spiritus Dei.

O dulcissima
atque amantissima mater, salve,
que natum tuum de celo missum
mundo edidisti:

Quem inspiravit
Spiritus Dei.

Gloria Patri et Filio
et Spiritui sancto.

Quem inspiravit
Spiritus Dei.

---

2 o *om.* V^2; autrix V^2 3 reedifficando D, R^c 9 concasti R^c 10 Filium Dei *om.* R^c 11 inspiravit] implevit S, V^2 14 amatissima D 15 de celo missum] celo fixum R^b, V^2 17 inspiravit] inplevit D 17–22 *om.* R^b, S, V^2

8. Responsory for the Virgin

Mary!
Death heard your steps and fled,
troubled. The house of life
lay in ruins. But you—
you built it new.
Stiff-necked Eve,
swollen with her own
importance,
courted the serpent. But you
crushed him completely
when you conceived the Son of heaven
whom the Spirit of God inspired.

Tender one, hail!
Hail mother of love!
You bore for the world
a child sent from heaven
whom the Spirit of God inspired.

Glorify the Father,
the Spirit and the Son
whom the Spirit of God inspired.

Hail Mary, / author of life, / rebuilding salvation. / You confounded death / and crushed the serpent / to whom Eve reached up, / her neck outstretched / with the swelling of pride. / You trampled him / when you bore the Son of God from heaven, // Whom the Spirit of God / inspired. // Hail, most tender / and most loving mother! / You bore for the world / your Child sent from heaven, // Whom the Spirit of God / inspired.

9. O clarissima mater

O clarissima mater
sancte medicine,
tu ungenta
per sanctum Filium tuum
infudisti
in plangentia vulnera mortis,
que Eva edificavit
in tormenta animarum.
Tu destruxisti mortem,
edificando vitam.

Ora pro nobis
ad tuum natum,
stella maris,
Maria.

O vivificum instrumentum
et letum ornamentum
et dulcedo omnium deliciarum,
que in te non deficient.

Ora pro nobis
ad tuum natum,
stella maris,
Maria.

Gloria Patri et Filio
et Spiritui sancto.

Ora pro nobis
ad tuum natum,
stella maris,
Maria.

---

6 plangencia V² 11 nobis] populo S, V² 17 delitiarum S 19–28 *om.* Rᵇ, S, V²

9. Responsory for the Virgin

Radiant
mother of sacred healing!
you poured salve on the sobbing
wounds that Eve sculpted
to torment our souls.
For your salve is your son and you
wrecked death forever,
sculpturing life.

Pray for us to your child,
Mary, star of the sea.

O life-giving source and gladdening
sign and sweetness of all
delights that flow unfailing!

Pray for us to your child,
Mary, star of the sea.

Glorify the Father,
the Spirit and the Son.

Pray for us to your child,
Mary, star of the sea.

O radiant Mother / of sacred healing! / Through your holy Son, / you poured ointments / on the sobbing wounds of death / that Eve built / into torments for souls. / You destroyed death, / building up life. // Pray for us / to your Child, / Mary, / star of the sea. // O life-giving instrument / and joyful ornament / and sweetness of all delights / that in you shall never fail. // Pray for us / to your Child, / Mary, / star of the sea.

10. O splendidissima gemma

O splendidissima gemma
et serenum decus solis
qui tibi infusus est,
fons saliens
de corde Patris,
quod est unicum Verbum suum,
per quod creavit
mundi primam materiam,
quam Eva turbavit.

Hoc Verbum effabricavit tibi
Pater hominem,
et ob hoc es tu illa lucida materia
per quam hoc ipsum Verbum exspiravit
omnes virtutes,
ut eduxit in prima materia
omnes creaturas.

---

8 prima D

10. Antiphon for the Virgin

Resplendent jewel and unclouded brightness
of the sunlight streaming through you,
know that the sun is a fountain leaping
from the father's heart,
his all-fashioning word.
He spoke and the primal matrix
teemed with things unnumbered—
but Eve unsettled them all.

To you the father spoke again
but this time
the word he uttered was a man
in your body.
Matrix of light! through you he breathed forth
all that is good,
as in the primal matrix he formed
all that has life.

O resplendent jewel / and unclouded beauty of the sun / poured into you: / a fountain springing / from the Father's heart. / This is his only Word, / by which he created / the primal matter of the world, / which Eve threw into chaos. // For you, the Father fashioned / this Word into a man. / So you are that luminous matter / through which the Word breathed forth / all virtues, / as in the primal matter / he brought forth all creatures.

11. Hodie aperuit

Hodie aperuit nobis
clausa porta
quod serpens in muliere suffocavit,
unde lucet in aurora
flos de Virgine Maria.

1 Hodie] Nunc R^b, R^c, S, V^2; nobis] mundo R^b, S, V^2

12. Quia ergo femina

Quia ergo femina mortem instruxit,
clara virgo illam interemit,
et ideo est summa benedictio
in feminea forma
pre omni creatura,
quia Deus factus est homo
in dulcissima et beata virgine.

2 virga D, S; illum D, R^c

11. Antiphon for the Virgin

Today a closed portal
has opened to us the door
the serpent slammed on a woman:
the flower of the maiden Mary
gleams in the dawn.

Today a closed gate / has opened to us / that which the serpent choked in a woman. / So the flower of the Virgin Mary / gleams in the dawn.

12. Antiphon for the Virgin

Because it was a woman
who built a house for death
a shining girl tore it down.
So now
when you ask for blessings
seek the supreme one
in the form of a woman
surpassing all that God made
since in her
(O tender! O blessed!)
he became one of us.

Because a woman constructed death, / a bright virgin demolished it. / Therefore the supreme blessing / comes in the form of a woman / beyond all creation: / for God became man / in the Virgin, most sweet and blessed.

13. Cum processit factura

Cum processit factura digiti Dei,
formata ad imaginem Dei
in ortu mixti sanguinis
per peregrinationem casus Ade,
elementa susceperunt
gaudia in te,
o laudabilis Maria,
celo rutilante
et in laudibus sonante.

6 in te] vite R^c 9 sonant te R^c

14. Cum erubuerint

Cum erubuerint
infelices in progenie sua,
procedentes in peregrinatione casus,
tunc tu clamas clara voce,
hoc modo homines elevans
de isto malicioso
casu.

4 clara] vora D

13. Antiphon for the Virgin

Self-portrait of the maker,
masterpiece of his hand—
how is it, man, that you come
into your world through bestial
coupling, mingling of blood?

You are exiled
because Adam fell.

But in you the elements,
excellent Mary,
recovered joy.

At daybreak the heavens blaze
and ring with praise.

While the handiwork of God's finger, / formed after the image of God, / was born of the mingling of blood / through the exile of Adam's fall, / the elements received / joy in you, / O Mary all-praised, / as heaven blushed / and resounded in praise.

14. Antiphon for the Virgin

Banished Eve and Adam blushing
watched as their children fell,
helplessly rushing
toward hell.

Mary!
you plead for all:
lift up your voice and carry
our souls above on the wings of your call.

While the unhappy parents were blushing / at their offspring, / walking in the exile of the fall, / then you cry out with a clear voice, / lifting humankind in this way / from that malicious / fall.

15. O frondens virga

O frondens virga,
in tua nobilitate stans
sicut aurora procedit:
nunc gaude et letare
et nos debiles dignare
a mala consuetudine liberare
atque manum tuam porrige
ad erigendum nos.

---

2 stas R^b, V^2 5 nos] tuos R^b, V^2 7 tuam *om.* V^2 8 nos] eos V^2

16. O quam magnum miraculum

O quam magnum miraculum est
quod in subditam femineam formam
rex introivit.
Hoc Deus fecit
quia humilitas super omnia ascendit.
Et o quam magna felicitas est
in ista forma,
quia malicia,
que de femina fluxit—
hanc femina postea detersit,
et omnem suavissimum odorem virtutum
edificavit,
ac celum ornavit
plus quam terram prius turbavit.

---

5 quia] quod V^2 8 maliciam R^b, V^2 malitia S 10 hanc] hec S 14 turbaverit R^b

15. Antiphon for the Virgin

Morning bursts into light,
the golden bough into green.
Let grief be put to flight—
exult, virgin queen!
Lend your hand with a shout
of high auroral praise,
and lift us frail ones out
of our old bad ways.

O leafy branch, / standing in your nobility / as the dawn breaks: / Now rejoice and be glad, / and deign to set us frail ones free / from our bad habits, / and stretch forth your hand / to raise us up.

16. Antiphon for the Virgin

O wonder!
To a submissive
woman
the king came bowing.
This is what God did
because meekness
mounts higher than all.

"But malice flowed from woman?"
So from woman felicity
overflows.
Do you see? She makes goodness
sweeter than perfume,
brings more grace to heaven
than ever disgrace to earth.

O what a great miracle! / Into a submissive feminine form / the King has entered. / This is what God did / because humility mounts above all. / And O what felicity / resides in this form, / for malice, / which flowed from woman— / woman thereafter blotted it out. / She has built / all the sweetest fragrance of virtues, / and beautified heaven / more than she formerly marred the earth.

17. Ave generosa

1. Ave generosa,
gloriosa et intacta puella.
Tu pupilla castitatis,
tu materia sanctitatis,
que Deo placuit.

2. Nam hec superna infusio
in te fuit,
quod supernum Verbum
in te carnem induit.

3. Tu candidum lilium
quod Deus ante omnem creaturam
inspexit.

4. O pulcherrima et dulcissima,
quam valde Deus in te delectabatur,
cum amplexionem caloris sui
in te posuit,
ita quod Filius eius
de te lactatus est.

5. Venter enim tuus gaudium habuit
cum omnis celestis symphonia de te sonuit,
quia virgo Filium Dei portasti,
ubi castitas tua in Deo claruit.

6. Viscera tua gaudium habuerunt
sicut gramen super quod ros cadit
cum ei viriditatem infundit,
ut et in te factum est,
o mater omnis gaudii.

7. Nunc omnis ecclesia in gaudio rutilet
ac in symphonia sonet
propter dulcissimam Virginem
et laudabilem Mariam,
Dei Genitricem.
Amen.

---

2. hec *om.* R[b] 4. est] sit V[2] 5. simphonia D; Filium Dei] Dei Filium V[2] 6. ei *om.* V[2]; infudit D, R[c] 7. ac] et R[b]; simphonia D; propter dulcissimam] text in D breaks off at this point; Amen *om.* R[b], V[2]

17. Hymn to the Virgin

In the pupil of chastity's eye
I beheld you
untouched.
Generous maid! Know that it's God
who broods over you.

For heaven flooded you like
unbodied speech
and you gave it a tongue.

Glistening
lily: before all worlds
you lured the supernal one.

How he reveled
in your charms! how your beauty
warmed to his caresses
till you gave your breast to his child.

And your womb held joy when heaven's
harmonies rang from you,
a maiden with child by God,
for in God your chastity blazed.

Yes your flesh held joy like the grass
when the dew falls, when heaven
freshens its green: O mother
of gladness, verdure of spring.

Ecclesia, flush with rapture! Sing
for Mary's sake, sing
for the maiden, sing
for God's mother. Sing!

Hail, high-born, / glorious, inviolate Maid! / You are the pupil of chastity, / the matrix of sanctity, / pleasing to God. // For this supernal flood / was within you, / as the supernal Word / put on flesh in you. // You are the shining lily / on which God gazed / before all creation. // O fairest and sweetest one, / how greatly God delighted in you / when he set within you / the embrace of his warmth, / so that his Son / took milk from you. // For your womb held joy / when all the harmony of heaven resounded

18. O virga mediatrix

Alleluia!
O virga mediatrix,
sancta viscera tua
mortem superaverunt
et venter tuus
omnes creaturas illuminavit
in pulcro flore
de suavissima integritate
clausi pudoris tui orto.

---

1 Alleluia *om.* R^b, S, V^2 2 virgo V^2 7 pulchro S, V^2

from you; / for as a virgin, you bore God's own Son / when your chastity shone bright in God. // Your flesh held joy / like the grass when the dew falls / and floods it with living green. / So it was in you also, / O Mother of all joy. // Now let the whole Church flush with gladness / and resound in harmony / for the sake of the Virgin, sweetest / Mary, deserving all praise, / the Mother of God. / Amen.

18. Alleluia-verse for the Virgin

Alleluia! light
burst from your untouched
womb like a flower
on the farther side
of death. The world-tree
is blossoming. Two
realms become one.

Alleluia! / O branch, mediatrix, / your holy body / overcame death, / and your womb / illumined all creatures / with the beautiful flower / born from the sweetest integrity / of your chaste honor.

19. O viridissima virga

1. O viridissima virga, ave,
que in ventoso flabro sciscitationis
sanctorum prodisti.

2. Cum venit tempus
quod tu floruisti in ramis tuis,
ave, ave fuit tibi,
quia calor solis in te sudavit
sicut odor balsami.

3. Nam in te floruit pulcher flos
qui odorem dedit
omnibus aromatibus
que arida erant.

4. Et illa apparuerunt omnia
in viriditate plena.

5. Unde celi dederunt rorem super gramen
et omnis terra leta facta est,
quoniam viscera ipsius frumentum protulerunt
et quoniam volucres celi
nidos in ipsa habuerunt.

6. Deinde facta est esca hominibus
et gaudium magnum epulantium.
Unde, o suavis Virgo,
in te non deficit ullum gaudium.

7. Hec omnia Eva contempsit.

8. Nunc autem laus sit Altissimo.

---

2. fuit] sint R^b, sit R^c 6. epulantibus V^2

19. Song to the Virgin

Never was leaf so green,
for you branched from the spirited
blast of the quest
of the saints.

When it came time
for your boughs to blossom
(I salute you!)
your scent was like balsam
distilled in the sun.

And your flower made all spices
fragrant
dry though they were:
they burst into verdure.

So the skies rained dew on the grass
and the whole earth exulted,
for her womb brought forth wheat,
for the birds of heaven
made their nests in it.

Keepers of the feast, rejoice!
The banquet's ready. And you
sweet maid-child
are a fount of gladness.

But Eve?
She despised every joy.
Praise nonetheless,
praise to the Highest.

1. Hail, O greenest branch! / You came forth in the windy blast / of the questioning of saints. 2. When the time came / for you to blossom in your branches, / "hail" was the word to you, / for the heat of the sun distilled in you / a fragrance like balsam. 3. For in you bloomed the beautiful flower / that gave fragrance / to all the spices / that had grown dry. 4. And they all appeared / in

20. O virga ac diadema

1a. O virga ac diadema
purpure regis,
que es in clausura tua
sicut lorica:

1b. Tu frondens floruisti
in alia vicissitudine
quam Adam omne genus humanum
produceret.

2a. Ave, ave, de tuo ventre
alia vita processit
qua Adam filios suos
denudaverat.

2b. O flos, tu non germinasti de rore
nec de guttis pluvie,
nec aer desuper te volavit,
sed divina claritas
in nobilissima virga te produxit.

3a. O virga, floriditatem tuam
Deus in prima die
creature sue previderat.

3b. Et te Verbo suo
auream materiam,
o laudabilis Virgo, fecit.

full verdure. 5. So the skies rained dew on the grass / and the whole earth exulted, / for her womb brought forth wheat, / and the birds of heaven / made their nests in it. 6. Then food was prepared for humans / and great joy for the banqueters. / So in you, sweet Virgin, / no joy ever fails. 7. Eve despised all these things! 8. But now, praise be to the Most High.

20. Sequence for the Virgin

A royal scepter and a crown
of purple, a fortress
strong as mail! O fortress
of maidenhood, scepter
all verdant:

The way you bloomed would have startled
the grandsire of us all,
for the life father Adam
stripped from his sons (praise
to you!) slid from your loins.

You never sprang from the dew,
my blossom, nor from the rain—
that was no wind that swept
over you—for God's
radiance opened you
on a regal bough. On the morn

of the universe he saw you
blossoming, and he made you
a golden matrix, O maid
beyond praise, for his word.

Strong rib of Adam! Out of you
God sculpted woman: the mirror
of all his charms, the caress
of his whole creation. So voices

chime in heaven and the whole
earth marvels at Mary,
beloved beyond measure.

4a. O quam magnum est
in viribus suis latus viri,
de quo Deus formam mulieris produxit,
quam fecit speculum
omnis ornamenti sui
et amplexionem
omnis creature sue.

4b. Inde concinunt celestia organa
et miratur omnis terra,
o laudabilis Maria,
quia Deus te valde amavit.

5a. O quam valde plangendum et lugendum est
quod tristicia in crimine
per consilium serpentis
in mulierem fluxit.

5b. Nam ipsa mulier
quam Deus matrem omnium posuit
viscera sua
cum vulneribus ignorantie decerpsit,
et plenum dolorem
generi suo protulit.

6a. Sed, o aurora,
de ventre tuo
novus sol processit,
qui omnia crimina Eve abstersit
et maiorem benedictionem per te protulit
quam Eva hominibus nocuisset.

6b. Unde, o Salvatrix,
que novum lumen
humano generi protulisti:
collige membra Filii tui
ad celestem armoniam.

1a. dyadema V[2] 2b. desuper] super R[b], V[2]; davina V[2]; claritas] fragmentary text in D begins here 3a. virgo V[2] 3b. te] de D, R[c] 5a. O *om.* R[c]; plagendum D; est et lugendum V[2] 5b. ignorantie et R[b] 6a. nocuisset hominibus V[2] 6b. o *om.* V[2]; armonyam V[2]

Cry, cry aloud! A serpent
hissed and a sea of grief
seeped through his forked
words into woman. The mother

of us all miscarried.
With ignorant hands she
plucked at her womb and bore
woe without bounds.

But the sunrise from your thighs
burnt the whole of her guilt away.
More than all that Eve lost
is the blessing you won.

Mary, savior,
mother of light:
may the limbs of your son be the chords of the song
the angels chant above.

1a. O branch and diadem / of royal purple, / you stand fast in your cloister / like a breastplate. 1b. Unfolding your leaves, you blossomed / in another way / than Adam brought forth / the whole human race. 2a. Hail, hail! From your womb / came another life, / the life that Adam / stripped from his children. 2b. O flower, you did not spring from the dew, / nor from drops of rain, / nor did an airy wind fly over you, / but the divine radiance / brought you forth on the noblest bough. 3a. O branch, God foresaw / your blossoming / on the first day of his creation. 3b. And he made you as a golden matrix / for his Word, / O all-praised Virgin. 4a. O how great / in its strength is the side of man, / from which God produced the form of woman. / He made her the mirror / of all his beauty / and the embrace / of his whole creation. 4b. So the instruments of heaven chime / and the whole earth marvels, / O Mary all-praised, / for God has greatly loved you. 5a. O how we must weep and mourn / because, through the serpent's counsel, / sadness flowed with guilt / into woman. 5b. For the woman / God made to be mother of all / plucked at her womb / with the wounds of ignorance, / and bore consummate pain / for her kind. 6a. But from your womb, / O dawn, / has come forth a new sun / that cleansed all the guilt of Eve, / and through you, brought humans a blessing greater / than the harm that Eve did. 6b. O saving Lady, / you who bore the new light / for humankind: / gather the members of your Son / into celestial harmony.

21. O tu suavissima virga

O tu suavissima virga
frondens de stirpe Iesse,
o quam magna virtus est
quod divinitas
in pulcherrimam filiam aspexit,
sicut aquila in solem
oculum suum ponit:

Cum supernus Pater claritatem Virginis
adtendit
ubi Verbum suum
in ipsa incarnari voluit.

Nam in mistico misterio Dei,
illustrata mente Virginis,
mirabiliter clarus flos
ex ipsa Virgine
exivit:

Cum supernus Pater claritatem Virginis
adtendit
ubi Verbum suum
in ipsa incarnari voluit.

Gloria Patri et Filio
et Spiritui sancto,
sicut erat
in principio.

Cum supernus Pater claritatem Virginis
adtendit
ubi Verbum suum
in ipsa incarnari voluit.

---

12 mystico mysterio R[a]

21. Responsory for the Virgin

Slender branch
from the stump of Jesse,
God gazed at you like an eagle
staring into the sun.
Daughter of Zion! such daring!
the supernal father
saw a maiden's splendor
and her mortal flesh spoke his word.

In the depth of mystery her
mind was illumined
and bright was the rose that
sprang from that maiden
when the supernal father
saw her virgin splendor
and her mortal flesh spoke his word.

Glorify the Father,
the Spirit and the Son.
As it was in the beginning
so it is now
and so be it ever.

The supernal father
saw a maiden's splendor
and her mortal flesh spoke his word.

O sweetest branch / budding from the stock of Jesse, / what a mighty work this is! / God gazed / on his fairest daughter / as an eagle / sets its eye upon the sun: // When the supernal Father / saw the Virgin's splendor / and wished his Word / to take flesh in her. // For in the mystical mystery of God, / the Virgin's mind was illumined, / and a wondrously bright flower / came forth / from that Maid. // When the supernal Father / saw the Virgin's splendor / and wished his Word / to take flesh in her.

22. O quam preciosa

O quam preciosa est virginitas
virginis huius
que clausam portam habet,
et cuius viscera
sancta divinitas calore suo
infudit,
ita quod flos in ea crevit.

Et Filius Dei
per secreta ipsius
quasi aurora exivit.

Unde dulce germen,
quod Filius ipsius est,
per clausuram ventris eius
paradisum aperuit.

Et Filius Dei
per secreta ipsius
quasi aurora exivit.

13 ventris] mentis R[c] 14 paradysum R[b], V[2] 15–17 *om.* R[b], S, V[2]

22. Responsory for the Virgin

Priceless integrity!
Her virgin gate
opened to none. But the Holy One
flooded her with warmth
until a flower sprang in her womb
and the Son of God came forth
from her secret chamber like the dawn.

Sweet as the buds of spring, her
son opened paradise
from the cloister of her womb.
And the Son of God came forth
from her secret chamber like the dawn.

O how precious is the virginity / of this virgin! / Her portal is closed, / and her womb / the holy Godhead / flooded with his warmth, / so a flower grew within her. // And the Son of God came forth / from her secret chamber / like the dawn. // Thus the tender shoot / that is her Son / opened paradise / through the cloister of her womb. // And the Son of God came forth / from her secret chamber / like the dawn.

23. O tu illustrata

O tu illustrata
de divina claritate,
clara Virgo Maria,
Verbo Dei infusa,
unde venter tuus floruit
de introitu Spiritus Dei,
qui in te sufflavit
et in te exsuxit
quod Eva abstulit
in abscisione puritatis,
per contractam contagionem
de suggestione diaboli.

Tu mirabiliter abscondisti in te
inmaculatam carnem
per divinam racionem,
cum Filius Dei
in ventre tuo floruit,
sancta divinitate eum educente
contra carnis iura
que construxit Eva,
integritati copulatum
in divinis visceribus.

---

3 virga S 4 Deo V^2 6 Dei] sancti V^2 8 in te te R^c; exuxit S 13 Tu] R^c has rubric *Versus* 14 immaculatam S 15 rationem S 16 cum] cuius V^2 18 deducente R^b, V^2 21 copulatim R^c

23. Antiphon for the Virgin

Pierced by the light of God,
Mary Virgin,
drenched in the speech of God,
your body bloomed,
swelling with the breath of God.

For the Spirit purged you
of the poison Eve took.
She soiled all freshness when she caught
that infection
from the devil's suggestion.

But in wonder within you
you hid an untainted
child of God's mind
and God's Son blossomed in your body.

The Holy One was his midwife:
his birth broke the laws
of flesh that Eve made. He was coupled
to wholeness
in the seedbed of holiness.

O radiant Virgin Mary, / illumined / by divine radiance, / flooded with the Word of God: / your womb blossomed / at the entrance of God's Spirit. / He breathed upon you / and, within you, sucked out / what Eve bore off / in the breach of purity, / through the infection contracted / from the devil's suggestion. // You wondrously hid within you / immaculate flesh / through divine Reason, / when the Son of God / blossomed in your womb, / and the holy Divinity brought him forth / against the laws of flesh / that Eve built, / united to wholeness / in the bosom of God.

III
The Holy Spirit

24. Spiritus sanctus vivificans vita

Spiritus sanctus vivificans vita,
movens omnia,
et radix est in omni creatura
ac omnia de inmunditia abluit,
tergens crimina,
ac ungit vulnera,
et sic est fulgens ac laudabilis vita,
suscitans et resuscitans
omnia.

---

4 inmundicia D

25. Karitas habundat

Karitas
habundat in omnia,
de imis excellentissima
super sidera
atque amantissima
in omnia,
quia summo regi osculum pacis
dedit.

---

1 Karitas] initial *om.* D

24. Antiphon for the Holy Spirit

The Spirit of God
is a life that bestows life,
root of the world-tree
and wind in its boughs.

Scrubbing out sins,
she rubs oil into wounds.

She is glistening life
alluring all praise,
all-awakening,
all-resurrecting.

The Holy Spirit is a life-giving life, / moving all things: / it is the root of the whole creation / and cleanses all things from impurity, / scrubbing out sins / and anointing wounds. / So it is a glistening life and worthy of praise, / arousing and resurrecting / all.

25. Antiphon for Divine Love

Charity rising
from the vast abyss
past the stars above
abounds in all worlds,
unbounded love,
and with spousal kiss
disarms the sky-king.

Charity / abounds toward all, / most exalted from the depths / above the stars, / and most loving / toward all, / for she has given / the High King the kiss of peace.

26. Laus Trinitati

Laus Trinitati
que sonus et vita
ac creatrix omnium
in vita ipsorum est,
et que laus angelice turbe
et mirus splendor archanorum,
que hominibus ignota sunt, est,
et que in omnibus vita est.

27. O ignee Spiritus

1. O ignee Spiritus, laus tibi sit,
qui in timpanis et citharis
operaris.

2. Mentes hominum de te flagrant
et tabernacula animarum eorum
vires ipsarum continent.

3. Inde voluntas ascendit
et gustum anime tribuit,
et eius lucerna est desiderium.

4. Intellectus te in dulcissimo sono advocat
ac edificia tibi
cum racionalitate parat,
que in aureis operibus sudat.

26. Antiphon for the Trinity

To the Trinity be praise!
  God is music, God is life
  that nurtures every creature in its kind.
Our God is the song of the angel throng
  and the splendor of secret ways
  hid from all humankind,
But God our life is the life of all.

To the Trinity be praise! / It is sound and life / and creator of all beings / in their life. // It is the praise of the angelic host / and the wondrous splendor of mysteries / unknown to humankind: / It is the life in all.

27. Hymn to the Holy Spirit

Praise to you
Spirit of fire!
to you who sound the timbrel
and the lyre.

Your music sets our minds
ablaze! The strength of our souls
awaits your coming
in the tent of meeting.

There the mounting will
gives the soul its savor
and desire is its lantern.

Insight invokes you in a cry
full of sweetness, while reason
builds you temples as she labors
at her golden crafts.

5. Tu autem semper gladium
habes illud abscidere
quod noxiale pomum
per nigerrimum homicidium profert,

6. Quando nebula voluntatem
et desideria tegit,
in quibus anima volat
et undique circuit.

7. Sed mens est ligatura
voluntatis et desiderii.

8. Cum vero animus se ita erigit,
quod requirit pupillam mali videre
et maxillam nequicie,
tu eum citius in igne comburis
cum volueris.

9. Sed et cum racionalitas
se per mala opera
ad prona declinat,
tu eam, cum vis,
stringis et constringis et reducis
per infusionem experimentorum.

10. Quando autem malum
ad te gladium suum educit,
tu illud in cor illius refringis
sicut in primo perdito angelo fecisti,
ubi turrim superbie illius
in infernum deiecisti.

11. Et ibi aliam turrim
in publicanis et peccatoribus elevasti,
qui tibi peccata sua
cum operibus suis confitentur.

But sword
in hand you stand poised
to prune shoots of the poisoned
apple—
scions of the darkest
murder—

when mist overshadows the will.
Adrift in desires the soul is spinning
everywhere. But the mind
is a bond
to bind will and desire.

When the heart yearns to look
the Evil One in the eye,
to stare down the jaws of
iniquity, swiftly
you burn it in consuming
fire. Such is your wish.

And when reason doing ill
falls from her place, you
restrain and constrain her as you will
in the flow of experience until
she obeys you.

And when the Evil One brandishes
his sword against you,
you break it in his own
heart. For so you did
to the first lost angel,
tumbling the tower of his
arrogance to hell.

And there you built a second
tower—traitors and sinners
its stones. In repentance
they confessed all their crafts.

12. Unde omnes creature
que de te vivunt, te laudant,
quia tu preciosissimum ungentum es
fractis et fetidis vulneribus,
ubi illa in preciosissimas gemmas convertis.

13. Nunc dignare nos omnes
ad te colligere
et ad recta itinera dirigere.
Amen.

---

1. item laus R^b; tympanis et cytharis R^b, V^2 3. Inde] Unde D 4. te in] in *om.* V^2 5. gladium semper V^2 6. Quando] no cap. in R^b, V^2; et desideria *om.* R^b; tegit] regit R^b, V^2 8. ita se V^2; videre mali V^2; nequitie R^b; cicius D, V^2; conburis V^2 9. Sed et] Sed V^2 constringis] confringis all MSS. 10. educit] deducit R^b; refringis] refingis D, R^b, R^c; illius *om.* R^b 11. suis *om.* V^2 13. nos omnes] homines R^b, V^2; Amen *om.* R^b, V^2

So all beings that live by you
praise your outpouring
like a priceless salve upon festering
sores, upon fractured
limbs. You convert them
into priceless gems!

Now gather us all to yourself
and in your mercy guide us
into the paths of justice.

1. O fiery Spirit, praise to you / who play / upon the timbrel and the lyre. 2. The minds of men catch fire from you, / and the tents of their souls / contain their forces. 3. Thence the will mounts up / and gives the soul a savor: / desire is its lantern. 4. The intellect invokes you with the sweetest sound / and prepares for you temples / with the power of reason, / which labors in golden works. 5. But you hold a sword ever / ready to cut off / what the poisonous apple / brings forth through the blackest murder, 6. When a cloud shadows / the will and its desires. / Amid them the soul flies about / and circles everywhere. 7. But the mind is the bond / of will and desire. 8. But when the spirit lifts itself up, / longing to see the pupil of the Evil One's eye / and the jaws of wickedness, / you swiftly consume it in fire / as you have willed. 9. But when rationality / falls prostrate / through evil works, / you strain and constrain and recall it / as you will, / through a flood of experiences. 10. But when evil / draws its sword against you, / you shatter it in its own heart, / as you did to the first lost angel / when you cast the tower of his pride / into hell. 11. And there you raised a second tower / in publicans and sinners, / who confess to you their sins / with their works. 12. So all creatures / that have life from you, praise you, / for you are a priceless ointment / for broken and fetid wounds: / You convert them into priceless gems. 13. Now deign to gather us all / to yourself, / and guide us in the paths of righteousness. / Amen.

28. O ignis Spiritus Paracliti

1a. O ignis Spiritus Paracliti,
vita vite omnis creature,
sanctus es vivificando formas.

1b. Sanctus es ungendo
periculose fractos,
sanctus es tergendo
fetida vulnera.

2a. O spiraculum sanctitatis,
o ignis caritatis,
o dulcis gustus in pectoribus
et infusio cordium
in bono odore virtutum.

2b. O fons purissime,
in quo consideratur
quod Deus alienos colligit
et perditos requirit.

3a. O lorica vite
et spes compaginis membrorum omnium
et o cingulum honestatis:
salva beatos.

3b. Custodi eos qui carcerati sunt
ab inimico,
et solve ligatos
quos divina vis salvare vult.

4a. O iter fortissimum,
quod penetravit omnia
in altissimis et in terrenis
et in omnibus abyssis,
tu omnes componis et colligis.

28. Sequence for the Holy Spirit

Fiery Spirit,
fount of courage,
life within life
of all that has being!

Holy are you, transmuting the perfect
   into the real.
Holy are you, healing
   the mortally stricken.
Holy are you, cleansing
   the stench of wounds.

O sacred breath O blazing
love O savor in the breast and balm
flooding the heart with
the fragrance of good,

O limpid mirror of God
who leads wanderers
home and hunts out the lost,

Armor of the heart and hope
of the integral body,
sword-belt of honor:
save those who know bliss!

Guard those the fiend holds
imprisoned,
free those in fetters
whom divine force wishes to save.

O current of power permeating all
in the heights upon the earth and
in all deeps:
you bind and gather
all people together.

4b. De te nubes fluunt, ether volat,
lapides humorem habent,
aque rivulos educunt,
et terra viriditatem sudat.

5a. Tu etiam semper educis doctos
per inspirationem Sapientie
letificatos.

5b. Unde laus tibi sit,
qui es sonus laudis
et gaudium vite,
spes et honor fortissimus,
dans premia lucis.

1a. O tu V²; Paraclyti V² 2a. initial *om.* D; et *om.* D 2b. purissimus D, R^c 3a. conpaginis V² 3a–b. et o cingulum . . . solve ligatos *om.*V² 4a. penetrasti V²; tu omnes iuste V² 4b. sudatt D

Out of you clouds
come streaming, winds
take wing from you, dashing
rain against stone;
and ever-fresh springs
well from you, washing
the evergreen globe.

O teacher of those who know,
a joy to the wise
is the breath of Sophia.

Praise then be yours!
you are the song of praise,
the delight of life,
a hope and a potent honor
granting garlands of light.

1a. O fire of the Spirit, the Comforter, / life of the life of all creation, / holy are you, giving life to the Forms. 1b. Holy are you, anointing / the dangerously broken; / holy are you, cleansing / the fetid wounds. 2a. O breath of sanctity, / O fire of charity, / O sweet savor in the breast / and balm flooding hearts / with the fragrance of virtues. 2b. O limpid fountain, / in which it is seen / how God gathers the strays / and seeks out the lost: 3a. O breastplate of life / and hope of the bodily frame, / O sword-belt of honor: / save the blessed! 3b. Guard those imprisoned / by the foe, / free those in fetters / whom divine force wishes to save. 4a. O mighty course / that penetrated all, / in the heights, upon the earth, / and in all abysses: / you bind and gather all people together. // 4b. From you clouds overflow, winds take wing, / stones store up moisture, / waters well forth in streams— / and earth swells with living green. 5a. You are ever teaching the learned, / made joyful by the breath / of Wisdom. 5b. Praise then be yours! / You are the song of praise, / the delight of life, / a hope and a potent honor, / granting rewards of light.

IV
The Celestial Hierarchy

29. O gloriosissimi lux vivens angeli

O gloriosissimi lux vivens angeli,
qui infra divinitatem
divinos oculos
cum mistica obscuritate
omnis creature aspicitis
in ardentibus desideriis,
unde numquam potestis saciari:

O quam gloriosa gaudia illa
vestra habet forma,
que in vobis est intacta
ab omni pravo opere,
quod primum ortum est
in vestro socio,
perdito angelo,
qui volare voluit
supra intus latens
pinnaculum Dei,
unde ipse tortuosus
dimersus est in ruinam,
sed ipsius instrumenta casus
consiliando facture
digiti Dei instituit.

---

1 O *om.* D 4 mystica R^{a} 19 demersus R^{a}; est *om.* D

29. Antiphon for the Angels

Spirited light! on the edge
of the Presence your yearning
burns in the secret darkness,
O angels, insatiably
into God's gaze.

Perversity
could not touch your beauty;
you are essential joy.
But your lost companion,
angel of the crooked
wings—he sought the summit,
shot down the depths of God
and plummeted to hell,
hissing counsels of ruin
in the ears of God's new
creation.

O most glorious angels, living light: / beneath the Divinity / you gaze on the eyes of God / within the mystical darkness / of all creation / in ardent desires, / so you can never be satiated. // O how glorious are those joys / that belong to your form, / which in you is untouched / by all the wicked work / that first arose / in your companion, / the lost angel, / who wished to fly / above the pinnacle hidden / in the depths of God. / So he crookedly / plunged into ruin— / but by his counsel, / he supplied the means of his fall / to the handiwork of God's finger.

30. O vos angeli

O vos angeli
qui custoditis populos,
quorum forma fulget
in facie vestra,
et o vos archangeli
qui suscipitis
animas iustorum,
et vos virtutes,
potestates,
principatus, dominationes
et troni,
qui estis computati
in quintum secretum numerum,
et o vos cherubin
et seraphin,
sigillum secretorum Dei:

Sit laus vobis,
qui loculum antiqui cordis
in fonte asspicitis.

Videtis enim
interiorem vim Patris,
que de corde illius spirat
quasi facies.

Sit laus vobis,
qui loculum antiqui cordis
in fonte asspicitis.

---

5 anchangeli D 11 throni R[a] 19 aspicitis R[a]

30. Responsory for the Angels

Angels that guard the nations
(the form of them gleams in your faces),

Archangels that welcome
souls of the just,

Thrones, dominations, princedoms, virtues, powers,
reckoned in the mystic five,

And cherubim, O seraphim,
seal upon the secret things of God:

All praise! you behold in the fountain
the place of the everlasting heart.

For your eyes are fixed on the father's pulse
as on a face that breathes from his soul.

All praise! you behold in the fountain
the place of the everlasting heart.

O angels / that guard the peoples, / whose form gleams / in your faces; / and O archangels / that receive / the souls of the just; / and you virtues, / powers, / princedoms, dominations / and thrones, / who are reckoned / in the mystical number of five; / and O you cherubim / and seraphim, / seal upon the secret things of God: // Praise to you, / who behold in the fountain / the little place of the ancient heart. // For you see / the inmost strength of the Father, / which breathes from his heart / like a face. // Praise to you, / who behold in the fountain / the little place of the ancient heart.

31. O spectabiles viri

O spectabiles viri
qui pertransistis occulta,
aspicientes per oculos spiritus
et annuntiantes
in lucida umbra
acutam et viventem lucem
in virga germinantem,
que sola floruit
de introitu radicantis luminis:

Vos antiqui sancti,
predixistis salvationem
exulum animarum
que inmerse fuerant morti,
qui circuisti ut rote,
mirabiliter loquentes mistica montis
qui celum tangit,
pertransiens ungendo multas aquas,
cum etiam inter vos
surrexit lucida lucerna,
que ipsum montem precurrens ostendit.

---

1 O *om.* R[c] 2 pertranssistis D 4 annunciantes R[a] 15 mimibiliter R[c]; mystica R[a] 19 surrexxit D

31. Antiphon for Patriarchs and Prophets

Spectacular men! you see
with the spirit's eyes,
piercing the veil.
In a luminous shade you proclaim
a sharp living brightness
that buds from a branch
that blossomed alone
when the radical light took root.

Holy ones of old! you foretold
deliverance for the souls
of exiles
slumped in the dead lands.

Like wheels you
spun round in wonder as you spoke
of the mysterious mountain
at the brink of heaven
that stills many waters, sailing
over the waves

And a shining lamp
burned in the midst of you!
Pointing,
he runs to that mountain.

O clear-sighted men! / you have pierced the mysteries, / seeing with the spirit's eyes / and proclaiming / in luminous shadow / a keen and living light / budding on a branch / that blossomed alone / from the entrance of the Light taking root. // You ancient saints, / you foretold the salvation / of exiled souls / who had been plunged in death. / You circled like wheels, / wondrously telling the mysteries of the mountain / that touches heaven, / crossing and anointing many waters, / when even in the midst of you / arose a shining lantern / that, racing ahead, reveals that mountain.

32. O vos felices radices

O vos felices radices
cum quibus opus miraculorum
et non opus criminum
per torrens iter
perspicue umbre
plantatum est,
et o tu ruminans ignea vox,
precurrens limantem lapidem
subvertentem abyssum:

Gaudete in capite vestro.

Gaudete
in illo quem non viderunt
in terris multi
qui ipsum ardenter vocaverunt.

Gaudete in capite vestro.

---

9 vertentem D; abissum R^a 15 *om.* R^c

32. Responsory for Patriarchs and Prophets

O flourishing
roots of the tree of wonders
(no longer the tree of crimes),
a cascade of dappled shadow
rained on your planting.

And you, fire-breathing
voice, chewing
the cud of the word, racing
to the touchstone that
topples hell:
rejoice in your captain.

Rejoice in him whom many
though they called on him ardently
saw not upon earth.
Rejoice in your captain.

O you happy roots, / with whom the work of miracles / was planted— / and not the work of crimes— / in a rushing course / of translucent shadow. / And you, O fiery, ruminating voice, / racing before the filing-stone / that topples the abyss: // Rejoice in your captain. // Rejoice / in him whom many / that called on him ardently / did not see upon earth. // Rejoice in your captain.

33. O cohors milicie floris

O cohors milicie floris virge
non spinate,
tu sonus orbis terre,
circuiens regiones
insanorum sensuum
epulantium cum porcis,
quas expugnasti
per infusum adiutorem,
ponens radices
in tabernacula
pleni operis Verbi Patris.

Tu etiam nobilis es gens Salvatoris,
intrans viam regenerationis aque
per Agnum,
qui te misit in gladio
inter sevissimos canes,
qui suam gloriam destruxerunt
in operibus digitorum suorum,
statuentes non manufactum
in subiectionem manuum suarum,
in qua non invenerunt eum.

---

1 choors D chohors R[c] 6 portis D, R[c] 7 quos R[a], R[c] 9 ponentis MSS.
21 quo D, R[c]

33. Antiphon for the Apostles

O soldiers of the flower
from the branch without thorns,
you are the voice of the universe,
circling lands where madmen rave,
feasting with swine.
But the Spirit
fell upon you as you stormed
their tents, striking root
in the fort of the utmost
work of the word.

Aristocrats of Christ!
you were reborn in water
for the lamb who sent you
with his sword among savage
dogs. For they ravaged
their glory with the works
of their hands, making man,
the creature not made with hands,
submit to their handiwork—
and they found no God.

O legion of the army of the flower of the branch / without thorns: / you are the voice of the whole world, / circling regions / where mad senses rave, / feasting with swine. / These regions you stormed / through the Helper infused in you, / striking roots / in the tents / of the perfect work of the Father's Word. // You are the noble lineage of the Savior, / entering on the way of rebirth by water / through the Lamb, / who sent you with a sword / among the most savage dogs. / They destroyed their own glory / with the works of their fingers, / setting the creature not made with hands / in subjection to [the work of] their hands, / and in this they did not find Him.

34. O lucidissima apostolorum turba

O lucidissima
apostolorum turba,
surgens in vera agnitione
et aperiens
clausuram magisterii
diaboli,
abluendo captivos
in fonte viventis aque,
tu es clarissima lux
in nigerrimis tenebris,
fortissimumque genus columnarum,
sponsam Agni sustentans
in omnibus ornamentis ipsius:

Per cuius gaudium
ipsa mater et virgo est vexillata.

Agnus enim inmaculatus
est sponsus ipsius sponse
inmaculate.

---

4 aperriens D 11 columpnarum R[a]

34. Responsory for the Apostles

O scintillating throng,
O apostles
who teach without lying:
you fling wide the doors
of the devil's schoolroom
and cleanse his captives in a spring
of live water.
You are radiant light
in thick darkness,
pillars of the colonnade
where the Lamb's bride leans in her beauty.

Mother and maid, she rejoices,
bearing his banner:
for the unspotted Lamb is the bridegroom
of his spotless bride.

O most luminous / band of apostles, / arising in true knowledge / and opening / the enclosure / of the devil's teaching, / washing his captives / in a font of living water: / you are the most radiant light / in the blackest darkness. / You are a mighty row of pillars / supporting the Lamb's bride / in all her beauty. // Through his joy, / she is mother and standard-bearing virgin. // For the immaculate Lamb / is the bridegroom of his / immaculate bride.

35. O speculum columbe

O speculum columbe
castissime forme,
qui inspexisti misticam largitatem
in purissimo fonte:

O mira floriditas
que numquam arescens cecidisti,
quia altissimus plantator misit te:

O suavissima quies
amplexuum solis:
tu es specialis filius Agni
in electa amicicia
nove sobolis.

35. Antiphon for Saint John the Evangelist

O mirror of the dove, the all-chaste beauty,
you who saw the secret largesse
at its limpid source:

O wondrous blossom,
you who never withered, never faded,
since the gardener of Eden planted you:

O sweet refreshment in the sun's embraces:
you are the Lamb's special son,
beloved among the chosen
friends of the age to come.

O mirror of the dove / of most chaste beauty, / you looked upon the mystic largesse / in the purest source. / O wondrous flower, / you never withered or wilted / because the highest Gardener planted you. / O sweetest rest / in the sun's embraces, / you are the special son of the Lamb / in the chosen friendship / of a new generation.

36. O dulcis electe

O dulcis electe,
qui in ardore ardentis
effulsisti, radix,
et qui in splendore Patris
elucidasti mistica,
et qui intrasti cubiculum castitatis
in aurea civitate
quam construxit rex,
cum accepit sceptrum regionum:

Prebe adiutorium peregrinis.

Tu enim auxisti pluviam
cum precessoribus tuis,
qui miserunt illam
in viriditate pigmentariorum.

Prebe adiutorium peregrinis.

36. Responsory for Saint John the Evangelist

The fire you flashed
from the blaze of God!
Chosen and tender you
struck root in light,
in the Father's splendor you
enlightened depths.

You who had entry
to the bower of chastity
in the golden city the king built
when he came to his throne:
guide us wayfarers home.

With the eleven before you
you sent torrents from heaven,
you brought rain to the garden
where spices grow green.
Guide us wayfarers on.

O tender, chosen one, / in the ardor of the Ardent One / you flashed forth as a root, / and in the Father's splendor / you made mysteries clear. / You entered the bridal chamber of chastity / in the golden city / that the King built / when he received the scepter of the provinces: // Lend your aid to pilgrims. // For you increased the rainfall / along with your precursors, / who sent rain / upon the verdure of the spice-dealers. // Lend your aid to pilgrims.

37. O victoriosissimi triumphatores

O victoriosissimi triumphatores,
qui in effusione sanguinis vestri
salutantes edificationem
ecclesie,
intrastis
sanguinem Agni,
epulantes
cum vitulo occiso:

O quam magnam mercedem habetis,
quia corpora vestra viventes despexistis,
imitantes Agnum Dei,
ornantes penam eius,
in qua vos introduxit
in restaurationem
hereditatis.

---

7 epulantis R[c] 10 viventis D

37. Antiphon for Martyrs

O conquerors!
in your utmost triumph,
as you sent Ecclesia's builders
your tidings of blood,
you entered into the blood of the Lamb
to feast on the fatted calf.

Consider your crowns!
Since you despised your living flesh
to follow God's Lamb and
embellish his anguish,
his pain has restored you:
you have your inheritance.

O most victorious conquerors, / who in the shedding of your blood / greeted the upbuilding / of the Church: / you have entered / into the blood of the Lamb, / feasting / on the slaughtered calf. // O how great a reward you have, / since you despised your living bodies, / imitating the Lamb of God, / embellishing his pain. / In this he has brought you / into the restoration / of your inheritance.

38. Vos flores rosarum

Vos flores rosarum,
qui in effusione sanguinis vestri
beati estis,
in maximis gaudiis redolentibus
et sudantibus in emptione
que fluxit
de interiori mente consilii
manentis ante evum:

In illo, in quo non erat constitutio
a capite.

Sit honor in consortio vestro,
qui estis instrumentum ecclesie
et qui in vulneribus
vestri sanguinis undatis:

In illo, in quo non erat constitutio
a capite.

38. Responsory for Martyrs

Blessed are you bleeding roses:
  your scent is surpassing joy,
  your fragrance redemption;
before time it came streaming
  from the heart of the purpose
  of him who had no beginning.

May the Church give you glory,
for you grant her grace
  as you surge amid the sea of your bleeding
  in him who had no beginning.

Blessed are you / roses / in the shedding of your blood, / fragrant with supreme delight, / distilling the purchase / that flowed / from the inmost heart of the purpose / that abides before time: // In the Uncreated One / who had no beginning. // Honor be to your company! / you are an instrument for the Church / and you surge in the wounds / of your bleeding, // In the Uncreated One / who had no beginning.

39. O vos imitatores

O vos imitatores excelse persone,
in preciosissima
et gloriosissima significatione,
o quam magnus est vester ornatus,
ubi homo procedit,
solvens et stringens in Deo
pigros et peregrinos:

Etiam ornans candidos et nigros
et magna onera
remittens.

Nam et angelici ordinis
officia habetis,
et fortissima fundamenta prescitis,
ubicumque constituenda sunt,
unde magnus est vester honor.

Etiam ornans candidos et nigros,
et magna onera
remittens.

---

2 pretiosisima S 8 ornas S 10 remitens D restituens S

39. Responsory for Confessors

Superlative actors! how noble
the play, how splendid
your costume, how lofty
your role! See how a man
plays Christ. He steps forth
to bind and to loose
the wayward
with the wayfaring.
To white and to black
he gives beauty,
he lifts burdens away.

Not only with angels
do you sing your part,
but you know the sites
of the firmest foundations
before you have built them.
Great is your honor!
To white and to black
you give beauty,
you lift burdens away.

O you imitators of the most exalted person, / in the most precious / and glorious symbolic act: / How great is your beauty / when a man steps forth, / binding and loosing in God / the wayward and the wayfarers: // Making white and black beautiful, / and lifting great burdens / away. // For you both share the duties / of the angelic order / and foreknow the firmest foundations, / wherever they are to be laid, / so great is your honor. // Making white and black beautiful, / and lifting great burdens / away.

40. O successores

O successores
fortissimi leonis,
inter templum et altare
dominantes in ministratione eius,
sicut angeli sonant in laudibus
et sicut assunt populis in adiutorio,
vos estis inter illos
qui hec faciunt,
semper curam habentes in officio Agni.

40. Antiphon for Confessors

In the tracks of
the mighty Lion,
you pass between
temple and altar,
lords in his service.
As angels sing praises,
assisting the nations,
you stand among them
painstaking always
to serve the Lamb.

O successors / of the most mighty lion, / between temple and altar / you are lords in his service. / As the angels resound in praise / and assist the peoples with their aid, / you stand among them / who do these things, / always taking pains in the service of the Lamb.

V
Patron Saints

41. O mirum admirandum

O mirum admirandum
quod absconsa forma precellit,
ardua in honesta statura,
ubi vivens altitudo
profert mistica.
Unde, o Disibode,
surges in fine,
succurrente flore
omnium ramorum mundi,
ut primum surrexisti.

---

6 dysibode V[1] 7 surge D

41. Antiphon for Saint Disibod

O wonder! the one
who was hidden scales
the summit
of the cliffs of integrity
where the living Majesty
utters mysteries.

So you, Disibod,
shall arise in the end
as you rose in the beginning
when the blossom that sustains you blooms
on all the boughs in the world.

O marvelous wonder! / A hidden figure towers high, / steep on the honorable height / where the living Majesty / utters mysteries. / So you, Disibod, / shall arise in the end / as you first arose / with the aid of the flower / of all the boughs in the world.

42. O viriditas digiti Dei

O viriditas digiti Dei,
in qua Deus constituit plantationem
que in excelso resplendet
ut statuta columna:

Tu gloriosa in preparatione Dei.

Et o altitudo montis
que numquam dissipaberis
in discretione Dei,
tu tamen stas a longe ut exul,
sed non est in potestate
armati
qui te rapiat.

Tu gloriosa in preparatione Dei.

Gloria Patri et Filio
et Spiritui sancto.

Tu gloriosa in preparatione Dei.

---

4 columpna V^1 5 gloriosa es V^1 8 discretione] differentia D, R^c 13–16 *om.* D, V^1

42. Responsory for Saint Disibod

Green
finger of God:
the vineyard you planted
glistens in heaven
like a pillar of light.
In preparing for God is your glory.

When he levels the mountains
you shall not be brought low,
O exalted one,
yet you stand afar off
like an exile
though the armed man has no strength to seize you.
In preparing for God is your glory.

Glorify the Father,
the Spirit and the Son.
In preparing for God is your glory.

O living green of God's finger, / with which God planted a vineyard / that glistens on high / like a pillar: // You are glorious in God's preparation. // O mountaintop, / you shall never be dispersed / in the judgment of God, / yet you stand afar off like an exile. / But it does not lie in the power / of the armed man / to seize you. // You are glorious in God's preparation.

43. O felix anima

O felix anima
cuius corpus
de terra ortum est,
quod tu cum peregrinatione
huius mundi conculcasti:

Unde de divina
racionalitate,
que te speculum suum fecit,
coronata es.

Spiritus sanctus etiam te
ut habitaculum suum
intuebatur.

Unde de divina
racionalitate,
que te speculum suum fecit,
coronata es.

Gloria Patri et Filio
et Spiritui sancto.

44. O beata infantia

O beata infantia
electi Disibodi,
que a Deo ita inspirata est
quod postea sanctissima opera
in mirabilibus Dei
ut suavissimum odorem
balsami
exsudasti.

43. Responsory for Saint Disibod

O happy soul,
a pilgrim in this world, you trod
your earth-born body underfoot,
so your crown is the mind of God
which made you its mirror.

And the Holy Spirit saw you
as his own habitation,
so your crown is the mind of God
which made you its mirror.

Glorify the Father,
the Spirit and the Son.
Your crown is the mind of God
which made you its mirror.

O happy soul, / whose body / was born of earth: / in the pilgrimage of this world, / you trampled it down. // So you are crowned / by the divine / rationality, / which made you its mirror. // The Holy Spirit also / looked upon you / as his own habitation. // So you are crowned / by the divine / rationality, / which made you its mirror.

44. Antiphon for Saint Disibod

Disibod,
God's chosen!
Because the breath divine
breathed on your infancy,
holiness flowed from you like perfume
when you were grown,
sweet as balm were the wonders
you wrought in God.

Blessed was the childhood / of the chosen Disibod, / so inspired by God / that afterward, / amid the marvels of God, / you exuded the most holy deeds / like the sweetest fragrance / of balsam.

45. O presul vere civitatis

1a. O presul vere civitatis,
qui in templo angularis lapidis
ascendens in celum,
in terra prostratus fuisti
propter Deum.

1b. Tu, peregrinus a semine mundi,
desiderasti exul fieri
propter amorem Christi.

2a. O mons clause mentis,
tu assidue pulcram faciem aperuisti
in speculo columbe.

2b. Tu in absconso latuisti,
inebriatus odore florum,
per cancellos sanctorum
emicans Deo.

3a. O culmen in clavibus celi,
quod propter perspicuam vitam
mundum vendidisti:
hoc certamen, alme confessor,
semper habes in Domino.

3b. In tua enim mente
fons vivus clarissima luce
purissimos rivulos eduxit
per viam salutis.

4a. Tu magna turris
ante altare summi Dei,
et huius turris culmen obumbrasti
per fumum aromatum.

4b. O Disibode,
in tuo lumine
per exempla puri soni
membra mirifice laudis edificasti
in duabus partibus
per Filium hominis.

45. Sequence for Saint Disibod

Prelate of the true City, soaring
to heaven in the temple
of the cornerstone:
on earth you fell prostrate
for the sake of God.

Estranged from the seed of this world,
you longed to become an exile
for the love of Christ.

O mountain of a cloistered mind!
your face never ceased to shine
in the mirror of the dove.

You dwelt in a secret place,
drunk with the scent of flowers,
aglow before God
through a trellis of saints.

O gabled roof upon heaven's gates!
because you sold this world
for the life translucent,
the prize is yours forever,
gracious confessor.

In your mind the living fountain
welled forth in unclouded rivers,
rivers of light
that stream toward salvation.

You are a lofty tower before the altar
of God Most High:
its turret is shaded
by the smoke of spices.

In your brightness, O Disibod,
with exemplars of pure sound
you built a body of wondrous praise,
song in two choirs for Christ, God and man.

5a. In alto stas,
non erubescens ante Deum vivum,
et protegis viridi rore
laudantes Deum ista voce.

5b. O dulcis vita
et o beata perseverantia
que in hoc beato Disibodo gloriosum lumen
semper edificasti
in celesti Ierusalem.

6a. Nunc sit laus Deo
in forma pulcre tonsure
viriliter operante.

6b. Et superni cives gaudeant
de his qui eos
hoc modo imitantur.

2a. asidue V[1] 3a. habens V[1] 4b. O Disibode] the remainder of this strophe is missing at this point in D, but appears at the end of the sequence. 6a. pulchre D

In the heights you stand unashamed
before the living God
and with life-giving dew you protect
those who sing his praise.

O sweet is the life, O blessed the endurance
that in Disibod the blessed
built a light forever famous
in celestial Jerusalem!

Praise God who worked like a man
in the beauty of a tonsured monk,
and may the citizens of the skies rejoice
in those who imitate their lives.

1a. O prelate of the true City, / ascending to heaven / in the temple of the cornerstone, / on earth you were prostrate / for the sake of God. 1b. A stranger to the seed of this world, / you longed to become an exile / for the love of Christ. 2a. O mountain of a cloistered mind! / you constantly displayed a fair face / in the mirror of the dove. 2b. You dwelt in a hidden place, / drunk with the scent of flowers, / flashing before God / through a lattice of saints. 3a. O roof in the keys of heaven, / because you sold the world / for a translucent life, / the prize of this contest, gracious confessor, / is yours forever in the Lord. 3b. For in your mind / the living fountain poured out the purest streams / in radiant light / along the way of salvation. 4a. You are a lofty tower / before the altar of God Most High, / and you have shaded the roof of this tower / with the smoke of incense. 4b. O Disibod, / in your light, / with exemplars of pure sound, / you built up a body of wondrous praise / in two parts / through the Son of man. 5a. You stand on high, / unashamed before the living God, / and with life-giving dew you protect / those who praise God in this song. 5b. O sweet life, / O blessed perseverance! / In this blessed Disibod / you have built a light forever glorious / in celestial Jerusalem. 6a. Now praise be to God / working like a man / in the figure of a beautiful tonsured monk. 6b. And may the supernal citizens rejoice / in those who imitate them / in this manner.

46. O felix apparicio

O felix apparicio,
cum in amico Dei Ruperto
flamma vite choruscavit,
ita quod caritas Dei
in corde eius fluxit,
timorem Domini amplectens.
Unde etiam agnitio eius
in supernis civibus
floruit.

---

1 apparitio R^b 2 roberto R^b Ruopperto V^2 3 flama D; coruscavit R^b 7 agnicio V^2

47. O beatissime Ruperte

O beatissime Ruperte,
qui in flore etatis tue
non produxisti
nec portasti vicia diaboli,
unde naufragum mundum
reliquisti:
nunc intercede
pro famulantibus tibi in Deo.
Alleluia.

---

1 roberte R^b Ruopperte V^2 4 dyaboli V^2 9 Alleluia *om.* D, R^b, V^2

46. Antiphon for Saint Rupert

Rupert, the friend of God—
he feasts the eyes, he glints
like flame.
Tongues of charity
fired his heart; he feared God.
All saints
in Paradise cheered his name.

O happy apparition, / when the flame of life glinted / in Rupert, the friend of God, / so that God's charity / flowed in his heart, / embracing the fear of the Lord. / And so the knowledge of him / flourished / among the supernal citizens.

47. Antiphon for Saint Rupert

Joy to you, Rupert!
Leaving the shipwrecked
world behind you,
you scorned Satan's lures,
even in youth. May God's
servants and yours
reach port by your prayers.

O most blessed Rupert! / In the flower of your age, / you neither produced / nor bore the devil's vices. / So you abandoned / the shipwrecked world. / Intercede now / for those who serve you in God. / Alleluia.

48. Quia felix puericia

Quia felix puericia
in laudabili Ruperto
ad Deum anhelavit
et mundum reliquit,
ideo ipse in celesti armonia
fulget,
et ideo etiam angelica turba
Filium Dei
laudando concinit.

---

1 Quia a R[c]

49. O Ierusalem

1a. O Ierusalem, aurea civitas
ornata regis purpura:

1b. O edificatio summe bonitatis,
que es lux numquam obscurata:

1c. Tu enim es ornata
in aurora et in calore solis.

2a. O beata puericia
que rutilas in aurora,
et o laudabilis adolescentia
que ardes in sole.

2b. Nam tu, o nobilis Ruperte,
in his sicut gemma fulsisti,
unde non potes abscondi stultis hominibus
sicut nec mons valli celatur.

3a. Fenestre tue, Ierusalem,
cum topazio et saphiro
specialiter sunt decorate.

48. Antiphon for Saint Rupert

Rupert,
the wise child,
sighed for God and forsook the world:
so he gleams amid heaven's choirs
and commands our praise as the angels
praise the immortal Child.

Because in Rupert, worthy of praise, / a happy childhood / sighed for God / and renounced the world, / he now gleams / amid celestial harmony, / and the angelic host also / sings in concord, / praising the Son of God.

49. Sequence for Saint Rupert

Jerusalem! royal city,
walls of gold and purple banners,

building of utmost bounty,
light never darkened,

lovely at dawn,
ablaze at noon.

Blessed be your childhood
that glimmers at dawn,
praised be your vigor
that burns in the sun.

O Rupert! Pearl
of the morning, diamond
at noon, ever sparkling!
Fools cannot hide you,
nor the vale the mountain.

Jerusalem! In the frames
of your windows glisten your gems,
lapis lazuli with topaz,

3b. In quibus dum fulges, o Ruperte,
non potes abscondi tepidis moribus,
sicut nec mons valli
coronatus rosis, liliis et purpura
in vera ostensione.

4a. O tener flos campi
et o dulcis viriditas pomi
et o sarcina sine medulla,
que non flectit pectora in crimina.

4b. O vas nobile,
quod non est pollutum
nec devoratum
in saltatione antique spelunce,
et quod non est maceratum
in vulneribus antiqui perditoris:

5. In te symphonizat Spiritus sanctus,
quia angelicis choris associaris
et quoniam in Filio Dei ornaris,
cum nullam maculam habes.

6. Quod vas decorum tu es,
o Ruperte,
qui in puericia
et in adolescentia tua
ad Deum anhelasti in timore Dei
et in amplexione caritatis
et in suavissimo odore bonorum operum.

7. O Ierusalem,
fundamentum tuum positum est
cum torrentibus lapidibus,
quod est cum publicanis et peccatoribus
qui perdite oves erant,
sed per Filium Dei invente,
ad te cucurrerunt
et in te positi sunt.

Rupert among them,
a light never quenched.
Indifference cannot hide you,
nor the vale the mountain—
rose-crowned and purple-mantled,
lily-veiled,
the mount of vision.

O delicate
bloom of the field, green
as of fruit before harvest, sheaf
without pith: your ripeness
weighs lightly, burdens no hearts.

Your body's a chalice,
its wine never drained
in the ancient cave dance.
The ancient foe could not ravish
or scar your flesh.

In your soul the Spirit's
symphonies ring, you sing
with angels, join their carols,
Christ your radiance,
pure your song.

Chalice of honor! Child
and youth, you sighed
after God, feared and embraced him
whose bounty lured yours
like a rare perfume.

O Jerusalem! founded
on glowing stones, shooting
stars, sheep lost and found:
Christ called and publicans raced,
sinners made haste
to your walls to be laid in their place.

8. Deinde muri tui
fulminant vivis lapidibus,
qui per summum studium bone voluntatis
quasi nubes in celo volaverunt.

9. Et ita turres tue,
o Ierusalem,
rutilant et candent per ruborem
et per candorem sanctorum
et per omnia ornamenta Dei,
que tibi non desunt, o Ierusalem.

10. Unde vos, o ornati
et o coronati
qui habitatis in Ierusalem,
et o tu Ruperte,
qui es socius eorum
in hac habitatione,
succurrite nobis famulantibus
et in exilio laborantibus.

1b. bonitatatis R[c]; lux *om.* V[2] 2a. adolescencia V[2]; que ardes in sole] text in D breaks off here. 2b. roberte R[b] Ruopperte V[2]; hys V[2] 3a. topazyo et saphyro V[2]; spelialiter R[c] 3b. roberte R[b] Ruopperte V[2]; in vera ostensione] after these words R[b] and V[2] insert an extra strophe (see Commentary). 4a. flexit R[b], V[2] 5. simphonizat R[b] 6. roberte R[b] ruopperte V[2]; adolescencia V[2]; in suavissimo] in *om.* V[2] 7. tuum] totum V[2]; torrencium V[2] 8. nubes *om.* V[2] 9. tue] tui R[b], V[2] 10. o coronati] o *om.* V[2]; o tu] o R[b] tu o V[2]; roberte R[b] Ruopperte V[2]

Like clouds they coursed
through the skies, the living
stones, on wings of goodwill,
to gleam in your walls.

Blood-red beacons
of martyrs flash there, candor
of virgins, splendor
of saints without number,
flashing forever—
in your turrets, Jerusalem.

Hear, O crowned ones,
O radiant-gowned ones,
you who dwell in Jerusalem!
And Rupert, helper and friend,
remember and send
for your servants in exile
when exile has end.

1a. O Jerusalem, golden city / decked with royal purple: 1b. O building of supreme goodness, / light never darkened: 1c. You are made lovely / at dawn and in the sun's heat. 2a. O blessed childhood, / you glow ruddy at dawn, / O praiseworthy youth, / you burn in the sun. 2b. For you, noble Rupert, / shone in these like a gem. / So you cannot be hidden by fools, / as a mountain cannot be concealed by a valley. 3a. Your windows, Jerusalem, / are specially embellished / with topaz and sapphire. 3b. While you gleam among them, O Rupert, / you cannot be hidden by tepid ways, / nor the mountain by the valley— / the mountain crowned with roses, lilies, and purple / in a true revelation. 4a. O tender flower of the field, / O sweet green of the apple, / O burden without pith, / not bowing the breast with sins. 4b. O noble vessel, / neither polluted / nor devoured / in the dance of the ancient cave, / nor weakened / by the ancient destroyer's wounds: 5. In you the Holy Spirit makes symphony, / for you are joined to the angelic choirs / and adorned in the Son of God, / since you have no stain. 6. What a beautiful vessel you are, / O Rupert! / In childhood / and in your youth / you sighed for God in the fear of God, / in the embrace of charity, / and in the sweetest

50. Mathias sanctus

1a. Mathias, sanctus per electionem,
vir preliator per victoriam,
ante sanguinem Agni electionem non habuit,
sed tardus in scientia fuit
quasi homo qui perfecte
non vigilat.

1b. Donum Dei illum excitavit,
unde ipse pre gaudio sicut gygas
in viribus suis surrexit,
quia Deus illum previdit
sicut hominem
quem de limo formavit
cum primus angelus cecidit,
qui Deum negavit.

2a. Homo qui electionem vidit—
ve, ve, cecidit!
Boves et arietes habuit,
sed faciem suam ab eis
retrorsum duxit
et illos dimisit.

fragrance of good works. 7. O Jerusalem, / your foundation is laid / with glowing stones— / with publicans and sinners / who had been lost sheep. / But, found by the Son of God, / they raced to you / and were placed in you. 8. So your walls / gleam with living stones / that flew like clouds in the sky / through the supreme zeal of goodwill. 9. So your towers, / O Jerusalem, / gleam ruddy and bright with the rosy glow / and the sparkling white of the saints, / and with all the ornaments of God / which you do not lack, O Jerusalem. 10. O adorned ones, / O crowned ones, / you who dwell in Jerusalem, / and you, Rupert, / their companion / in that dwelling: / help us who serve / and labor in exile.

50. Hymn to Saint Matthias

Matthias the fighting man
won this victory: he became a saint
by lot.
Before the Lamb died
he had no call: he came late
to his knowledge
like one half-sleeping.

God's gift aroused him!
He leapt for joy like a giant
in his prime—
for Providence knew him well—
waking just like Adam
from the slime
when the angel of denial fell.

The one God elected then—
alas! he had oxen
and rams for sacrifice
yet he turned his face
from the altar and fell.

2b. Unde foveam carbonum invasit,
et desideria sua osculatus
in studio suo,
illa sicut Olimpum
erexit.

3a. Tunc Mathias per electionem divinitatis
sicut gygas surrexit,
quia Deus illum posuit
in locum
quem perditus homo noluit.
O mirabile miraculum
quod sic in illo resplenduit!

3b. Deus enim ipsum previdit
in miraculis suis
cum nondum haberet meritum operationis,
sed misterium Dei
in illo gaudium habuit,
quod idem per institutionem suam
non habebat.

4a. O gaudium gaudiorum
quod Deus sic operatur,
cum nescienti homini gratiam suam impendit,
ita quod parvulus nescit
ubi magnus volat,
cuius alas Deus parvulo tribuit.

4b. Deus enim gustum in illo habet
qui seipsum nescit,
quia vox eius
ad Deum clamat
sicut Mathias fecit,
qui dixit:
O Deus, Deus meus, qui me creasti,
omnia opera mea tua sunt.

Instead of God he embraced
his desires, made
his wishes his idols. There
in a coalpit, he raised
his Olympus.

It was then that Matthias,
God's choice, rose like a giant.
God gave him the place
the lost one voided—and there
(O amazement!) his grace
dazzled our eyes.

For the God of wonders
saw his worth before he earned it.
In him the Mysterious One
took joy, not in Judas.

O joy of all joys that our God
gives grace to the ignorant!
The babe has no notion
where the mighty man flies—
yet God grants him his wings.

That man pleases God
who forgets himself,
who cries like Matthias:
O God, my God, you who made me—
all my works are yours.

5. Nunc ergo gaudeat omnis ecclesia
in Mathia,
quem Deus
in foramine columbe ṣic elegit.
Amen.

2a. retrosum R[c]

Let Matthias, God's choice,
be a joy to his Church, be a dove
in the clefts of his holy mountain.

1a. Matthias, a saint by election, / a warrior by victory, / was not chosen before the Lamb shed his blood. / Rather he was delayed in knowledge, / like a man who is not fully / awake. 1b. God's gift aroused him, / so he rose for joy like a giant / in his strength, / since God had foreseen him / just as he foresaw / the man he formed out of clay / when the first angel fell— / the one who denied God. 2a. The man who had seen election— / alas, alas, he fell! / He had oxen and rams, / yet he turned his face from them / and sent them away. 2b. So he plunged into a coalpit / and, embracing his desires / in his zeal, / he raised them up / like Olympus. 3a. Then Matthias arose like a giant / by divine election, / for God set him / in the place / that the lost man did not want. / O marvelous miracle / that he shone so brightly in it! 3b. For God foresaw him / in his miracles / when he did not yet have the merit of action, / but the mystery of God / took a joy in him / that he did not have / in his original plan. 4a. O joy of joys / that God acts thus! / He bestows his grace on one who is unaware, / as a little child does not know / where a great man is flying, / yet God grants his wings to the child. 4b. For God savors the man / who forgets himself, / because his voice / cries to God / as Matthias did / when he said: / "O God, my God, who created me, / all my works are yours." 5. Now then let the whole Church rejoice / in Matthias, / whom God chose this way / in the cleft of the dove. / Amen.

51. O Bonifaci

O Bonifaci,
lux vivens vidit te
similem viro sapienti,
qui puros rivulos
ex Deo fluentes
ad Deum remisisti,
cum viriditatem florum rigasti.
Unde es amicus Dei viventis
et cristallus lucens
in benivolentia
rectarum viarum,
in quibus sapienter
cucurristi.

51. Antiphon for Saint Boniface

The living light
watched you water your gardens
as a wise man hastens
the course of pure streams
that flow from God back to God.
Saint Boniface!
friend of the living God,
your goodwill gleams
in our path like crystal
lighting ways you traveled
in zeal for right.

O Boniface, / the living light saw you / as a wise man / who sent the pure streams / that flow from God / back to God, / when you watered the verdure of the flowers. / So you are a friend of the living God, / a crystal gleaming / with goodwill / along the righteous paths / where you wisely / ran.

52. O Euchari columba

O Euchari,
columba virtutem illius
in signis tibi dedit,
qui olim in medio rote clamitavit:

Quem cum amplius
corporaliter non vidisti,
plena signa in umbra illius
perfecisti.

Et sic in pectore eius fulsisti
ac in cherubin sigillum fecisti.

Quem cum amplius
corporaliter non vidisti,
plena signa in umbra illius
perfecisti.

52. Responsory for Saint Eucharius

Eucharius!
The dove made you mighty in signs
through the might of Christ
whose shout rang out from Ezekiel's wheel.
When his body slipped away in light
you wrought signs in his shadow.

So the brilliance of your soul
flashed a brightness like the seal
in the mirror-eyes of the cherubim.
When his body slipped away in light
you wrought signs in his shadow.

O Eucharius, / the dove gave you the power / in signs / of him who once cried out in the middle of the wheel. // When you saw him no longer / in the body, / you accomplished perfect signs / in his shadow. // And thus you shone on his breast / and set a seal among the cherubim. // When you saw him no longer / in the body, / you accomplished perfect signs / in his shadow.

53. O Euchari in leta via

1a. O Euchari,
in leta via ambulasti
ubi cum Filio Dei mansisti,
illum tangendo
et miracula eius que fecit videndo.

1b. Tu eum perfecte amasti
cum sodales tui exterriti erant,
pro eo quod homines erant,
nec possibilitatem habebant
bona perfecte intueri.

2a. Tu autem in ardenti amore plene caritatis
illum amplexus es,
cum manipulos preceptorum eius
ad te collegisti.

2b. O Euchari,
valde beatus fuisti
cum Verbum Dei te in igne columbe imbuit,
ubi tu quasi aurora illuminatus es,
et sic fundamentum ecclesie
edificasti.

3a. Et in pectore tuo
choruscat dies
in quo tria tabernacula
supra marmoream columpnam stant
in civitate Dei.

3b. Per os tuum Ecclesia ruminat
vetus et novum vinum,
videlicet poculum sanctitatis.

4a. Sed et in tua doctrina
Ecclesia effecta est racionalis,
ita quod supra montes clamavit
ut colles et ligna se declinarent
ac mamillas illius sugerent.

53. Sequence for Saint Eucharius

Eucharius!
you walked blithely when you stayed
with the Son of God,
touching him, watching
his miracle-working.

You loved him with a perfect love
when terror fell on your friends—
who being human had no
strength to bear the brightness
of the good.

But you—in a blaze of utmost love—
drew him to your heart
when you gathered the sheaves
of his precepts.

Eucharius!
when the Word of God possessed you
in the blaze of the dove,
when the sun rose in your spirit,
you founded a church in your bliss.

Daylight shimmers in your heart
where three tabernacles stand
on a marble pillar
in the city of God.

In your preaching Ecclesia
savors old wine with new—
a chalice twice hallowed.

And in your teaching Ecclesia
argued with such force
that her shout rang over the mountains,
that the hills and the woods might bow
to suck her breasts.

4b. Nunc in tua clara voce
Filium Dei ora pro hac turba,
ne in cerimoniis Dei deficiat,
sed ut vivens holocaustum
ante altare Dei fiat.

2a. ardente R[c]

Pray for this company now,
pray with resounding voice
that we forsake not Christ
in his sacred rites,
but become before his altar
a living sacrifice.

1a. O Eucharius, / you walked on a joyful path / when you stayed with the Son of God, / touching him / and seeing the miracles he did. 1b. You loved him perfectly / when your companions were terrified / because they were human / and had no power / to gaze perfectly upon the good. 2a. But you embraced him / in the ardent love of full charity, / when you gathered to yourself / the sheaves of his commandments. 2b. O Eucharius, / you were greatly blessed / when the Word of God steeped you in the fire of the dove. / You were illumined there like the dawn, / and thus you built the foundation / of a church. 3a. And in your breast / shimmers the daylight / where three tabernacles / stand on a marble pillar / in the city of God. 3b. Through your mouth the Church savors / old and new wine— / the chalice of holiness. 4a. But in your teaching / the Church was made rational, / so she cried out above the mountains, / that the hills and the woods might bow / and suck her breasts. 4b. Now in your clear voice / pray to the Son of God for this flock / that it may not fail in the rites of God, / but become a living sacrifice / before God's altar.

54. Columba aspexit

1a. Columba aspexit
per cancellos fenestre,
ubi ante faciem eius
sudando sudavit balsamum
de lucido Maximino.

1b. Calor solis exarsit
et in tenebras resplenduit,
unde gemma surrexit
in edificatione templi
purissimi cordis benivoli.

2a. Iste, turris excelsa
de ligno Libani et cipresso facta,
iacincto et sardio ornata est,
urbs precellens artes
aliorum artificum.

2b. Ipse, velox cervus,
cucurrit ad fontem purissime aque
fluentis de fortissimo lapide,
qui dulcia aromata irrigavit.

3a. O pigmentarii,
qui estis in suavissima viriditate
hortorum regis,
ascendentes in altum
quando sanctum sacrificium
in arietibus perfecistis:

3b. Inter vos fulget hic artifex,
paries templi,
qui desideravit alas aquile,
osculando nutricem Sapientiam
in gloriosa fecunditate
Ecclesie.

54. Sequence for Saint Maximin

A dove gazed in
through a latticed window:
there balm rained down on her face,
raining from lucent
Maximin.

The heat of the sun blazed out
to irradiate the dark:
a bud burst open, jewel-like,
in the temple of his heart
(limpid and kind his heart).

A tower of cypress is he,
and of Lebanon's cedars—
rubies and sapphires frame his turrets—
a city passing the arts
of all other artisans.

A swift stag is he
who ran to the fountain—
pure wellspring from a stone
of power—to water
sweet-smelling spices.

O perfumers! you who dwell
in the luxuriance of royal
gardens, climbing high
when you accomplish the holy
sacrifice with rams:

Among you this architect
is shining, a wall
of the temple, he who longed
for an eagle's wings as he kissed
his foster-mother Wisdom
in Ecclesia's garden.

4a. O Maximine,
mons et vallis es,
et in utroque alta
edificatio appares,
ubi capricornus
cum elephante exivit,
et Sapientia
in deliciis fuit.

4b. Tu es fortis et suavis
in cerimoniis
et in choruscatione altaris,
ascendens ut fumus aromatum
ad columpnam laudis:

5. Ubi intercedis pro populo
qui tendit ad speculum lucis,
cui laus est in altis.

1a. sudavit] sudan R^c

O Maximin,
mountain and valley,
on your towering height
the mountain goat leapt
with the elephant,
and Wisdom was in rapture.

Strong and sweet in the sacred
rites and in the shimmer
of the altar,
you rise like incense
to the pillar of praise—

where you pray for your people
who strive toward the mirror
of light. Praise him!
Praise in the highest!

1a. A dove gazed in / through the lattice of a window, / where before her face / a dripping balm dripped down / from lucent Maximin. 1b. The heat of the sun blazed out / and shone in the darkness, / so that a gem arose / in the building of the temple / of the most pure, benevolent heart. 2a. He, a lofty tower / built from the wood of Lebanon and cypress, / is adorned with jacinth and ruby: / a city surpassing the arts / of other artisans. 2b. He, a swift stag, / ran to the spring of purest water / flowing from the mighty stone, / the spring that watered sweet spices. 3a. O spice-dealers! / you who dwell in the sweetest foliage / of the King's gardens, / mounting on high / when you have accomplished / the holy sacrifice with rams: 3b. Among you shines this architect, / a wall of the temple, / he who longed for an eagle's wings / as he kissed his foster-mother Wisdom / amid the glorious fruitfulness / of the Church. 4a. O Maximin, / you are a mountain and a valley, / and in both you appear / as a lofty structure / where the mountain goat / walked with the elephant, / and Wisdom / was in rapture. 4b. You are strong and sweet / in the rites / and in the shimmer of the altar, / rising like the smoke of incense / to the pillar of praise, 5. Where you intercede for the people / who strive toward the mirror of light. / Praise to him in the highest!

VI
Virgins, Widows, and Innocents

55. O pulcre facies

O pulcre facies,
Deum aspicientes
et in aurora edificantes,
o beate virgines,
quam nobiles estis,
in quibus rex se consideravit
cum in vobis
omnia celestia ornamenta
presignavit,
ubi etiam suavissimus hortus estis,
in omnibus ornamentis
redolentes.

---

1 pulche D 10 ortus D, R^c 12 redolentis D

56. O nobilissima viriditas

O nobilissima viriditas,
que radicas in sole
et que in candida serenitate
luces in rota
quam nulla terrena excellentia
comprehendit:

Tu circumdata es
amplexibus divinorum
ministeriorum.

Tu rubes ut aurora
et ardes ut solis flamma.

---

5 excellencia R^c 7 est D 9 misteriorum R^a

55. Antiphon for Virgins

Exquisite
eyes fixed on God,
blithe noble virgins,
beholding him and building
at dawn:
the king saw his image
in your faces
when he made you mirrors of
all heaven's graces,
a garden of surpassing
sweetness, a fragrance
wafting all graciousness.

O beautiful faces, / beholding God / and building in the dawn! / O blessed virgins, / how noble are you, / in whom the King contemplated himself / when he sealed in you / beforehand / all the beauties of heaven. / So you are the sweetest garden, / fragrant / with all beauties.

56. Responsory for Virgins

Most noble
evergreen with your roots
in the sun:
you shine in the cloudless
sky of a sphere no earthly
eminence can grasp,
enfolded in the clasp
of ministries divine.

You blush like the dawn,
you burn like a flame
of the sun.

O most noble greenness, / you are rooted in the sun, / and you shine in bright serenity / in a sphere / no earthly eminence / attains. // You are enfolded / in the embraces of divine / ministries. // You blush like the dawn / and burn like a flame of the sun.

57. O dulcissime amator

1. O dulcissime amator,
o dulcissime amplexator:
adiuva nos custodire
virginitatem nostram.

2. Nos sumus orte in pulvere,
heu, heu,
et in crimine Ade.
Valde durum est contradicere
quod habet gustus pomi.
Tu erige nos, Salvator Christe.

3. Nos desideramus ardenter te sequi.
O quam grave nobis miseris est
te immaculatum et innocentem
regem angelorum imitari.

4. Tamen confidimus in te,
quod tu desideres gemmam requirere
in putredine.

5. Nunc advocamus te,
sponsum et consolatorem,
qui nos redemisti
in cruce.

6. In tuo sanguine
copulate sumus tibi
cum desponsatione,
repudiantes virum
et eligentes te,
Filium Dei.

7. O pulcherrima forma,
o suavissime odor
desiderabilium deliciarum,
semper suspiramus post te
in lacrimabili exilio.
Quando te videamus
et tecum maneamus?

57. Symphony of Virgins

Sweet lover! you of the sweet
embraces! help us keep
our virginity.

We were born in dust,
alas! and in the guilt
of Adam.
Not easy to resist
what tastes of the apple.
Lift us up, O Christ,
Savior!

How we long to pursue you—
and how hard for us wretches
to follow the blameless one,
the chaste king of angels.

Yet we trust you,
for we know that you long
to redeem your gem from the slime.

We call you now as bridegroom
for you bought us on the cross:
we call you to comfort us.

You pledged us in your blood,
we were married! we are yours,
we'll have no husbands:
we choose God's Son.

O your beauty! O the fragrance
of the joys we yearn for!
we sigh for you always,
banished, weeping—
when can we see you,
remain with you?

8. Nos sumus in mundo
et tu in mente nostra,
et amplectimur te in corde
quasi habeamus te presentem.

9. Tu fortissimus leo
rupisti celum,
descendens in aulam Virginis,
et destruxisti mortem,
edificans vitam in aurea civitate.

10. Da nobis societatem cum illa
et permanere in te,
o dulcissime sponse,
qui abstraxisti nos de faucibus diaboli,
primum parentem nostrum seducentis.

---

1. o dulcissime amplexator] et o R^b, V^2 2. Valde] et ideo valde R^b, V^2; est *om.* V^2; Tu] Sed tu R^b, V^2 3. Nos] Nos enim R^b, V^2; inmaculatum R^b 7. O pulcherrima] O *om.* R^c; suavissimus D, R^c; suspiravimus V^2 9. destruxxisti V^2; ediffICANS D 10. dyaboli V^2; seducentem D, R^b, V^2

We live in the world
and you in our minds:
we embrace you at heart
as if we held you.

A ferocious lion,
you shattered the sky and came down
to the Virgin's palace:
you vanquished death and built
life in the golden city.

Grant us her friendship
and help us abide in you,
our beloved, you who snatched us
from the devil's jaws,
from the fiend that seduced our mother.

1. O sweetest lover, / O giver of sweetest embraces, / help us keep / our virginity. 2. We were born in dust, / alas, alas! / and in the guilt of Adam. / It is very hard to resist / what tastes of the apple. / Lift us up, O Savior Christ! 3. We long ardently to follow you. / O how hard it is for us wretches / to imitate you, the immaculate / and innocent King of angels. 4. Yet we trust in you, / that you long to seek your gem / in the slime. 5. Now we call on you, / our bridegroom and comforter, / you who redeemed us / on the Cross. 6. In your blood / we were married to you / with a pledge of betrothal, / renouncing a husband / and choosing you, / the Son of God. 7. O fairest form, / O sweetest fragrance / of longed-for delights! / We sigh for you always / in tearful exile. / When may we see you / and remain with you? 8. We are in the world / and you in our mind: / we embrace you at heart / as if we held you present. 9. A mighty lion, / you burst through heaven, / coming down to the Virgin's palace, / and you destroyed death, / building up life in the golden city. 10. Grant us companionship with her / and let us abide in you, / O sweetest bridegroom, / you who snatched us from the devil's jaws, / from him who seduced our first parent.

58. O Pater omnium

1. O Pater omnium
et o rex et imperator gentium,
qui constituisti nos in costa prime matris,
que construxit nobis magnum casum erumpne,
et nos secute sumus illam
in propria causa in exilio,
sociantes nos illius dolori.

2. O tu nobilissime genitor,
per summum studium currimus ad te,
et per dilectissimam
atque per dulcissimam penitentiam
que nobis per te venit,
anhelamus ad te
et post dolorem nostrum
devotissime amplectimur te.

3. O gloriosissime
et o pulcherrime Christe,
qui es resurrectio vite,
nos reliquimus propter te
fertilem amatorem coniunctionis,
et comprehendimus te
in superna caritate
et in virginea virga nativitatis tue,
ac in altera vice copulate sumus tibi
quam prius essemus secundum carnem.

4. Adiuva nos perseverare
et tecum gaudere
et a te numquam separari.

---

1. gencium V[2]; erumne D 2. penitenciam V[2] 3. et o] o *om.* R[b], V[2]; amatorem] R[c] reads amorem *corrected to* amatorem; conprehendimus V[2]; karitate R[c]; ac] et R[b]; tibi interlinear R[b], *om.* V[2] 4. nos] nos tecum R[b], V[2]

58. Symphony of Widows

Father of all and king
and emperor above all kings!
In Adam's rib, first of mothers,
you formed us: but she carved
an abyss of woe—and we
raced after her, embraced
her exile, made her pain
our own.

O first of fathers! Now we race
after you with our final effort,
delighting in penance
(so lovely and so longed-for)
as we sigh for your love:
after our pain
we devoutly embrace you.

Christ of glory, Christ
of beauty! resurrection
into life! for you we left
marriage, turned from fertility:
we embrace you in charity
like the people of heaven,
O child of the virgin:
when you wed us in the spirit
you divorced us from our flesh.

Help us to be faithful
until we rejoice with you,
never to leave you.

1. O Father of all, / O King and Emperor of nations, / you created us in the rib of the first mother, / she who built for us a great fall into affliction. / And we followed her / in our own right into exile, / uniting ourselves with her pain. 2. O most noble Father! / With a supreme effort we race to you, / and we sigh for you / with the loveliest / and sweetest penance / that comes to us from you. / After our pain / we devoutly embrace

59. Rex noster promptus

Rex noster promptus est
suscipere sanguinem innocentum.
Unde angeli concinunt
et in laudibus sonant.

Sed nubes super eundem sanguinem
plangunt.

Tirannus autem
in gravi somno mortis
propter maliciam suam
suffocatus est.

Sed nubes super eundem sanguinem
plangunt.

Gloria Patri et Filio
et Spiritui sancto.

Sed nubes super eundem sanguinem
plangunt.

you. 3. O most glorious, / O most beautiful Christ! / You are the resurrection into life. / For your sake we have renounced / a fertile lover in marriage, / and we have clasped you / in supernal charity / and in the virginal branch of your birth. / We are married to you in a different way / than we were before according to the flesh. 4. Help us to persevere / and rejoice with you, / and never to be parted from you.

59. Responsory for the Holy Innocents

Our king is swift to receive
the blood of innocents:
angels in concert chime their praise.

But for blood that was spilled
the clouds are grieving.

In a grave dream the tyrant
was choked for his malice.

But for blood that was spilled
the clouds are grieving.

Glorify the Father,
the Spirit and the Son.

But for blood that was spilled
the clouds are grieving.

Our king is swift / to receive the blood of innocents. / So the angels sing / and resound in praise. // But over that blood / the clouds are grieving. // The tyrant / was choked / on account of his malice / in the heavy sleep of death. // But over that blood / the clouds are grieving.

VII

Saint Ursula and Companions

60. Spiritui sancto

Spiritui sancto
honor sit,
qui in mente Ursule virginis
virginalem turbam
velut columbas
collegit.
Unde ipsa patriam suam
sicut Abraham reliquit.

Et etiam propter amplexionem Agni
desponsationem viri sibi
abstraxit.

Nam iste castissimus
et aureus exercitus
in virgineo crine
mare transivit.
O quis umquam talia
audivit?

Et etiam propter amplexionem Agni
desponsationem viri sibi
abstraxit.

Gloria Patri et Filio
et Spiritui sancto.

Et etiam propter amplexionem Agni
desponsationem viri sibi
abstraxit.

21–25 *om.* D

60. Responsory for Saint Ursula

Hail to the Holy Spirit!
In the mind of Ursula,
maiden, a flock
of maidens gathered like doves
and she left the land of her fathers
like another Abraham.

And she left the man who had pledged her
to lie in the arms of the Lamb.

So that golden, chaste armada,
army of unveiled maids,
sailed over the sea.
Who ever heard such tales?

For she left the man who had pledged her
to lie in the arms of the Lamb.

Glorify the Father,
the Spirit and the Son.

She left the man who had pledged her
to lie in the arms of the Lamb.

Honor be / to the Holy Spirit! / In the mind of Ursula the virgin / he gathered / a virginal flock / like doves. / And so like Abraham / she left her fatherland. // For the sake of the Lamb's embrace / she tore herself away / from betrothal to a man. // For that most chaste / and golden army / crossed over the sea / with virginal hair [unbound]. / O who ever heard / such things? // For the sake of the Lamb's embrace / she tore herself away / from betrothal to a man.

61. O rubor sanguinis

O rubor sanguinis,
qui de excelso illo fluxisti
quod divinitas tetigit:
tu flos es
quem hyems de flatu serpentis
numquam lesit.

---

5 hyemps R^{c}

61. Antiphon for Saint Ursula

Red river falling
from the touch of God,
a flower of blood,
serpentine winter's
winds cannot wilt you.

O redness of blood, / you flowed from that lofty height / that Divinity touched: / you are a flower / that the winter of the serpent's breath / has never harmed.

62. Favus distillans

Favus distillans
Ursula virgo fuit,
que Agnum Dei amplecti
desideravit,
mel et lac sub lingua eius:

Quia pomiferum hortum
et flores florum
in turba virginum
ad se collegit.

Unde in nobilissima
aurora
gaude, filia Syon.

Quia pomiferum hortum
et flores florum
in turba virginum
ad se collegit.

Gloria Patri et Filio
et Spiritui sancto.

Quia pomiferum hortum
et flores florum
in turba virginum
ad se collegit.

62. Responsory for Saint Ursula

A dripping honeycomb
was Ursula, virgin,
who yearned to lie with God's lamb,
honey and milk beneath her tongue.

For she gathered around her
a flock of virgins,
a fruit-bearing orchard,
a garden in bloom.

Rejoice, daughter of Zion,
in the exalted dawn!

For she gathered around her
a flock of virgins,
a fruit-bearing orchard,
a garden in bloom.

Glorify the Father,
the Spirit and the Son.

She gathered around her
a flock of virgins,
a fruit-bearing orchard,
a garden in bloom.

A dripping honeycomb / was Ursula the virgin, / who yearned / to embrace the Lamb of God, / honey and milk beneath her tongue. // For she gathered to herself / a fruitful garden / and the choicest flowers / in a flock of virgins. // So rejoice, daughter of Zion, / in the most noble / dawn. // For she gathered to herself / a fruitful garden / and the choicest flowers / in a flock of virgins.

63. In matutinis laudibus

1. Studium divinitatis
in laudibus excelsis osculum pacis
Ursule virgini
cum turba sua
in omnibus populis dedit.

2. Unde quocumque venientes
perrexerunt,
velut cum gaudio celestis paradisi
suscepte sunt,
quia in religione morum
honorifice apparuerunt.

3. De patria etiam earum
et de aliis regionibus
viri religiosi
et sapientes
ipsis adiuncti sunt,
qui eas in virginea custodia servabant
et qui eis in omnibus ministrabant.

4. Deus enim
in prima muliere presignavit
ut mulier a viri custodia
nutriretur.

5. Aer enim volat
et cum omnibus creaturis
officia sua exercet,
et firmamentum eum sustinet
ac aer in viribus istius pascitur.

6. Et ideo puelle iste
per summum virum sustentabantur,
vexillate in regali prole
virginee nature.

7. Deus enim rorem in illas misit,
de quo multiplex fama crevit,
ita quod omnes populi
ex hac honorabili fama
velut cibum gustabant.

63. Antiphons for Saint Ursula

1. Praise rang in heaven
when God kissed his virgins,
Ursula and her flock—
a kiss of peace in the sight
of all peoples.

2. Wherever they came they were welcomed
as if they brought paradise
down from above—their lives,
their religion,
seemed rich in honor.

3. From England and every land
monks joined their band,
with learned men who served them
and preserved their virginity.

4. For a woman deserves
a man's care and protection—
God revealed it through Eve.

5. The life-giving wind
that sustains all creation
is itself sustained by the vault
of heaven, and feeds
on heaven's strength.

6. Even so these maids
were sustained by the greatest
man of all: they bore the standard
of the Virgin's royal child.

7. So God watered them
with dew, good report
grew around them,
and their fame was bread to all lands.

8. Sed diabolus in invidia sua
istud irrisit,
qua nullum opus Dei
intactum dimisit.

---

2. paradysi R^c 3. eis] eas D 5. ac] aer D 8. unnvidia R^c; qua] quod D

---

64. O Ecclesia

1. O Ecclesia,
oculi tui similes
saphiro sunt,
et aures tue monti Bethel,
et nasus tuus est
sicut mons mirre et thuris,
et os tuum quasi sonus
aquarum multarum.

8. Only the devil laughed
honor to scorn:
in his envy he left
no work of God untouched.

1. Divine zeal / gave the virgin Ursula / with her flock / a kiss of peace amid the highest praises / before all peoples. 2. So wherever they came, / they were received / as with the joy of celestial paradise, / for in the religious life / they appeared full of honor. 3. Both from their fatherland / and from other regions, / religious / and learned men / were joined with them. / These men protected them in virginal custody / and served them in all things. 4. For God / signified in the first woman / that a woman should be nurtured / by the protection of a man. 5. For the air flies / and fulfills its offices / with all creatures / and the firmament supports it; / the air is nourished by its powers. 6. And so these girls, / bearing the standard of the royal Child / of virginal nature, / were supported by the supreme man. 7. For God sent a dew upon them, / from which their fame grew so manifold / that all peoples / tasted of this honorable fame / as of a food. 8. But the devil in his envy / made a mockery of it: / by envy he has left no work of God / untouched.

64. Sequence for Saint Ursula

Ecclesia! your eyes
are like sapphires, your ears
like Mount Bethel, your nose
like a mountain of incense and myrrh,
your voice like the sound of many waters.

2. In visione vere fidei
Ursula Filium Dei amavit
et virum cum hoc seculo reliquit
et in solem aspexit
atque pulcherrimum iuvenem
vocavit, dicens:

3. In multo desiderio
desideravi ad te venire
et in celestibus
nuptiis tecum sedere,
per alienam viam ad te currens
velut nubes que in purissimo aere
currit similis saphiro.

4. Et postquam Ursula
sic dixerat,
rumor iste
per omnes populos exiit.
Et dixerunt:
Innocentia puellaris ignorantie
nescit quid dicit.

5. Et ceperunt ludere cum illa
in magna symphonia,
usque dum ignea sarcina
super eam cecidit.
Unde omnes cognoscebant
quia contemptus mundi est
sicut mons Bethel.

6. Et cognoverunt etiam
suavissimum odorem
mirre et thuris,
quoniam contemptus mundi
super omnia ascendit.

7. Tunc diabolus
membra sua invasit,
que nobilissimos mores
in corporibus istis
occiderunt.

Ursula fell in love
with God's Son in a vision:
her faith was true. She rejected
her man and all the world
and gazed straight into the sun,
crying out to her beloved,
fairest of the sons of men:

With yearning I have yearned
to come to you and sit by you
at our wedding in heaven!
Let me race to you strangely,
chase you like a sapphire cloud
where the sky is purest.

When Ursula had spoken,
all people heard her and answered:
how naive she is! the girl
has no notion what she means!

And they began
to mock her in harmony—
until the burden of flame
fell upon her. Then they learned
how scorn for the world is like Mount Bethel.

And they discovered
the fragrance of incense and myrrh—
because scorn for the world
mounts above all.

Then the devil possessed his own.
In those virgin bodies they
slaughtered nobility.

8. Et hoc in alta voce
omnia elementa audierunt
et ante thronum Dei
dixerunt:

9. Wach!
rubicundus sanguis innocentis agni
in desponsatione sua
effusus est.

10. Hoc audiant omnes celi
et in summa symphonia
laudent Agnum Dei,
quia guttur serpentis antiqui
in istis margaritis
materie Verbi Dei
suffocatum est.

---

1. saphyro R[c] 4. Et dixerunt] capital marks new stanza in R[c] 5. simphonia D; Unde] capital R[c] 8. trhonum D 10. simphonia D; matherie D

And all the elements heard
the clamor of their blood and cried
before the throne of God:

Ach! the scarlet
blood of an innocent lamb
is spilled at her wedding.

Let all the heavens hear it
and praise God's Lamb in great harmony—
for the neck of the ancient serpent
is choked in these pearls
strung on the Word of God.

1. O Church, / your eyes / are like sapphire, / and your ears like Mount Bethel, / your nose / like a mountain of incense and myrrh, / and your mouth like the sound / of many waters. 2. In a vision of true faith, / Ursula fell in love with the Son of God / and renounced a husband along with this world. / She gazed upon the sun / and called to the fairest youth, / saying: 3. In great yearning / I have yearned to come to you / and sit with you / at the heavenly wedding feast, / racing to you by a strange path / like a cloud that, in the purest sky, / races like sapphire. 4. And after Ursula / had spoken thus, / this report / went out among all peoples. / And they said: / In the innocence of girlish ignorance, / she knows not what she says. 5. And they began to sport with her / in great harmony, / until the fiery burden / fell upon her. / Then all people recognized / that scorn for the world is / like Mount Bethel. 6. And they recognized also / the sweetest fragrance / of incense and myrrh, / because scorn for the world / mounts above all. 7. Then the devil / entered into his members, / who, in those bodies, / slaughtered / the noblest way of life. 8. And all the elements heard this / and said in a loud voice / before the throne of God: 9. Wach! / the scarlet blood of an innocent lamb / is spilled / at her betrothal. 10. Let all the heavens hear this / and in supreme harmony / praise the Lamb of God: / for the throat of the ancient serpent / is strangled / in these pearls / from the matter of the Word of God.

65. Cum vox sanguinis

1. Cum vox sanguinis
Ursule et innocentis turbe eius
ante thronum Dei sonuit,
antiqua prophetia venit
per radicem Mambre
in vera ostensione Trinitatis
et dixit:

2. Iste sanguis nos tangit,
nunc omnes gaudeamus.

3. Et postea venit congregatio Agni,
per arietem in spinis pendentem,
et dixit:

4. Laus sit in Ierusalem
per ruborem huius sanguinis.

5. Deinde venit sacrificium vituli
quod vetus lex ostendebat,
sacrificium laudis
circumamicta varietate,
et que faciem Dei Moysi obnubilabat,
dorsum illi ostendens.

6. Hoc sunt sacerdotes
qui per linguas suas Deum ostendunt
et perfecte eum videre non possunt,
et dixerunt:

7. O nobilissima turba,
virgo ista que in terris Ursula vocatur
in summis Columba nominatur,
quia innocentem turbam
ad se collegit.

8. O Ecclesia, tu es laudabilis
in ista turba.

65. Hymn to Saint Ursula

When the voice of Ursula's blood
and the blood of her innocent
flock cried like Abel's
before the throne of God,
an ancient prophet came forth—
he who saw the truth
of the Trinity by the oaks
of Mamre—and he said:

This blood is touching us!
Let us all rejoice!

Then came the company of the Lamb,
foreshadowed by the ram
that hung amid thorns—and they said:

By the redness of this blood,
let praise be sung in Jerusalem!

Then came the sacrificial calf
of the ancient Law—a sacrifice
of praise in many colors.
For the Law showed Moses
God's back but veiled his face.

Understand by this the priests
who make God known with their words
yet cannot wholly see him.
And they said:

O noble flock! This maid
who on earth is called Ursula
is named in heaven Columba,
for she gathered around her
an innocent flock.

In that flock, O Ecclesia,
you have garnered praise!

9. Turba magna, quam incombustus rubus
(quem Moyses viderat) significat,
et quam Deus in prima radice plantaverat
in homine quem de limo formaverat,
ut sine commixtione viri viveret,
cum clarissima voce clamavit
in purissimo auro, thopazio,
et saphiro circumamicta in auro.

10. Nunc gaudeant omnes celi,
et omnes populi cum illis ornentur.
Amen.

---

3. Et] no capital in D 5. vittuli R[c] 7. virgo] virga D 8. *om.* R[c] 9. auro] agno D

The bush that Moses saw in flames,
burning but not consumed,
signifies this flock, this root
of healing in the human stock
that God modeled from clay
to live without coupling. Clear
rang their voices in a cry
of fine gold, topaz
and sapphire set in rings of gold.

Let all the heavens
make merry, let all the nations
put on these jewels!

1. When the voice of Ursula's blood / and the blood of her innocent flock / resounded before the throne of God, / the ancient prophecy came forth / in a true revelation of the Trinity / by the root of Mamre, / and said: 2. This blood is touching us! / Now let us all rejoice. 3. And then came the congregation of the Lamb, / [figured by] the ram hanging among thorns, / and said: 4. Let there be praise in Jerusalem / through the redness of this blood! 5. Next came the sacrifice of the calf / that the Old Law revealed— / a sacrifice of praise / clothed in many colors. / The Law hid God's face from Moses in a cloud, / showing him God's back. 6. This refers to the priests / who reveal God by their language / and cannot perfectly see him. / And they said: 7. O most noble flock! / This virgin, who on earth is called Ursula, / is named in the heights Columba, / for she has gathered to herself / an innocent flock. 8. O Church, you deserve praise / in this flock! 9. The great flock, signified by the burning bush / that Moses saw, / is the flock God had planted in the primal root, / in the human being he had formed out of clay / to live without the commingling of man. / With the clearest voice the flock cried out / in the purest gold, in topaz / and sapphire surrounded by gold. 10. Now let all the heavens rejoice, / and all the peoples be adorned with these. / Amen.

VIII
Ecclesia

66. O virgo Ecclesia

O virgo Ecclesia,
plangendum est,
quod sevissimus lupus
filios tuos
de latere tuo abstraxit.
O ve callido serpenti!
Sed o quam preciosus est sanguis
Salvatoris,
qui in vexillo regis
Ecclesiam ipsi desponsavit,
unde filios
illius requirit.

66. Antiphon for Dedication of a Church

Ecclesia, mourn!
Virgin, lament!
That savage
wolf—shame
on that snake!—
has snatched your sons.
Cursed be his cunning!
But the savior
raises his
standard,
he ransoms
all with his blood—
he makes you his bride!

O virgin Church, / we must grieve / because a most savage wolf / has snatched your children / from your side. / O woe to the cunning serpent! / But O how precious is the blood / of the Savior, / who betrothed the Church to himself / with the King's standard. / Therefore he is seeking / her children.

67. Nunc gaudeant

Nunc gaudeant materna viscera
Ecclesie,
quia in superna simphonia
filii eius
in sinum suum collocati sunt.
Unde, o turpissime serpens,
confusus es,
quoniam quos tua estimatio
in visceribus suis habuit
nunc fulgent in sanguine Filii Dei,
et ideo laus tibi sit,
rex altissime.
Alleluia.

---

1 Nunc] Nunc autem R^b, V^2 3 symphonia R^b, V^2 13 Alleluia *om.* R^b, V^2

68. O orzchis Ecclesia

O orzchis Ecclesia,
armis divinis precincta
et iacincto ornata,
tu es caldemia stigmatum loifolum
et urbs scientiarum.
O, o, tu es etiam crizanta
in alto sono
et es chorzta gemma.

---

1 O orzchis] orhchis S 4 caldemya V^2; sticmatum R^b, V^2; loiffolum S, V^2 6 cryzanta V^2

67. Antiphon for Dedication of a Church

Let Mother Ecclesia
sing for joy!
Her children are found,
she gathers them home
to celestial harmony.
But you, vile serpent,
lie low! For those
your jealousy held in its maw
now shine in the blood of Christ.
Praise to our King,
praise to the Highest!
Alleluia.

Now let the motherly heart / of the Church rejoice, / for in supernal symphony / her children / are gathered into her bosom. / So you, shameful serpent, / are confounded, / for those your jealousy / held in its maw / now gleam in the blood of God's Son. / Praise then be yours, / O King Most High! / Alleluia.

68. Antiphon for Dedication of a Church

Ecclesia! maiden
tall beyond measure, clad
in God's armor, your gems
the color of heaven:
you are the fragrance
of the wounds of nations,
the city of knowledge.
O lady, O jewel
ever sparkling:
such music
sounds at your crowning!

O measureless Church, / girded with divine armor / and adorned with jacinth, / you are the fragrance of the wounds of nations, / the city of sciences. / O, O, you are anointed / amid lofty song: / you are a sparkling gem.

69. O choruscans lux stellarum

O choruscans lux stellarum,
o splendidissima specialis forma
regalium nuptiarum,
o fulgens gemma:
tu es ornata in alta persona
que non habet maculatam rugam.
Tu es etiam socia angelorum
et civis sanctorum.
Fuge, fuge speluncam
antiqui perditoris,
et veniens veni in palatium regis.

69. Antiphon for Dedication of a Church

O glistening starlight,
O royal bride-elect,
resplendent, O sparkling
gem: you are robed
like a noble lady
without spot or wrinkle.
Companion of angels,
fellow citizen with saints—
flee, flee the ancient
destroyer's cave and come—
come into the palace of the King!

O glistening starlight, / O resplendent, special form / of the royal nuptials, / O sparkling gem: / you are arrayed as a noble person / without blemish or wrinkle. / You are a companion of angels / and a citizen of the holy places. / Flee, flee the cave / of the ancient destroyer, / and come, come into the palace of the King.

Four Songs without Music

O Verbum Patris

O Verbum Patris,
tu lumen prime aurore
in circulo rote es,
omnia in divina vi operans.
O tu prescientia Dei,
omnia opera tua previdisti,
sicut voluisti,
ita quod in medio potencie tue latuit
quod omnia prescivisti,
et operatus es
quasi in similitudine rote
cuncta circueuntis,
que inicium non accepit
nec in fine prostrata est.

---

8 quod] ut R^b; potentie R^b 9 quod] quia R^b 11 similitudinem V^2 12 circueunte R^b, V^2

Song to the Creator

You, all-accomplishing
Word of the Father,
are the light of primordial
daybreak over the spheres.
You, the foreknowing
mind of divinity,
foresaw all your works
as you willed them,
your prescience hidden
in the heart of your power,
your power like a wheel around the world,
whose circling never began
and never slides to an end.

O Word of the Father, / you are the light of the primal dawn / in the rim of a wheel, / accomplishing all things in divine power. / O foreknowledge of God, / you foresaw all your works / as you willed, / so in the midst of your power it lay hidden / that you foreknew them all, / and you acted / as if in the likeness of a wheel / encompassing all, / a sphere that had no beginning / nor is it cast down in the end.

O Fili dilectissime

O Fili dilectissime,
quem genui in visceribus meis
de vi circueuntis rote
sancte divinitatis,
que me creavit
et omnia membra mea ordinavit
et in visceribus meis
omne genus musicorum
in omnibus floribus tonorum
constituit,
nunc me et te,
o Fili dulcissime,
multa turba virginum sequitur,
quas per adiutorium tuum salvare
dignare.

---

6 et] ac V2 12 o *om.* V2

Song of the Virgin to Her Son

O beloved son
whom I bore in my womb
by the might of the circling
wheel of the holy
God who created me
and formed all my limbs
and laid in my womb
all manner of music
in all the flowers of sound:
now a flock
of virgins follows
me and you:
help and save them,
dearest son.

O beloved Son, / whom I bore in my womb / by the might of the circling wheel / of the holy Godhead, / who created me / and arranged all my limbs, / and laid in my womb / all manner of music / in all the flowers of the tones: / Now a great flock of virgins / follows me and you, / O sweetest Son. / Deign by your help to save them.

O factura Dei

O factura Dei
que es homo,
in magna sanctitate edificata es,
quia sancta divinitas in humilitate
celos penetravit.
O quam magna pietas est
quod in limo terre deitas claruit,
et quod angeli Deo ministrantes
Deum in humanitate vident.

---

4 in humilitate *om.* V^2

Song to the Redeemer

O handiwork of God,
O human form divine!
In great holiness
you were fashioned,
for the Holy One pierced the heavens
in great humility
and the splendor of God shone forth
in the slime of the earth:
the angels that minister on high
see heaven clothed in humanity.

O handiwork of God / which is man: / in great holiness you were built, / for the holy Godhead / pierced the heavens in humility. / O what great kindness it is / that Deity shone forth in the slime of the earth, / and the angels who minister to God / see God in humanity.

O magna res

1a. O magna res
que in nullo constituto latuit,
ita quod non est facta
nec creata ab ullo,
sed in se ipsa permanet.

1b. O vita
que surrexisti in aurora,
in qua magnus rex sapientiam
que in antiquo
apud virum sapientem fuit
misericorditer manifestavit,
quia mulier per foramen antiqui perditoris
mortem intravit.

2a. O luctus! Ach meror! He planctus,
qui in muliere edificati sunt!

2b. O aurora, hec abluisti
in forma prime coste.

3a. O feminea forma, soror Sapientie,
quam gloriosa es,
quoniam fortissima vita
in te surrexit,
quam mors nunquam suffocabit.

3b. Te Sapientia erexit,
ita quod omnes creature
per te ornate sunt,
in meliorem partem
quam in primo acciperent.

1a. se ipsa] semetipsa V² 1b. aput V³ 2b. abluisti] abstulisti V² 3b. sapiencia V²; creature] create S; acceperunt S

Song to the Virgin

No creature
concealed the great wonder.
Nobody made it,
nobody formed it:
it abides in itself.

But life sprang up at daybreak
when the High King in mercy
unveiled the wisdom
of the ancient sage—
because a woman opened the door
of the ancient fiend
and entered death's kingdom.

O the grief! the tears! the mourning
that were built in that woman!
But you, the daybreak—
you washed them away
in the figure of Adam's rib.

O form of woman, sister of Wisdom,
great is your glory!
For in you there sprang a life unquenchable
that death shall never stifle.

Wisdom exalted you to make
all creatures fairer through your beauty
than they were when the world was born.

1a. O greatness / that lay hidden in no created thing, / so that it was neither made / nor created by anyone, / but abides in itself. 1b. O life / that arose in the dawn, / in which the great King / mercifully revealed the wisdom / that the wise man possessed / of old, / because a woman entered into death / through the ancient destroyer's passage. 2a. O the grief! Ah, the sorrow! Alas, the mourning / that were built in the woman! 2b. O dawn, you washed them away / in the form of the primal rib. 3a. O feminine form, sister of Wisdom, / how glorious you are, / for in you has arisen / the mightiest life / that death shall never stifle. 3b. Wisdom exalted you / so that, by you, all creatures / are made more beautiful / with a better share / than they received in the beginning.

Commentary

After each title I have listed the genre of the piece, its subject or rubric as given in the manuscripts, and its locations. The B-R numbers in parentheses identify the location of each song in Pudentiana Barth, M-I. Ritscher, and Joseph Schmidt-Görg, eds., *Hildegard von Bingen: Lieder* (Salzburg, 1969). In the commentary I have dealt with obscure and difficult passages, scriptural allusions, related texts in Hildegard's oeuvre, distinctive poetic features, and other material that will help the reader form a just appreciation. I have not tried to provide an exhaustive reading of each poem, nor have I dealt with the relationship between text and music. References are given in short form; full information may be found in the bibliography.

1. O vis eternitatis (B-R 58)
Responsory.
R^b 405va; R^c 466ra; V^2 156va

This responsory, which opens the *Symphonia* in R, begins as a prayer to the Father but modulates into a joyful confession of faith. Its grandiose and simple theme, setting the tone for all that follows, is the fulfillment of God's eternal design through creation by the Word and recreation by the Word-made-flesh. Typically,

Hildegard celebrates the Incarnation itself, not Christ's death, as the central liberating moment in history; and she sees the fallen world freed not so much from sin as from suffering. In fact, she passes silently over the crucial event of Adam's fall. In her symbolic idiom, "garments" represent the body, but the repetenda or refrain is cunningly positioned so that Adam's clothing in the first response becomes Christ's in the second, in token that the Savior has "put on" human flesh. By a similar transposition, the "form / that was taken from Adam," a circumlocution for Eve, is used by extension of all womankind and hence of Mary. The psalmlike shift from second to third person is one of Hildegard's literary mannerisms.

2. **O virtus Sapientie (B-R 59)**
Votive antiphon.
R^c 466rb

Divine Wisdom—Sophia or Sapientia—is a many-splendored biblical personage (see Prov. 8–9, Ecclus. 24, Wisd. of Sol. 7–8). In Hildegard's visions she often appeared as a radiant female figure. But in this evocative antiphon, Wisdom takes a more abstract form. The three-winged figure invites comparison with a visually similar image in *Scivias* III.5. In that vision, however, the winged form is terrible and represents the jealousy of God (*zelum Dei*); posted like a gargoyle at the corner of a church, it beats its wings in fury. Here, its gentler analogue recalls the six-winged seraph of Isaiah 6; "with two wings he covered his face, and with two he covered his feet, and with two he flew." Another source for the image is the figure of Wisdom the creatrix, who "circled the vault of heaven alone, and pierced into the depth of the abyss" (Ecclus. 24:8). Or the three wings can be taken as emblems of the three divine Persons: the Father in heaven, the Son upon earth, and the ubiquitous Spirit. *Sudat,* a double-edged verb (l. 7), suggests Christ's agonized sweat in Gethsemane (Luke 22:44) even as it evokes an older affinity between Wisdom and Nature, which "exudes" everything lush, green, and fruitful.

3. O quam mirabilis (B-R 60)
Votive antiphon.
R^{c} 466^{rb-va}

Hildegard dwelt frequently and joyfully on the theme of predestination, which for her meant the eternal existence of the world in the mind of God before it emerged in time, when the Father uttered the Word. Man, the microcosm, occupies a central place in the newborn cosmos, as he is God's image and consummate work. In him the angelic and material creations meet, and with the coming of the God-man and the descent of the Holy Spirit, all creation is destined to attain union with the Creator through the redeemed human race. In the antiphon, God looks at the newly created Adam and affirms his sublime potential.

4. O pastor animarum (B-R 61)
Votive antiphon.
R^{b} 405va; R^{c} 466va; V^{2} 156va

A prayer to Christ. In the miscellany this and the following antiphon have been revised to eliminate the first-person forms and to address God the Father instead of the Son.

5. O cruor sanguinis (B-R 77)
Votive antiphon.
R^{b} 405va; R^{c} 466va; V^{2} 156va

This grotesquely beautiful prayer belongs to the same poetic realm as the antiphon for Saint Ursula (no. 61) and the sequence "O Ecclesia" (no. 64). Its literal meaning derives from Gospel accounts of the earthquake, the eclipse, and other miracles that accompanied Christ's death: the event was of such stupendous magnitude that nature itself revolted, bearing witness to its God. But the power and immediacy of this lyric may stem from a more private inspiration. Hildegard's visions involved a kind of synesthesia, as she explained in a celebrated letter to Guibert of

Gembloux: "I see, hear and know all at once. . . . And the words of this vision are . . . like a shimmering flame or like a cloud" (Pitra 333). In the same act of imagination, she mystically "sees" the shedding of sacred blood and "hears" the cry of the outraged earth, so that blood and sound flow in a single stream, rising with the terror of the earth and descending with the pity of heaven.

6. O magne Pater (B-R 1)
Psalm antiphon.
D 153^{r}; R^{b} 405rb; R^{c} 466^{ra-b}; S 28^{r}; V^{2} 156ra

This antiphon is the first piece that remains in the fragmentary D manuscript. The liturgical diction is, for Hildegard, unusually formal, with three parallel subjunctives. God's *adiutorium* (l. 11) is his creative Word or name, both his "helper" and ours. The language echoes Genesis 2:18, where Eve is identified as the "help" of Adam.

7. O eterne Deus (B-R 2)
Psalm antiphon.
D 153^{r}; R^{c} 466rb

This is a fervent prayer based on Paul's conception of the Church as the cosmic body of Christ, "the fullness of him who fills all in all" (Eph. 1:22–23). Because God foreknew the elect "before the foundation of the world," they are everlasting limbs of Christ's body, yet vexed in time by the "need" that is Hildegard's way of characterizing the slings and arrows of outrageous fortune. Here she prays that what is already true in eternity may become empirically true in the present, as her nuns grow more fully into their stature as members of Christ. Lines 6–8 allude to the biblical affirmation, "I bore you from the womb before the morning star" (Vulg. Ps. 109:3). The dawn was one of Hildegard's favorite images for the Virgin, so this piece leads fittingly into the next section of the *Symphonia*, which celebrates Mary's role in the Incarnation.

8. Ave Maria (B-R 3)
Responsory for the Virgin.
D^{153r-v}; R^{b} 407rb; R^{c} 467^{va-b}; S 54^{r-v}; V^{2} 158^{rb-va}

In more than two-thirds of her Marian lyrics, Hildegard rings changes on the ancient contrast between Mary and Eve: the one was seduced by Satan and brought death into the world, but the other became the bride of God and gave birth to life. In this responsory, Mary is celebrated for her victory over Eve's foe, the serpent, whose head she has crushed by her childbearing (Gen. 3:15). Less conventionally, Hildegard also portrays the Virgin as a builder (l. 3). The abbess herself founded two monasteries, and when she began to compose the *Symphonia,* her convent at the Rupertsberg was under construction, so architectural metaphors came easily to her. Part III of the *Scivias,* written in the same period, constitutes a vast allegory of the building of salvation, which is both the body of Christ and the new Jerusalem. In this responsory and the next, Mary figures as architect of the City of God, just as Eve before her had "constructed death" (no. 12).

9. O clarissima mater (B-R 4)
Responsory for the Virgin.
D 153^{v}–154^{r}; R^{b} 407rb; R^{c} 467vb–468ra; S 54^{v}; V^{2} 158va

The first lines of this responsory illustrate Hildegard's taste for the mixed metaphors that give her poems some of their freshness and quirkiness. Five hundred hymnodists might point out that Eve inflicted wounds on the soul, but only Hildegard would say that she built them, and only she would hear not the victim but the wounds themselves sobbing. Such compressions seem to arise spontaneously from the intense and synesthetic character of her perceptions. Mary then becomes the physician and Christ the cure for the disease of mortality—a conventional figure but also a reminder of Hildegard's personal interest in medicine. *Instrumentum* in l. 15 is shorthand for "instrument of the Incarnation" or, more broadly, "means of grace" (cf. "Vos flores rosarum," no.

38). In the repetenda, *stella maris* is a classic Marian title popularized by Saint Bernard's second Homily in Praise of the Virgin Mother (trans. M.-B. Said and Grace Perigo in *Magnificat* [Kalamazoo, 1979], 15–31).

10. O splendidissima gemma (B-R 5)
Psalm antiphon for the Virgin.
D 154^{r-v}; R^a 132va; R^c 466vb

The conceit of the gem or crystal was one of the many such devices, beloved of medieval poets, used as analogies for the Virgin Birth. Adam of St. Victor, a hymnographer contemporary with Hildegard, employed the same conceit in a Christmas sequence:

Si crystallus sit humecta	If a crystal is moistened
Atque soli sit obiecta,	and placed in the sunlight,
Scintillat igniculum;	it emits a little spark of fire;
Nec crystallus rumpitur,	the crystal is not shattered,
Nec in partu solvitur	nor is the seal of chastity broken
Pudoris signaculum.	in [the Virgin's] childbearing.

(Adam, *Sämtliche Sequenzen*, ed. F. Wellner, 42–44)

In her more concentrated and elliptical style, Hildegard leaps from this image of the Virgin Birth to the creation of the world, the Fall, and the restoration of life through Mary. The Virgin is the golden matter or matrix (*materia*) for the rebirth of heavenly virtues upon earth—in contrast to the *prima materia*, a philosophical term for the formless matter out of which God created the world. The association of this *prima materia* with Eve entails a play on *mater* (mother).

Lines 10 and 11 are difficult. *Pater* may be taken as a vocative: "For you, Father, this Word fashioned man"—but that reading would entail a sudden and awkward shift of subject in the next line, where *tu* plainly refers to Mary. It seems better to take *Pater* as the subject, making Mary the privileged woman for whom God "fashioned [his] Word as a man."

11. Hodie aperuit (B-R 6)
Psalm antiphon for the Virgin.
D 154^{v}; R^{b} 407rb; R^{c} 467ra; S 54^{v}; V^{2} 158va

For medieval students of the Bible, the closed gate of the temple in Ezekiel's vision was a sign of Mary's perpetual virginity, "for the Lord, the God of Israel, has entered by it; therefore it shall remain shut. Only the prince may sit in it" (Ezek. 44:2–3). In this antiphon the closed gate, which is Mary's womb, opens paradise; and through its portals the faithful can glimpse the sunrise of a new creation lighting its first vernal blossom. The image is crisp and startling, though muted by the indefinite *quod* of line 3. The initial *hodie* in D strikes a note of liturgical immediacy which would be proper to a specific feast, such as Annunciation or Christmas. In the other MSS. this hint of a precise liturgical setting is suppressed.

12. Quia ergo femina (B-R 7)
Psalm antiphon for the Virgin.
D 154^{v}; R^{o} 407rb; R^{c} 467^{ra-b}; S 54^{v}; V^{2} 158va

This antiphon is the sequel to "Hodie aperuit," as signaled by the *ergo*. Together with "O quam magnum miraculum" (no. 16) and the spectacular sequence "O virga ac diadema" (no. 20), it proclaims the exaltation of woman per se on account of Mary. The phrase *feminea forma* (l. 4) is one of Hildegard's leitmotivs; it denotes both the Platonic idea and the physical beauty of woman, although it could also have the connotations of humility and weakness, traits that medieval writers generically ascribed to women.

13. Cum processit factura (B-R 8)
Psalm antiphon for the Virgin.
D 154^{v}; R^{c} 467rb

A difficult piece. Like its sequel, "Cum erubuerint" (no. 14), this antiphon refers in a highly oblique fashion to the Fall. "The handiwork of God's finger" is man, and lines 3 and 4 evoke his fallen state as revealed by his origin from "mingled blood," that is, sexual intercourse. The biological basis of this theory is spelled out in *Causae et curae,* pp. 59–61 and 67. But Hildegard also believed that, if Eve had remained in Paradise, she would have conceived Adam's children without the "defilement" of sexual embraces or the loss of virginity. Thus a contrast between fallen sexuality and Mary's purity underlies the sonnet-like volta of line 5. As the elements, which share intimately in human fate, were to lament at Christ's passion, they also rejoice at his birth. In the elegant final cadence, an ablative absolute modulates from the past tense into an eternal present of festal praise.

14. **Cum erubuerint** (B-R 9)
Psalm antiphon for the Virgin.
D 155^{r}; R^{c} 467rb

A companion piece to "Cum processit factura," with a falling and rising movement reminiscent of Herbert's "Easter Wings." There is an even more striking tense change from the perfect subjunctive to the present in line 4. The *infelices* are Adam and Eve.

15. **O frondens virga** (B-R 10)
Psalm antiphon for the Virgin.
D 155^{r}; R^{b} 405vb; V^{2} 156vb

This antiphon (with "Laus Trinitati," no. 26) is one of only two pieces that appear in the earlier manuscript D but not in R. Peter Dronke has suggested that Hildegard chose to exclude them on poetic grounds ("Composition" 389). "O frondens virga," like "O pastor animarum" (no. 4), is an almost unadorned prayer of a sort rare in the *Symphonia.* But note the triple rhyme in lines 4–6.

16. **O quam magnum miraculum** (B-R 11)
Psalm antiphon for the Virgin.
D 155^{r-v}; R^{b} 407rb; R^{c} 467^{rb-va}; S 54^{r}; V^{2} 158rb

A celebration of Mary's (and by extension of womankind's) humility, which "ascends over all" as Ursula's contempt for the world does in "O Ecclesia" (no. 64). The exceptional feature of this antiphon is not the contrast but the seeming identification between Eve and Mary; it is grammatically the same *femina* who formerly disgraced the earth that has now graced the heavens. Hildegard is also alluding to the *felix culpa* (fortunate fall), the ancient teaching that humanity is actually happier on account of Adam's fall because it "merited so great a Redeemer." As a later Middle English poet would put it,

Ne hadde the apple taken been,
the apple taken been,
Ne hadde nevere Oure Lady
ybeen hevene Queen.

Lines 8–10 display the figure of *anacoluthon* or broken syntax, which the redactors of R^b and S have tried to correct. The last three lines again feature a triple rhyme.

17. Ave generosa (B-R 12)
Hymn to the Virgin.
D 155^v; R^b 405vb–406ra; R^c 474^{va-b}; V^2 156vb

A paean to the bride of God. Mary's predestined role is celebrated in stanza 3, and she is hailed in the first stanza as "matrix of sanctity" (cf. "O splendidissima gemma," no. 10). Hildegard blends her master images of flowering and music with great finesse. It is Christ himself, the New Song, who unfolds in Mary, so her womb contains in essence the complete consort of celestial music. The hymn is structured so that stanzas honoring the chastity of Mary alternate with those describing her union with God in the conception of their Son. The chaste eroticism of such lyrics is a characteristic medieval mood, no less fervent for being virginal, nor less delicate for being ardent. As a widely used antiphon for Marian feasts proclaims:

Ante torum hujus virginis frequentate nobis dulcia cantica dramatis.

(*Corpus antiphonalium* 3, no. 1438)

[Before the bridal couch of this virgin, perform for us the sweet songs of the drama.]

18. O virga mediatrix (B-R 70)

Alleluia-verse for the Virgin.

R^b 407ra; R^c 473vb; S 54^r; V^2 158rb; V^3 118^v

An alleluia-verse is a kind of mini-sequence with the same liturgical function: it precedes the Gospel reading at Mass. This one features a conventional play on *virgo* (virgin) and *virga* (branch), by which Mary came to be associated with the tree of life, the flowering branch of Aaron (Num. 17:1–11), and the branch from the root of Jesse (Isa. 11:1). Frequent MS. variants show that for copyists the two words were virtually interchangeable. Further implications of this play are expressed by the twelfth-century poet Alan of Lille:

> Et dum ex Evae matris floribus velut aurea rosa processit Virgo Maria, virga facta est Virgo; et alpha mutatum est in omega; quia principium factum finis, id est aeternus factus est temporalis. (PL 210, 201)

> [And when the Virgin Mary came forth like a golden rose out of the flowers of mother Eve, the *virga* became a *virgo* and the alpha was changed into an omega; for the beginning had become the end, that is, the Eternal One became temporal.]

19. O viridissima virga (B-R 71)

Free song to the Virgin.

R^b 407ra; R^c 474rb–va; S 54^r; V^2 158ra–b

A favorite motif in manuscript paintings and cathedral windows is the Tree of Jesse, which represents the genealogy of Christ. As the father of David lies sleeping, the Messiah's family tree is seen to rise from his loins, with prophets and ancestors of Christ seated on the several branches and pointing to Mary enthroned in the crown. The first stanza of this song is an analogous verbal icon. In the remainder of the lyric, the tree image is developed with skill and subtlety, enriched by a plethora of biblical echoes. The medieval singer or listener would no doubt recall the rich spices in the Song of Songs, Christ's parable of the green tree and the dry tree (Luke 23:31), the Advent antiphon beseeching dew from the heavens (Isa. 45:8), and the great tree of the Kingdom in which the birds of the air build their nests (Matt. 13:32). The "meal" of wheat bread is of course the Eucharist, which is also the heavenly wedding feast. In *Scivias* II.6.26 Hildegard explained that only wheat is used for the sacramental bread because it is a dry and pure grain, free from pith as Mary was free from "the pith of man."

20. O virga ac diadema (B-R 13)
Sequence for the Virgin.
D 156^{r-v}; R^b 406ra; R^c 473vb–474rb; V^2 156vb–157ra

When inquisitors came to Bingen after Hildegard's death to seek witnesses for her canonization, they found three nuns who swore they had seen their mistress illumined by the Holy Spirit as she walked through the cloister, chanting this sequence (PL 197, 133c). Hildegard had reason to be pleased with it, for it ranks with the finest of her work. The sequence falls logically into three parts, each composed of two strophic pairs, with a parallelism between the first and third parts. In 1b through 2b, Mary's childbearing is contrasted with natural generation, in particular with Adam's, while in 5a through 6a, Mary is compared with Eve, and the notion of fortunate fall is evoked. The initial salutation to a queenly figure (1a) is balanced by a final prayer to the Virgin as *salvatrix* or feminine savior (6b). In the central section, strophes 3 and 4, Hildegard returns to her theme of Mary as God's foreordained bride. The striking exclamation of 4a conflates Mary and Eve (cf. nos. 12 and 16); it is the "form of woman" which God has blessed in the one and the other, making it the centerpiece of the cosmos. *Organa* in 4b could refer in Hildegard's period either to musical instruments or to harmonized chant.

21. O tu suavissima virga (B-R 14)
Responsory for the Virgin.
D 156^{v}; R^a 132^{va-b}; R^c 468^{ra-b}

Another variant on the Tree of Jesse theme. Bestiary lore graced the eagle (l. 6) with the ability to look directly at the sun, making it a symbol of the contemplative soul fixed on God. In her first letter, Hildegard compared Saint Bernard, one of her heroes, to this bird (PL 197, 190c); and once as she lay on the brink of death she heard an angel calling to her in a vision, "Eagle, arise!" (PL 197, 110a). The curious twist in this piece is that God becomes the eagle and Mary the sun, as if her own brightness had magnetically drawn him down to earth. But in lines 12–13 the Virgin is also revealed as a contemplative who not only conceives but comprehends the Word that she bears. This responsory is the only one for which the manuscripts give the doxology in so complete a form.

22. O quam preciosa (B-R 63)
Responsory for the Virgin.
R^b 407^{rb-va}; R^c 468rb; S 54^v; V^2 158va

An expanded treatment of the themes of "Hodie aperuit" (no. 11). *Clausura,* "enclosure" (l. 13), has connotations of security and chastity; it was also a technical term for the claustration of nuns. The repetenda is of particular haunting beauty.

23. O tu illustrata (B-R 62)
Votive antiphon for the Virgin.
R^b 407rb; R^c 466vb–467ra; S 54^r; V^2 158rb

The theme of this antiphon is purity: the deliverance of the human race, through Mary, from what Hildegard saw as the satanic corruption of sex. The first six lines link the Virgin successively with the three persons of the Trinity: the Father who enlightened her, the Son whom she conceived, and the Holy Spirit who "came upon" her (Luke 1:35). Lines 7–12 render Mary's experience of purification almost clinically. In *Scivias* I.2 and in her *Causae et curae* (p. 36), Hildegard interpreted the forbidden fruit as a physical poison. Before Satan tempted Eve, he breathed upon the apple and defiled it with the filth of lust, which thus became the first symptom of the Fall. Therefore when the Holy

Spirit breathes upon Mary, he is counteracting this initial poisonous breath so that the fallen "laws of flesh" (l. 19) no longer obtain, and once again motherhood and virginity (*integritas*) meet.

24. Spiritus sanctus vivificans vita (B-R 15)
Psalm antiphon for the Holy Spirit.
D 157^{r}; R^{c} 466va

This antiphon with its accompanying hymn and sequence (nos. 27–28) are appropriate for Pentecost, the feast of the Holy Spirit. Like Wisdom in "O virtus Sapientie" (no. 2), the Spirit is here perceived as the source of life in nature, as well as the healer of wounds. The syntax is clumsy, but the parade of verbs and participles nonetheless reveals how deeply Hildegard associated the divine Spirit with *operatio* or action.

25. Karitas habundat (B-R 16)
Psalm antiphon.
D 157^{r}; R^{c} 466^{va-b}

Lady Love, or Charity, occupied a central place in Hildegard's visionary world. In the great cosmic vision that opens her last book, *On the Activity of God,* Caritas proclaims herself all but identical to the Trinity, but also to the *anima mundi* or world soul: "I am the supreme and fiery force who kindled every living spark, and I breathed forth no deadly thing . . . . And I am the fiery life of the essence of God: I flame above the beauty of the fields; I shine in the waters; I burn in the sun, the moon, and the stars" (PL 197, 743b). Sometimes she seems equivalent to Wisdom, and at other times to the Holy Spirit; in both *Symphonia* MSS. this antiphon directly follows "Spiritus sanctus vivificans vita." Here Caritas is in heaven what the Virgin Mary is on earth, the queen consort of God—that divinely feminine spirit whom no effort of doctrine could ever quite exclude from his throne.

26. Laus Trinitati (B-R 17)
Votive antiphon.
D 157^r

One of the composer's least effective lyrics, redundant and grammatically awkward. Its themes are more successfully treated in "O gloriosissimi lux vivens angeli" (no. 29).

27. O ignee Spiritus (B-R 18)
Hymn to the Holy Spirit.
D 157^v–158^r; R^b 406^{rb-va}; R^c 473^{rb-vb}; V^2 157va

In this sober hymn Hildegard reflects on moral psychology, the sphere in which the Holy Spirit interacts with the human spirit. The joyful first stanza recalls Psalm 150: "Praise the Lord . . . with lute and harp, praise him with timbrel and dancing! . . . Let every spirit praise the Lord." For the rest, Hildegard was inspired by that most famous of all hymns to the Spirit, the "Veni Creator" ascribed to Rabanus Maurus:

Veni Creator Spiritus,	Come, Creator Spirit!
Mentes tuorum visita,	Visit the minds of your people,
Imple superna gratia	Fill with celestial grace
Quae tu creasti pectora.	The hearts that you created.

The remaining stanzas trace the moral progress of a soul from the state of innocence through temptation and sin to repentance—a journey that Hildegard had also treated dramatically in her *Ordo virtutum* (*Play of Virtues*) and discursively in *Scivias* I.4, which provides a key to the terminology of this hymn. The "tabernacle" of the soul is its body, recalling the ancient Hebrew tabernacle that contained the ark of testimony and the mercy seat (Exod. 25–26). Hildegard saw the will (*voluntas*) and the understanding, or moral judgment (*intellectus*), as the two "arms" of the soul which motivate every action.

In the state of innocence (stanzas 3 and 4), reason and will work harmoniously together, illumined by holy desire. Stanzas 5 through 9 depict a soul beleaguered by temptation and a perverse longing for the knowledge of evil. To such a one, the Holy Spirit appears as a warrior, like the angel with a flaming sword at the gates of Eden. The eleventh stanza presents the sinner with a choice symbolized by the two towers: to remain obdurate like Satan, or else to repent like the publican and allow the Spirit to change the wounds of sin into jewels. This startling metamorphosis follows from the doctrine of the *felix culpa.* Hildegard captures in a vivid image what Julian of Norwich was to say in sober prose: "Right as different sins are punished by different pains, according to their grievousness, even so shall they be rewarded in heaven with different joys" (*Revelations of Divine Love,* chap. 38).

In stanza 9 I have emended *confringis* ("shatter") to the more plausible and easily miscopied *constringis* ("constrain"). The MSS. show a similar confusion in stanza 10 between *refingis* ("remake") and *refringis* ("break").

28. O ignis Spiritus Paracliti (B-R 19)
Sequence for the Holy Spirit.
D 158^{r-v}; R^{b} 406rb; R^{c} 473^{ra-b}; V^{2} 157^{rb-va}

A sharp contrast with the preceding hymn. The rhapsodic tone of this sequence is signaled by no fewer than eight appearances of the vocative, a mode that Hildegard could wear thin. Nevertheless, the sequence is compelling in its exuberance and breadth of vision. The author shows her colors as a Christian Platonist in her reference to the forms (1a) and more richly in her depiction of the Spirit as world soul (4a–b). This identification was made explicitly by Peter Abelard and William of Conches, and it was to the Paraclete that Abelard dedicated the convent he founded for Heloise.

The first strophic pair resembles a trope or elaboration on the triple Sanctus of the Mass ("Holy, holy, holy art Thou, Lord God of hosts"). There is a delicate balance of attributes: the Spirit is life-giver in the initial bounty of creation, while in the "stricken" world he (or she) is the source of healing. Strophes two and three continue this pattern of antithesis; in 2a and 3a the Spirit is seen as companion of the virtuous, in 2b and 3b as savior of the lost. The third strophic pair has a distinctly chivalric flavor. The play of images is mercurial, as if no single metaphor could capture the multiform Spirit: it is fire and fountain, perfume and armor and song—the binding force that unites both the members of the Church (3a) and the elements (4b) in one harmonious world.

Parts of this sequence were freely translated by Charles Williams as a choral refrain in his play *The House of the Octopus* (London, 1945):

> Fire of the Spirit, life of the lives of creatures,
> spiral of sanctity, bond of all natures,
> glow of charity, lights of clarity, taste
> of sweetness to sinners, be with us and hear us.
>
> Composer of all things, light of all the risen,
> key of salvation, release from the dark prison,
> hope of all unions, scope of chastities, joy
> in the glory, strong honour, be with us and hear us.

29. O gloriosissimi lux vivens angeli (B-R 20)
Votive antiphon for angels.
D 159^{r}; R^{a} 132vb; R^{c} 468^{rb-va}

The medieval heaven, like society on earth as theorists conceived it, followed strict principles of decorum and order. After God the Father, Christ the King, and Mary the Queen came the ranks of the blessed, all in their proper stations: first the nine orders of angels, then the saints in their several categories—patriarchs and prophets, apostles, martyrs, confessors or holy bishops, virgins, widows, and innocents. In the last vision of the *Scivias,* which honors the celestial hierarchy, Hildegard included one antiphon and one responsory for each group, with the exception of the lowly widows and innocents.

The *Scivias* cycle comprises nos. 10, 21, 29–34, 37–40, and 55–56 in this edition. These fourteen pieces, representing the earliest layer of the *Symphonia,* are distinguished by an opaque brilliance derived from the metaphorical density and convoluted syntax that characterize the *Scivias* as a whole.

Angels, for Hildegard, signified the perfection of praise. As pure mirrors of the eternal light, they provide images of the fulfillment that every soul desires. In a Miltonic vein, this antiphon contrasts the obedient angels with Satan. The construction of the first line is extremely odd, with its embedded vocative *lux vivens* serving as a compound adjective; one thinks of Hopkins's "dapple-dawn-drawn Falcon." The angels are presented as plural in their individual being, but singular in that they collectively reflect the "living light" on which they gaze in perpetual contemplation. *Forma* (l. 9) denotes both the angelic "form" or nature and its unsullied beauty in the loyalists.

The last three lines are grammatically tangled. Hildegard here turns from Satan's fall to Adam's, asserting that by his devious counsel (*consiliando*), the lost angel persuaded Adam and Eve ("the handiwork of God's finger") to join him in perdition. For the locution in lines 21-22, a paraphrase for "humankind," cf. "Cum processit factura" (no. 13).

30. O vos angeli (B-R 21)

Responsory for angels.
D 159^{r-v}; R^{a} 132vb; R^{c} 468^{va-b}

Ever since Pseudo-Dionysius the Areopagite, a sixth-century mystic, angel-watchers have acknowledged nine orders in ascending rank: ordinary angels, archangels, virtues, powers, princedoms, dominations (Vulg. Eph. 1:21), thrones, cherubim, and seraphim. In *Scivias* I.6 Hildegard recorded a vision of these orders, which the accompanying miniature illustrates as shimmering concentric circles around the white light of divinity. Although for the sake of numerology the angels were commonly divided into three groups of three, Hildegard counted them instead as two, five, and two. Allegorically the lower ranks, who deal most often with human beings, represent body and soul; the cherubim and seraphim, closest to the ineffable light, signify the knowledge and love of God; and the five orders in between (ll. 8–13) correspond to the five senses and the five wounds of Christ. Allegory aside, this responsory beautifully conveys the plenitude of the twelfth-century cosmos. Performed as an aid to contemplation, it can suggest the vertiginous ascent of the soul as it rises through splendor after splendor on its way to "the little place of the ancient heart."

31. O spectabiles viri (B-R 22)
Votive antiphon for patriarchs and prophets.
D 159^{v}–160^{r}; R^{a} 132vb; R^{c} 468vb–469ra

In this antiphon Hildegard achieves the cryptic intensity of a Blake or a Mallarmé by using her semi-private symbols as if they were common currency. In a sense they were, of course; but most medieval religious poets took pains to be understood, as Hildegard herself did in her prose works. In some of her lyrics, her mode of expression is closer to what Coleridge called symbolism rather than allegory. Yet like the latter, it lends itself readily to a kind of interpretation that verges on decoding, with Scripture and monastic liturgy as the code books. It is difficult to say whether a choir of twelfth-century monks or nuns, intimately acquainted with that code, would have found a piece like this genuinely obscure or merely eccentric.

The image underlying the first part is again the Jesse tree, with Mary as its topmost bough. The prophets are seen not in their Hebrew context but as witnesses to the Incarnation, perceiving Christ dimly through the half-light of Jewish revelation. Hildegard plays on the word *spectabiles* ("distinguished," but with the connotations of "far-seeing" or "visionary"), and again on *radicantis* (l. 9). The divine light, which is the "root" of all creation (cf. no. 24), is itself taking root in Mary; of its own accord the tree of life plants itself, germinates, and blossoms. In the last seven lines we find a kaleidoscope of mixed metaphors. The wheels of line 14 recall Ezekiel's vision, a frequent source for Hildegard (Ezek. 1:15–21), but also the ceaseless revolution of divine Wisdom. The "mountain that touches heaven" is Christ who, in the figure of Moses, parted the waters of the Red Sea; and the "shining lantern" is John the Baptist (John 5:35), the forerunner of Christ.

32. O vos felices radices (B-R 23)
Responsory for patriarchs and prophets.
D 160^{r-v}; R^a 132vb–133ra; R^c 469^{ra-b}

This elusive song closely follows its companion piece (no. 31) in its imagery and train of thought. In the first verse the Jesse tree or tree of life, whose roots are the patriarchs and whose fruit is Christ, is contrasted with that other tree which bore fruit in sin. The *iter perspicue umbre* evokes the prophets who tended this tree according to their lights. Next John the Baptist, last and greatest of prophets, is invoked as the fiery voice of one crying in the wilderness (Mark 1:3)—*ruminans* because, in medieval exegesis, to "chew the cud" (like the clean beasts under the Law) is to meditate deeply on the Word of God. The *limantem lapidem* (l. 8) is more eccentric. Although the phrase refers to Christ as the chief cornerstone-*cum*-stumbling block, an image derived ultimately from Isaiah 28:16–17, Hildegard adds the notion of a "filing stone" that can whittle away all that is unworthy of God's temple. The same versatile stone then transforms itself into a weapon for the overthrow of hell.

33. O cohors milicie floris (B-R 24)
Psalm antiphon for apostles.
D 160^{v}–161^{r}; R^a 133ra; R^c 469^{rb-va}

A welter of textual corruptions suggests that even Hildegard's scribes had trouble deciphering this poem. Despite its surrealistic effect, the antiphon is actually a narrative, though constructed wholly of images. In the first period, the apostles are revealed as a conquering army with Christ and the Holy Spirit as their generals. The singular forms emphasize the unity of this warrior band, which is at the same time "the voice of the whole world"—an echo of Psalm 18, prefiguring the Gospel proclaimed to the ends of the earth. Lines 4–6 allude to the prodigal son (Luke 15:15–16), whose sensuality and self-indulgence reduced him to hunger for pigs' swill—a type of the sinner's plight before he accepts the apostolic word. In line 9, the reader will not be surprised to find the inevitable tree, a sign that the word is indeed growing in the converts.

The second period, however, ends on a strangely inconclusive note, a reminder that not all accepted the apostles' preaching and that the apostles themselves were headed for martyrdom. *Gladio* (sword) in line 15 echoes the earlier military image and recalls the enigmatic text in which Christ tells his disciples to sell their mantles and buy swords (Luke 22:36). For they go forth to confront savage dogs, not unlike those who surround the dying Christ—the Lamb—in the ordinary gloss on Vulgate Psalm 21. These unregenerate beasts also hark back to the pigs in line 6. In the last five lines, beasts and beastlike men are condemned as Hildegard launches into an Old Testament polemic against idolatry, drawing on Wisdom 15:16–17 and Vulgate Psalm 134:15–18. But the theme of apostolic preaching points even more directly to Paul's famous speech on the Areopagus (Acts 17), in which he denied that God dwelt in temples made with hands. It is tempting to emend the frustratingly footloose *eum* in the last line to *deum,* for God is the only possible referent; but unfortunately there is no manuscript evidence for this reading.

The antecedent of *quas* in line 7 is probably *regiones,* not *sensuum*, which would yield the variant *quos*. I take the subject of *ponens* (l. 9) to be *tu* in line 3. Barth and Ritscher emend to *ponentem,* which gives good sense with *adiutorem* but does not follow as readily from the MSS. reading.

34. O lucidissima apostolorum turba (B-R 25)

Responsory for apostles.
D 161^{r-v}; R^{a} 133ra; R^{c} 469va

Described in both manuscripts as a responsory, this piece is not marked as such; evidently the repetenda (ll. 14–15) is to be sung again after the verse (ll. 16–18). More accessible than the preceding antiphon, it celebrates the apostolic band in counterpoint with the feminine figure of Ecclesia, the Church. As teachers, the apostles first overthrow the parodic *magisterium* of Satan (l. 5) and enlighten the pagans through baptism. Thereupon they become "pillars of the Church," a dead metaphor that Hildegard enlivens by taking it literally (for a visual equivalent of this image see *Scivias* II.4). Ecclesia, like Mary, is virgin and mother: virgin in the purity of her faith, but mother of many spiritual children. Her banner of triumph is the cross, recalling Solomon's bride "terrible as an army with banners" (Song 6:9), but also the ancient hymn "Vexilla regis prodeunt" ("The banners of the king go forth").

35. **O speculum columbe (B-R 26)**
Psalm antiphon for Saint John the Evangelist.
D 161^{v}; R^{c} 469vb

Saint John the Evangelist enjoyed a special place among the apostles because, although never martyred, he preserved lifelong virginity. In the twelfth-century *Mirror of Virgins*, a handbook for nuns, this evangelist took his place beside Christ, Mary, and John the Baptist as one of the four horses leading the triumphal chariot of virgins. His virginity was, for Hildegard, the source of his unique intimacy with Christ. Virginity is figured by the flower that never withers (cf. no. 61). As "the disciple that Jesus loved" (John 13:23), John also lay closest to him at the Last Supper and received a special privilege of contemplation, to which Hildegard alludes in the first and last sections. The "chosen . . . generation" (ll. 11–12) is the new elite of virgins and celibate clergy (*Scivias* II.5.15).

36. **O dulcis electe (B-R 27)**
Responsory for Saint John the Evangelist.
D 161^{v}–162^{r}; R^{c} 469vb–470ra

A lyrical piece with images faintly suggestive of the Apocalypse, John's visionary work par excellence. The repetenda (l. 10) locates the singer or hearer as a pilgrim on the way to that Jerusalem which the saint has already seen and entered. Characteristically, Hildegard draws on both the City and the Garden in her images of fulfillment. "The verdure of the spice-dealers" (l. 14) signifies the grace and vitality of the priesthood, which has been augmented by the apostle's teaching. In *Scivias* II.5.1 Hildegard explains that priests or spice-dealers (*pigmentarii*) "follow the apostolic doctrine, like priests under the law of the covenant, . . . to nourish the peoples with food for the inner self." John's "precursors" are probably the other apostles who watered the church by their martyrdom; the evangelist was held to be the youngest and the last to die.

37. O victoriosissimi triumphatores (B-R 31)
Psalm antiphon for martyrs.
D 163^{r-v}; R^a 133ra; R^c 470ra

"The blood of martyrs is the seed of the Church," according to an axiom drawn from Tertullian and echoed in this antiphon. Glorification of martyrs in the guise of victors had become so conventional by the Middle Ages that little sense of paradox remained. In lieu of pathos, Hildegard offers predictably jubilant praise, celebrating the martyrs' imitation of Christ which has brought them to his messianic banquet (for the slaughtered calf cf. Luke 15:23). Line 12 hints at the motif, developed in the songs to Saint Ursula, that the blood of martyrs is an ornament in heaven.

38. Vos flores rosarum (B-R 32)
Responsory for martyrs.
D 163^{r}; R^a 133ra; R^c 470^{ra-b}

This song represents Hildegard's poetry at its simultaneous best and worst: it is brimming with intensity and strangeness, but the startling images are sabotaged by unwieldy syntax. The baroque conceit will remind English-speaking readers of Crashaw: the saints' wounds become roses and their blood a fragrance. Although this topos was not new in the twelfth century, its conventionality in this context is undercut by the lack of direct allegorical "translation." In lines 6–8 the poet submerges an already strained, synesthetic image in a further metaphysical conceit. The scent of the roses, initially the blood of martyrs, now becomes Christ's blood and, more abstractly, his redemptive purpose "flowing" from before the foundation of the world (Eph. 1:4). *Undatis,* the surprising verb of line 14, extends the metaphor still more unnervingly. The martyrs, at first envisioned as blood-red flowers, are now likened to swimmers in the ocean of their own wounds, which is in turn subsumed into the bleeding heart of the Eternal.

39. O vos imitatores (B-R 33)
Responsory for confessors.
D 163^{v}–164^{r}; R^{a} 133rb; R^{c} 470rb; S 40^{v}

This unusual piece can be read in light of Hildegard's liturgical drama, the *Ordo virtutum.* In the play, the dramatis personae are allegorical virtues; here they are confessors or bishops, whom the composer sees as actors imitating Christ, the "most exalted person," in that precious symbolic representation (*significatio*) which is the Mass. Their gorgeous costumes or vestments (*ornatus*) suggest their spiritual beauty as they exercise the apostolic power of binding and loosing, delivering both the righteous and the repentant ("the white and the black") from the burden of sin. The phrase *pigros et peregrinos* also occurs in Hildegard's first letter to Frederick Barbarossa (c. 1155–1159), in which she told the emperor to "govern the sluggish, the straying, and the savage with the scepter of mercy" (PL 197, 187a).

It is possible that Hildegard understood "confessors" literally as "those who have the right to hear confessions." In the verse she calls to mind two additional privileges of these saints: they share in the angelic office, the singing of God's praise, and they found churches on sites that have been providentially revealed to them. The abbess may have been remembering her own vision of the Rupertsberg as a site for her new monastery.

40. O successores (B-R 34)

Psalm antiphon for confessors.

D 164^{r}; R^{a} 133^{ra-b}; R^{c} 470va

The confessors imitate Christ in his double role as Lion and Lamb, victor and victim. Although not actually called to be martyrs, they were nonetheless willing, like the righteous priest Zechariah, son of Barachiah, who was "slain between the temple and the altar" (Matt. 23:35). Following Christ's example and commandment, they exercised their spiritual lordship only through service (Luke 22:25–26). Once again they are linked with the angels, evidently those of the lowest order, who are assigned, in addition to praising God, to watch over the nations (no. 30).

41. O mirum admirandum (B-R 28)

Psalm antiphon for Saint Disibod.

D 162^{r}; R^{c} 470va; V^{l} 42^{v}–43^{r}

This antiphon, together with the responsory "O viriditas digiti Dei" (no. 42) and the sequence "O presul vere civitatis" (no. 45), was one of three songs commissioned by Kuno, abbot of Hildegard's original monastery of St. Disibod, in the early 1150s. Only a few years before, Kuno had vigorously opposed Hildegard's move to Bingen. Although she composed the songs he requested, she forwarded them to her ex-superior with a none-too-friendly letter of reproach (PL 197, 203–4).

Disibod's legend is recorded in a *vita* or life written by Hildegard in 1170 at the request of Kuno's successor Helenger. According to this text (PL 197, 1095–1116), the otherwise little-known seventh-century saint was an Irish bishop who, exiled from his see, traveled to Germany with three companions. There he built himself a hermitage on a wooded slope at the confluence of the Glan and the Nahe and later established a monastery on the summit of the mountain. Blessed with the gifts of healing and spiritual counsel, Disibod never entered the community he had founded, preferring to remain in a solitary life of rigorous asceticism. He died in the odor of sanctity at 81, and miraculous healings occurred at his tomb.

In this haunting and bewildering lyric, Hildegard contrasts the steep mountain of God, inhabited by the monks, with the saint's own preference for a lowly and "hidden" dwelling. Both the high mountain and the hermit's humble life are in different ways *ardua*—lofty and difficult to attain. So also is the meaning of the last five lines, which sound vaguely apocalyptic. The "flower of all the branches of the world" must be Christ. Perhaps Hildegard was looking forward to the saint's revealed glory on the day when the blossom of the dry branch, Mary, will flourish throughout the world and God will be all in all.

42. **O viriditas digiti Dei (B-R 29)**
Responsory for Saint Disibod.
D 162^{r-v}; R^{c} 470^{va-b}; V^{1} 42^{v}–43^{r}

God's life-creating finger, the Holy Spirit, works through the saint to establish a vineyard (*plantatio*)—a conventional metaphor for religious communities, but also the familiar dress of Hildegard's Rhineland mountains. This responsory, inspired by a passage in Isaiah, continues the themes of "O mirum admirandum" (no. 41). At the end of time, when every valley is exalted and every mountain brought low (Isa. 40:4), Disibod's mount will be exempted because he has already humbled himself, adopting the ascetic stance of exile even from his own community. The repetenda links him with John the Baptist, that archetypal exile who dwelt in the wilderness to prepare the way of the Lord (Isa. 40:3, Mark 1:3). In line 11 the "armed man" is Satan (cf. Matt. 12:29).

Although both *Symphonia* MSS. read *differentia* in line 8, the variant *discretione* in V^{1} is older and makes better sense.

43. **O felix anima (B-R 64)**
Responsory for Saint Disibod.
R^{c} 470vb

A generic eulogy that could serve for any ascetic saint. This piece represents the dualistic tendency in Hildegard's thought as she lauds the victory of soul over body, which enables the saint to become a temple of the Holy Spirit (1 Cor. 6:19). For the mirror, a sign of God's image and likeness restored in the creature through contemplation, compare "O speculum columbe" (no. 35).

44. O beata infantia (B-R 65)
Psalm antiphon for Saint Disibod.
R^c 470vb–471ra

Bowing to hagiographic convention, Hildegard wrote in her life of Saint Disibod that, along with "blessed Nicholas, blessed Benedict, and others like them" the future saint was a preternaturally good child, devoted to study, almsgiving, and prayer (PL 197, 1096–97). She had few concrete details to offer; Disibod was not among those rare babes who fasted from the breast on Wednesday and Friday. But the reader of Hildegard's own *Vita* will find a more remarkable instance of childhood precocity when the abbess tells her biographer how she enjoyed, or endured, her exceptional visions from the age of three (PL 197, 103a). Her awareness of being set apart from such an early age would have given her an unusually strong apprehension that the child is father (or mother) to the man. The "fragrance of balsam," according to the Romano-German Pontifical, "signifies a reputation for holy virtues spread far and wide by those who are anointed . . . with the active grace of the Holy Spirit" (*Pontifical Romano-Germanique* 2:83).

45. O presul vere civitatis (B-R 30)
Sequence for Saint Disibod.
D 162^{v}–163^{r}; R^c 475^{va-b}; V^1 43^{r-v}

This sequence, Hildegard's finest contribution to the cult of Saint Disibod, celebrates her patron as bishop-in-exile (1a–b), hermit and contemplative (2a–3b), priest (4a), monastic founder (4b), and intercessor in heaven (5a–b). The initial strophic pair establishes a pattern of exaltation through exile: cast out of his original see, the saint remains a prelate (*presul*) in the "true" city or see, identified at the end of 5b as celestial Jerusalem. As a wandering monk (*exul*), Disibod scales the heights of contemplation. His "cloistered mind" is the sign of spiritual virginity that enjoys the intimate delights of divine love, evoked in language echoing the Song of Songs (2:9–14) and the antiphon "O speculum columbe" (no. 35).

In 3a, because the hermit has exchanged earth for heaven, God exchanges his forest hideaway for the place of highest renown: he becomes a pinnacle on the gates of heaven. The image of the *culmen* is continued in 4a, which portrays the saint as priest. Disibod in this strophe is likened to a tower, but he is also a human being censing that tower. Hildegard frequently used such architectural paradoxes to signify the collaboration, or synergy, of God and man in the work of salvation. Every saint is both a builder of the Church and a living stone set into the building (1 Pet. 2:5)—a paradox developed in the visions of the second-century prophet Hermas, whose *Shepherd* Hildegard almost certainly knew.

The new Jerusalem is, like Tennyson's Camelot, a city built to music. Strophe 4b reveals Disibod as a mystical builder using light and sound, like the visionary poet herself, to construct "a body of wondrous praise...in two parts." Hildegard is here alluding to the threefold identity of the Church as mystical body, building, and chorus. Architecturally, the choir of the monastic church was divided into two parts for antiphonal chant and could allegorically denote the two natures of Christ, divine and human.

The remainder of the poem is less obscure. In 5a, Disibod as patron saint watches over the monks who praise God "in this very song"—a neat self-referential touch—provided that their admiration of the saint leads to imitation of his virtues (6b). Praise of God and praise of the saint are not severed, for salvation is achieved by "God working like a man" *within* a man (6a).

46. O felix apparicio (B-R 35)

Psalm antiphon for Saint Rupert.

D 164^{v}; R^{b} 404va; R^{c} 471ra; V^{2} 155ra

Little is known of Saint Rupert's cult before 1150, when Hildegard rebuilt his long-ruined church and moved there with her nuns. From that time she made the renewal of his cult a part of her mission. Her *Vita S. Ruperti* was probably written to arouse veneration for the saint at a time when the abbess was attempting (successfully) to transfer certain properties from the monks of St. Disibod to her nuns. Hildegard claimed that Rupert or Robert was the grandson of a Carolingian prince who owned vast estates near Bingen. The saint's father Robolaus was a pagan, his mother Bertha a Christian. After Robolaus's early death, Bertha adopted the life of a pious widow and raised her son in the fear of God. At the age of fifteen the boy made a pilgrimage to Rome and, upon his return, began giving his property to the poor and building churches throughout his lands. God brought this short but saintly career to an end when Rupert reached the age of twenty, lest he be corrupted by worldly friends. Bertha survived him for twenty-five years and founded a monastery at the site of his tomb, but this was destroyed by the Normans ca. 882 and remained desolate until the twelfth century.

In her life of Rupert, Hildegard recounts an anecdote to display the teen-aged saint's charity and fear of the Lord. When the boy was twelve years old, Bertha proposed to build an oratory for the salvation of their souls, but Rupert replied, "No, mother, first let us heed what the Gospel bids and the prophet says: 'Share your bread with the hungry, and bring the homeless poor into your house.'" So the joyful mother built hospices instead (PL 197, 1086c).

47. O beatissime Ruperte (B-R 36)
Psalm antiphon for Saint Rupert.
D 164^{v}; R^{b} 404va; R^{c} 471ra; V^{2} 155ra

A straightforward petition to the nuns' patron saint. The phrase *naufragum mundum* ("shipwrecked world," l. 5) is taken from Venantius Fortunatus's hymn, "Pange lingua gloriosi / prelium certaminis."

48. Quia felix puericia (B-R 66)
Psalm antiphon for Saint Rupert.
R^{c} 471^{ra-b}

Childhood inspiration was a favorite theme of Hildegard; compare "O beata infantia" (no. 44). In the *Vita S. Ruperti,* as in her medical writings, she observed that some people are born with constitutional inclinations toward malice, others toward sensuality, and others toward goodness. Those in the third group, which includes Rupert, possess a natural nobility; they are like rich and fruitful earth. Foreseeing their virtues, God often blesses them, like Jacob, even in their mothers' wombs (PL 197, 1085d; Pitra 490–91). As an aristocrat and a Benedictine, Hildegard tended to associate this nobility of grace and nature with the nobility of birth and fortune. In Saint Rupert's case, the great wealth he renounced provided him, through almsgiving, with his chief means of attaining heaven.

49. O Ierusalem (B-R 37)
Irregular sequence for Saint Rupert.
D 164^{v} (fragment); R^{b} 404^{rb-va}; R^{c} 476vb–477rb; V^{2} 154vb–155ra

On May 1, 1152, Hildegard's new monastic church at the Rupertsberg was consecrated to the Mother of God as well as Saints Philip and James, Martin and Rupert. This piece, the longest and most carefully crafted in the *Symphonia,* might have been composed for that festive occasion. Stanzas 7 and 8 echo the dedication hymn "Urbs beata Hierusalem":

Urbs beata Hierusalem,
dicta pacis visio,
Quae construitur in coelis
vivis ex lapidibus . . .

Tunsionibus, pressuris
expoliti lapides,
Suisque aptantur locis
per manum artificis,
Disponuntur permansuris
sacris aedificiis.
(*Analecta hymnica* 2:73, no. 93)

Jerusalem, blessèd city,
called "vision of peace,"
Which is built in the heavens
from living stones . . .

By hammering and beating
the stones are polished
And fitted for their places
by the Artificer's hand,
Laid in the everlasting
consecrated house.

Like the hymn, Hildegard's magnificent sequence commemorates not only Rupert but the whole communion of saints, the living stones in celestial Jerusalem, among whom the abbess and her nuns aspired to shine.

The peculiar numbering of stanzas reflects the highly unusual form of the piece. Its first three units (1a–1c) are musically parallel, like the stanzas of a hymn. There follow six paired strophes (2a–4b), with the two halves of each pair set to more or less the same melody as in a sequence (aa, bb, cc). Finally, the last six stanzas (5–10) are completely independent, each set to a melody of its own. The text, however, follows a different pattern: it begins and ends with visions of the new Jerusalem, while the central portion (2a–6) focuses specifically on Rupert. The teasing blend of pattern and asymmetry corresponds to a vision of beatitude which is artistically and theologically structured yet rhapsodically free in its expression.

For her image of the city, Hildegard draws on Apocalypse 21, in which the apostle John describes "the holy city Jerusalem coming down out of heaven from God, having the glory of God, its radiance like a most rare jewel." But she does not directly follow the apocalyptic text; in her vision there is no angel with a measuring rod, no sense of geometry and number. The texture is more impressionistic—a play of lights over jewel-encrusted walls, shimmering windows, flashing turrets. Jerusalem itself is a "light never darkened" (1b), but although its sun never sets, it does rise anew in the childhood of each saint, and Rupert in his youthful vigor is like its meridian blaze. The gemstones, also mentioned in John's vision, are not merely ornamental; each designates a particular virtue and has special healing powers, catalogued in the lapidaries of Marbod of Rennes and others. The sapphire or lapis lazuli, for instance, is associated with love of heaven, and the sparkling red and white jewels of stanza 9 (like the roses and lilies of 3b) suggest martyrdom and virginity.

In the preface to her own lapidary, Hildegard provided two explanations for the origin of precious stones, one scientific and the other theological (PL 197, 1247–50). According to the first theory, gems arise in the Orient where the tropical sun blazes down on the mountains, heating them to the melting point. When these mountains are washed by the flood of boiling rivers, the stone begins to foam, and this froth later crystallizes into jewels. These may be the molten or glowing stones (*torrentibus lapidi-*

bus) of stanza 7. *Lapides torrentes* occur liturgically in an antiphon for Saint Stephen:

> Lapides torrentes illi dulces fuerunt: ipsum sequuntur omnes animae justae.
>
> (*Corpus antiphonalium* 3, no. 3580)
>
> [The rushing stones were sweet to him: all righteous souls follow him.]

On the other hand, the living stones that fly through heaven like clouds (stanza 8) recall Hildegard's alternative notion that a shower of precious stones dropped from Satan when he fell, so that their beauty and virtue might be bestowed on the race of Adam.

Saint Rupert's history, set in counterpoint with the vision of Jerusalem, is closely tied to the history of his cult. Despite the "fools"—probably the Normans who destroyed his mother's monastery (2b)—and the indifferent generations who let it stand in ruins (3b), his light could not remain concealed; "a city set on a hill cannot be hid" (Matt. 5:14). In Hildegard's view, the fact that God had established her monastery on the Rupertsberg, "through a great miracle of mighty visions," was itself full proof of Rupert's sanctity (PL 197, 1083b). The "true revelation" (*vera ostensione*) mentioned in 3b is the vision in which she was instructed to leave the monastery of St. Disibod and move to the Rupertsberg. An additional verse at this point in the miscellany (perhaps the oldest version of the text) indicates that the flowers crowning Rupert's mountain are the congregation of nuns:

> Que dum in alia vinea plantate essent,
> ibi tulit eas Spiritus sanctus,
> et tibi eas nobiliter in misterio [V² ministerio] suo coniunxit.
>
> [While they were planted in another vineyard, / the Holy Spirit brought them there / and nobly united them to you in his mystery.]

The delicate imagery of 4a, redolent of the Song of Songs, alludes to Rupert's early death and perhaps also to his vernal feast day on May 15. The saint had attained maturity in spirit without losing the verdant freshness of youth. As in "O viridissima virga," Hildegard's images move from flower to fruit to a suggestion of harvest; the *sarcina sine medulla* is probably an allusion to Rupert's sexual purity (see above, note on no. 19). The next strophes also praise his virginity; his "vessel" or body remains undefiled, untouched by Satan, and like Mary he "has no stain" (Song 4:7). The tantalizing "dance of the ancient cave" (4b) remains unexplained, but as Peter Dronke has suggested, Hildegard seems to be juxtaposing an orgiastic pagan rite with the divine music and dance of the angels (*Poetic Individuality* 168). In the final stanzas, she returns in a highly ornamented language to the ornaments of the City of God.

50. **Mathias sanctus (B-R 72)**
Hymn to Saint Matthias.
R[c] 474[vb]–475[rb]

Saint Matthias, last of the apostles, was chosen by lot to replace Judas (Acts 1:21–26). Because the lot fell on this dark horse instead of the more plausible candidate, Joseph "the Just," medieval piety seized on Matthias as an instance of God's mysterious favor that chooses the humble and passes over the righteous. Legend enhanced the mystery by making Matthias a child, although his age is never mentioned in the New Testament. The saint's election is commemorated thus in the hymn "Diem angelicis solemnem choris" (*Analecta hymnica* 12:189), sung at the monastery of Saint Matthias in Trier:

Proditor numerum minuit sacrum Duodenarium apostolorum, Quem tu, parve Dei, restituisti.	The traitor diminished the sacred number Of twelve apostles, Which you, child of God, restored.
Sors apostolica duobus data Super te cecidit teque elegit Per gratiam Christi, quam meruisti.	The apostolic lot, given to two, Fell upon you and chose you Through the grace of Christ, which you merited.

O quam terribilis in consiliis Es super filios hominum, Deus, Dum parvi merito vincitur justus.	O how terrible in counsels are you, O God, above the children of men, When the just man is surpassed by the merit of a child.

This mysteriously chosen youth is also the Matthias of Hildegard's song (musically a true sequence, despite the misleading title in R). But, like the Paul of Romans, the abbess is equally concerned with a negative mystery—the rejection of grace. Matthias would not have been chosen had Judas not fallen, just as Adam would not have been created had Lucifer not sinned (1b). Yet each fall is predestined by God to be another's salvation; there can be more than one *felix culpa*. Every *institutio* or official plan (3b) can be superseded by uncovenanted mercies if it goes awry. Thus thc "man who saw election"—and rejected it—in strophes 2a–b is a composite figure representing Adam, the apostate Hebrews, and finally Judas. As the Jews betrayed God through their idolatry, so Judas betrayed Christ with a kiss, which is evoked in the remarkable collocation of 2b. The strophe is not without irony—a rare mood for Hildegard—and it contains one of her equally rare allusions to pagan mythology. The "coalpit" into which the apostate falls is reminiscent of *Scivias* III.1.14, in which Hildegard describes the fallen angels as extinguished coals cast into the abyss.

"Mathias sanctus" illustrates one of Hildegard's favorite strategies for depicting the paradox of holiness. Sharply contrasted, even incompatible images represent the saint on the one hand as a passive figure yielding to the divine initiative, on the other as a powerful actor. Thus Matthias in 1b and 3a is like a giant in his prime (cf. Vulg. Ps. 18:6), while in 4a he is a winged infant, a graceful *putto*. The humble saint *qui seipsum nescit* (4b) is not self-deceived but self-forgetful. In *De operatione Dei* 3.10.9, Matthias is characterized as "gentle and humble, with the manners of a dove . . . he did many signs and miracles in humility, as if unaware, and longed for martyrdom as for a banquet" (PL 197,

1008bc). The Spirit-dove in the last stanza has flown in from Song of Songs 2:14.

51. O Bonifaci (B-R 73)
Votive antiphon for Saint Boniface.
R^{c} 475^{rb-va}

Saint Boniface (680–755), the "Apostle of Germany," was an Anglo-Saxon monk and scholar who evangelized Bavaria, Franconia, and other regions. Consecrated bishop of Germany in 723, he founded the abbey of Fulda along with many other monasteries that he staffed with English monks and nuns. In 747 he became archbishop of Mainz and eight years later attained the martyr's crown at the ripe age of 75. Hildegard mentions him in her *Vita S. Disibodi* (PL 197, 1112bc) as presiding over the translation of Disibod's relics. Widely venerated throughout Germany, Boniface was a special patron of the Benedictines. "Watering the flowers" in this antiphon means caring for the monastic congregations (cf. 1 Cor. 3:6). They have come from God and return to God, in a Neoplatonic cycle, but the "wise man" can keep the pure streams from drying or straying.

52. O Euchari columba (B-R 74)
Responsory for Saint Eucharius.
R^{c} 475vb–476ra

The historical Eucharius, first bishop of Trier, lived in the late third century. In medieval legend, however, he was one of Christ's seventy-two disciples, sent by the apostle Peter to evangelize Gaul. The sequence "Almi colamus" (*Analecta hymnica* 44:127) claims that Eucharius served at the Last Supper and received the Holy Spirit on Pentecost; later he founded the church of St. John at Trier and worked many miracles there, including resuscitation of the dead.

Hildegard frequently corresponded with the monks of St. Eucharius in Trier, a foundation that was reconsecrated to Saint Matthias in 1148. It is likely that this piece, as well as the sequences "O Euchari in leta via" (no. 53) and "Mathias sanctus" (no. 50), were written for the monks, perhaps after Hildegard preached her public sermon at Trier in 1160. All three pieces appear only in R.

"O Euchari columba" celebrates the saint as miracle worker. Peter, Eucharius's companion, was said to heal by his mere shadow (Acts 5:15), and according to "Almi colamus" (12a) the younger saint performed the same feat:

Paralyticum	He restores the paralytic
signo crucis reparat,	with the sign of the cross,
sed signaculi	but with the shadow
umbra sacri defunctum	of the sacred sign,
repente vivificat.	he suddenly revives the dead.

Hildegard's imagery of the wheel and the cherubim comes from Ezekiel 10, a visionary passage famed for its obscurity and profundity. Medieval exegetes applied its mystical figures to the evangelists.

53. **O Euchari in leta via (B-R 75)**
Sequence for Saint Eucharius.
R^c 476^{ra-b}

A narrative sequence recalling the phases of Eucharius's life. As a young man he traveled with Christ (1a), and after the baptism of fire on Pentecost, he went to evangelize Trier and founded a church there (2b). The *sodales* of 1b are his missionary companions, Valerius and Maternus, portrayed as men of goodwill but insufficient courage in the face of martyrdom. Eucharius himself survived stoning by paralyzing his tormentors with a prayer; after they were converted, he released them. His fearful companions' inability to "gaze perfectly on the good" leads toward an evocation of the transfigured Christ, from whom the three chosen apostles had to avert their eyes. Peter nonetheless offered to build three tabernacles in the unearthly light (Matt. 17:4); in 3a Hildegard has transposed them from Mount Tabor into the City of God, where the saint now enjoys a lasting vision of Christ in glory. Strophes 3b and 4a recall his preaching: the "old and new wine" of Christ's parable (Matt. 9:17) stand for the Old and New Testaments, though the eucharistic chalice is also called to mind. In 4a the missionary merges with the powerful figure of Mother Church who nurses the world with the milk of doctrine, inverting the messianic promise of Isaiah 60:16.

54. Columba aspexit (B-R 76)

Sequence for Saint Maximin.
R[c] 476[rb – va]

Maximin or Maximinus, a fourth-century bishop of Trier, was historically important as a foe of Arianism and a supporter of the Nicene Creed. Like Matthias and Eucharius, he was the patron of a local monastery for which Hildegard probably wrote this sequence. But the saint's life and legend have little to do with her rich celebration of the priesthood and the beauty of holiness. As Christopher Page has pointed out (*Sequences and Hymns* 19), this sequence draws extensively on Old Testament depictions of worship, including the construction of Solomon's temple (1 Kings 6) and the eulogy of the high priest Simon, son of Onias (Ecclus. 50). Hildegard would have known these texts less through direct Bible study than through their liturgical refractions in the rites for ordination and the consecration of churches. Like the liturgy itself, her song is a tapestry of biblical images united by a common thread of symbolic interpretation.

The piece begins with a surrealistic echo of Isaiah 60:8 ("Who are these who fly like a cloud, and like doves to their windows?") and Song of Songs 2:9 ("My beloved . . . stands behind our wall, gazing in at the windows, looking through the lattice"). In the presence of the Spirit-dove, balm rains down from the praying saint, and divine light—within him and around him—floods the temple of his heart (1 Cor. 6:19). A *gemma* (1b) can be either a bud or a jewel; here it is both, and its mysterious "rising" begins a series of heavenward movements which continue with the building of the tower (2a), the priest's ascent to the altar (3a), the eagle's flight (3b), and the column of incense (4b). As in "O

Ierusalem" (no. 49), building and blossoming provide complementary images for the same process, the meeting of earth with heaven. In 2a the saint becomes the lofty tower or city that in 3b he is still helping to construct, both through his effort (as *artifex*) and in his very essence (as *paries templi*). Built of cedar and cypress, the Church reveals itself as the temple of Solomon as well as his bridal chamber (Vulg. Song 1:17). The swift stag of 2b also appears in the Song as an image of the Beloved, but conversely he recalls the Psalmist's metaphor of the soul thirsting for God (Vulg. Ps. 41:1) and drinking water from the rock (Ex. 17:1–7), which is Christ. For the *pigmentarii* or priests (3a), compare "O dulcis electe" (no. 36). As bishop, Maximin stands among his fellow clerics in the Church—"the verdure of the king's gardens"—as the high priest Aaron or Simon stood before the children of Israel; he offers the Lamb of God as the old priests offered the sacrificial rams.

In strophe 4a, the saint's exalted contemplative flight is balanced by an image of lowliness: he is both mountain and valley, like Disibod in "O mirum admirandum" (no. 41). The leaping mountain goat and the elephant reinforce this duality, like the giant and the infant in "Mathias sanctus" (no. 50). But the *capricornus* also harks back to the *cervus* of 2b, and the elephant may have been chosen because of its reputation for chastity. Hildegard's bestiary states that this animal always sniffs the earth for the fragrance of Paradise, and seldom mates (PL 197, 1313ab). Sporting with these symbolic beasts, mother Wisdom takes delight in her servant (Prov. 8:31). The sequence ends with two vignettes of Maximin, first as celebrant, his prayers rising to heaven like incense (Song 3:6), and then as patron of his aspiring monks. Patrick Diehl cites the last strophe as an example of *insinuatio* or indirect prayer (*Religious Lyric* 164–65).

55. O pulcre facies (B-R 38)

Psalm antiphon for virgins.

D 165^{r}; R^{a} 133rb; R^{c} 471rb

The image of Christian virginity remained remarkably constant from the third century up to the Second Vatican Council. However austere she may be outwardly, a consecrated virgin never withers; in her soul she embodies all that is fresh, vernal, and fragrant; her life on earth prefigures the bliss of heaven, as she contemplates and reflects the divine beauty. Hildegard always stressed the aesthetic rather than the ascetic qualities of a nun's life. Her virgins in this song are "building in the dawn," constructing the City of God through their chaste imitation of Christ and Mary. They are like the allegorical virtues in *Scivias* III.8.13—maidens who climb up and down the ladder of the incarnate Word, carrying the stones of good works. These ravishing female masons have been at work since the second-century *Shepherd* of Hermas (Similitude 9.3.4–5); and they appear two and a half centuries after Hildegard in Christine de Pizan's *Book of the City of Ladies*.

56. O nobilissima viriditas (B-R 39)
Responsory for virgins.
D 165^{r-v}; R^a 133rb; R^c 471^{rb-va}

This baffling and beautiful song is about Virginity, not virgins. As in her songs for the apostles (nos. 33–34), Hildegard uses singular forms for an entire group of saints to catch the essence of their particular type of holiness. Virginity for her reveals feminine beauty to be at one with all that is most promising in nature: it is verdant as the earth yet golden like sunlight and red as the dawn, sparkling in the white light of divinity. The iridescent play of colors recreates the burning bush, a figure of Mary. Or from another perspective, Virginity appears as the tree of life, but it grows in the celestial spheres instead of an earthly garden, and has angels to tend it instead of Adam.

Similar imagery appears in one of Hildegard's letters (Ep. 116), in which she explained to a critical abbess why she let the virgins of her convent wear special jewelry instead of ordinary veils. The veil of submission is for married women, she allowed, but the virgin may adorn herself for her Bridegroom because "the form of woman flashed radiant in the primal root, in . . . supernal beauty. What a marvelous thing is [Virginity], which laid a foundation in the sun and transcended the earth! . . . [The virgin] stands in the simplicity and integrity of a beautiful paradise which will never fade, but will remain ever verdant . . . Virgins are married in the Holy Spirit to holiness and the dawn of virginity" (PL 197, 337b–d).

As for no. 34, the manuscripts do not mark the repetenda (ll. 7–9), which should be repeated after the verse (ll. 10–11).

57. O dulcissime amator (B-R 40)
Symphonia virginum.
D 165^{v}–166^{r}; R^{b} 405ra; R^{c} 478^{ra-va}; V^{2} 155vb–156ra

This song and its companion piece, "O Pater omnium" (no. 58), are unique in Hildegard's oeuvre. Their manuscript titles, "symphony of virgins" and "symphony of widows," indicate that the abbess wrote them for choral performance by the two categories of nuns in her care. Thus they are direct expressions of the spirituality she wished to nurture, and also of the perceived difference between the "penitent" widows and the more exalted virgins, who had taken Christ for their first and only lover.

The virgins' song is suffused with a bridal spirituality modeled on the Song of Songs. This type of piety is thoroughly traditional; it can be traced back as far as the Song commentary of Origen in the third century. Contrary to widespread belief, nuptial piety was not the exclusive province of women or of Cistercians, although Saint Bernard's homilies on the Song of Songs did much to popularize it. Monks and nuns alike cultivated love for Christ as bridegroom of the soul; yet the consecrated virgin was the one who outwardly symbolized the inward devotion of both sexes. The nuns who performed this song were to identify themselves with Solomon's yearning bride: they praise their lover's beauty and lament his absence (stanzas 7–8), extol his superiority above all others (stanza 6), bewail their own weakness (stanzas 2–3), and above all, plead for his help (stanzas 1–2, 4–5, 10). But their love song is permeated with allusions to the Fall, the source of hated concupiscence, and the paradoxical opening prayer signals the markedly anti-erotic character of their eroticism. Stanza 2 evokes Song 8:5 (Vulgate), which is echoed once more in the closing lines: "Under the apple tree I raised you up; there your mother was corrupted, there she who bore you was defiled." Only with Christ's help can these daughters of Eve resist "the taste of the apple" and escape the fiend who seduced their mother. Stanza 9 recalls the victory already achieved through Mary.

58. O Pater omnium (B-R 41)

Symphonia viduarum.

D 166^{r-v}; R^{b} 405rb; R^{c} 478va; V^{2} 156ra

The widows' song is superficially parallel to the symphony of virgins. Yet, although both groups of women have become brides of Christ, the virgins dare to address him as lover and bridegroom, while the widows approach him more distantly as father and sire, emperor and king. The virgins feel and lament the effects of Eve's fall, but the widows have fallen in their own right; the first stanza indicates that they have not only inherited but also imitated her sin. Hildegard had ambivalent views on sexuality and marriage—a major theme of her *Causes and Cures*—but this song leans toward the negative side. On one hand, the love of marriage is "fertile," but on the other it is "pain" (*dolor,* the same word used in stanza 1 to describe Eve's punishment). Penitence, the cure for this pain, is by contrast lovely and sweet. The widows have exchanged their first marriage "according to the flesh" for a union in "supernal charity," which is not only purer but also sweeter.

This sense of monastic widowhood as a liberation from marriage was expressed even in the rite of consecration. A virgin becoming a nun had to receive her veil from the bishop's hands, but a widow was entitled to place it on her own head "because she is freed from the rule of man" (*soluta est a lege viri; Pontifical Romano-Germanique* 1:59). Heloise's famous act of profession bore dramatic and ironic witness to the difference.

There are several idiosyncrasies in Hildegard's diction. In line 3, the *costa prime matris* must of course be Adam's rib, not Eve's; the "rib of the first mother" is shorthand. *Amatorem* in stanza 3 is a peculiar substitution for *amorem*. The *virginea virga* is a circumlocution for Mary (cf. "O viridissima virga," no. 19), and the next two lines recall the formulations of "O virga ac diadema" (no. 20, 1b–2a).

59. Rex noster promptus (B-R 42)
Responsory for the Holy Innocents.
D 166^{v}–167^{r}; R^{c} 472rb

A solemn commemoration of the innocents slaughtered by King Herod (Matt. 2:16–18), whose festival on December 28 was observed as a Feast of Fools but also as a day of ill omen. This uncomplicated piece voices the pathos that Hildegard would not permit in her praise of martyrs (nos. 37–38). A song such as "O victoriosissimi triumphatores" makes no concession to human grief. But here, even as the angels sing their obligatory praise, the clouds—suspended between heaven and earth—are allowed to weep for the slaughtered children and give a voice to Rachel's woe. A rare simplicity enhances the effect.

60. Spiritui sancto (B-R 43)
Responsory for the 11,000 virgins.
D 167^{r}; R^{c} 471^{va-b}

Once upon a time there was a British princess named Ursula. Her father sought to marry her to a pagan prince, but in order to delay the marriage for three years she proposed a pilgrimage to Rome in the company of ten virgin companions. Each girl in turn had a thousand virginal handmaids. The eleven thousand maidens sailed for Rome, worshiped at the holy places, and persuaded the pope himself to join them on the return voyage. Embarking at Cologne, they were met by Attila the Hun and the entire company was martyred. Ursula revealed her special dedication when she refused to save herself by becoming Attila's concubine.

The kernel of this legend is found in a tenth-century *passio;* the story was retold in the eleventh century and again in the twelfth by Geoffrey of Monmouth. But the cult of Ursula and her companions did not begin to achieve its exceptional popularity until the mid-twelfth century. In 1106 workmen enlarging the walls of Cologne stumbled on an ancient Roman cemetery, and the bones were taken to be those of Ursula and her friends. A lively trade in relics ensued; some were acquired by Hildegard's monastery of St. Disibod. Fifty years later, a new exhumation of the graves led some to suspect that the relics were spurious, because the bones of men were found alongside those of the supposed virgins. But the cult was authenticated by the nun Elisabeth of Schönau, a friend and protégée of Hildegard. At the request of her abbot and several others, Elisabeth had visions to order, in which one of the martyred virgins appeared to her and explained their history, their family ties, and the details of their death and burial. Elisabeth represented herself as skeptical because her revelations diverged from the received legend; but the virgins explained to her that their male companions were devout bishops. These visions date from 1156–1157 and are recorded in *Elisabeth's Book of Revelations concerning the Sacred Army of Virgins of Cologne* (ed. F. W. E. Roth, *Die Visionen der heiligen Elisabeth* [Brünn, 1884], pp. 123–38).

Hildegard wrote more songs for Saint Ursula and her companions than for any other saint except the Mother of God. It is hard to say whether she was directly influenced by Elisabeth's visions. The nun of Schönau was interested in constructing a historically plausible legend, whereas Hildegard cared more about the symbolic meaning of martyrdom and virginity—although she did accept the new revelation that men were part of the company (no. 63, 3). But she was undoubtedly stirred by the general excitement that her friend's revelations fostered.

"Spiritui sancto" focuses on Ursula the pilgrim. A second Abraham, she leaves her betrothed and her native land to follow God's call. The passage of the "golden army" (l. 13) might recall the children of Israel crossing the Red Sea. *In virgineo crine* (l. 14) probably means "with unveiled hair, as befitting virgins" (see note on no. 56).

61. O rubor sanguinis (B-R 44)
Gospel antiphon (possibly to be sung with the Magnificat at vespers) for the 11,000 virgins.
D 167^{r}; R^{c} 471vb

Every hint of suffering or of history has been purged from this imagist piece. Closely related to "O cruor sanguinis" (no. 5) and "Vos flores rosarum" (no. 38), the antiphon transmutes the martyrs' blood into an immortal flower. Mingled with the blood of Christ, flowing from the heights of the eternal counsel, their shed blood becomes the ornament of their maidenhood, now saved forever from "the serpent's breath." Slaughtered, they cannot perish; fallen, they cannot wither.

62. Favus distillans (B-R 45)
Responsory for the 11,000 virgins.
D 167^{v}; R^{c} 471va

"Your lips distil nectar, my bride, honey and milk beneath your tongue. . . . A garden sealed is my sister, my bride, a garden sealed . . . with all choicest fruits" (Song 4:11–13). Ursula's maidens have become such a garden, a paradise where Christ may go walking at dawn. It is possible, but not necessary, to remember that the honeycomb could stand for Christ's body, the honey for his soul, and so forth. The images speak for themselves.

63. In matutinis laudibus (B-R 46–53)
Psalm antiphons for the 11,000 virgins.
D 167^{v}–168^{v}; R^{c} 471vb–472rb

These eight antiphons are labeled *In matutinis laudibus* ("for matins") in D and *Laudes* ("lauds" or "praises") in R. They are musically distinct, each with its own psalm differentia, but textually they make up a single narrative. The sixth is labeled *In evangelium,* like the antiphon "O rubor sanguinis" (no. 61). Since there is no Gospel canticle at matins, it may have been meant to accompany the Benedictus (Luke 1:68–79) at lauds. The exact liturgical setting of the pieces remains a puzzle; perhaps matins and lauds were sung consecutively as one service.

The antiphons relate Ursula's story from her initial call to a point just before her martyrdom. Two themes are singled out for emphasis: public response to the virgins' enterprise and the role of men in their company. Having led her own band of virgins to the Rupertsberg, in the face of strong opposition as well as support, Hildegard clearly sympathized with Ursula's venture. There is something Ursuline about her recollections of her own move to the new foundation: "by the archbishop's permission, with a vast escort of our kinsfolk and of other men, in reverence of God we came to this place. Then the ancient deceiver put me to the ordeal of great mockery, in that many people said: '. . . .Surely this will come to nothing!'" (*Vita* 2.22; ed. and trans. Peter Dronke, *Women Writers* 150, 233). In the same way Ursula's virgins are seen to be famous in the sight of "all peoples" and accompanied by an honorable escort, until the devil through his envy stirs up mockery.

Antiphons 3–6 justify the virgins' male companionship. Women, as the composer firmly believed, needed men to protect and care for them even—or especially—if they had chosen the life of virginity. In a Christmas sermon, she once preached that the Mother of God herself was wedded for the sake of humility: "if Mary had had no one to care for her, pride would easily have snatched her, as if she had not needed a husband to provide for her" (Pitra 245). The analogy of air and firmament (antiphon 5) draws on cosmology to support the interdependence of male and female. By means of the wholesome air, Hildegard observed, God sustains all life, growth, and verdure upon earth; but he also constructed the world so that the lower parts should be supported by the higher (see *De operatione Dei,* PL 197, 744b and 807d). Here woman is like the all-nurturing air and man like the solid, protective firmament above. Similar analogies appear frequently in the *Causes and Cures.*

The "kiss of peace" in the first antiphon recalls the theme of "Karitas habundat" (no. 25). In no. 6, the *summum virum* is probably Christ, although the pope who accompanied Ursula's troupe could also be intended.

64. O Ecclesia (B-R 54)
Irregular sequence for the 11,000 virgins.
D 168^{v}–169^{r}; R^{c} 477^{rb-vb}

One of Hildegard's most stunning poetic achievements, this song makes its premise the unity of Ursula—a naive, girlish figure—with Ecclesia, the cosmic and celestial Bride of Christ. It was Ecclesia—undefiled virgin, unblemished bride, mother of all the faithful—whom medieval exegetes found in the gorgeous imagery of the Song of Songs and who dominated five visions of Hildegard's *Scivias*. In the invocation of stanza 1 she is praised feature by feature, just like Solomon's bride, but the rhetoric teases; here is no woman's face but a sublime landscape of mountains and waterfalls. In echoes and figures the description of Ecclesia evokes the divine majesty: sapphire for the throne of God (Ezek. 1:26), Bethel for Jacob's vision (Gen. 28:11–22), incense and myrrh (Song 4:6) for priesthood and the passion of Christ, and the sound of many waters (Apoc. 1:15, 14:2) for the voice of the Lamb in judgment. Against the background of this colossal apparition, Ursula pours out her yearning, herself a bride and a figure of the Bride.

Hildegard makes her a visionary, eagle-eyed (see note on no. 21); dazzled by the sun, she can no longer look on the things of earth. Her outcry echoes Christ's words at the Last Supper (Luke 22:15): as he "desired with desire" to partake of the Passover before he suffered, she too yearns to pass over and partake of the celestial marriage feast. Dying means nothing to her: she will fly like a cloud (Isa. 60:8; cf. no. 49, 8) or become herself a sapphire, brilliant against heaven's blue, light against light.

A harsher reality intrudes. Stanza 4 introduces the theme of mockery which accounted for some of the composer's empathy with Ursula. No one takes the girl seriously; even their scoffing is a game, a kind of music. Then comes a hiatus before the slaughter, a moment of epiphany. Ursula awakens to the "fiery burden" she must bear, and her heroic *contemptus mundi* briefly astonishes the bystanders. For a fleeting moment their eyes are opened: they see her courage ascending like a mountain, her longing like a column of incense. The cosmic Ecclesia has become incarnate.

Biblical exegetes gave the devil a "body" to parody Christ's, and in stanza 7, Satan's "members" spring into action, seeking to annihilate all nobility and grace (*nobilissimos mores*) by destroying these virginal bodies. As in "O cruor sanguinis" (no. 5), the very elements echo the cry of their blood. *Wach* is a German exclamation of dismay and horror, a dissonant note in the symphony of angels. Like the weeping clouds in "Rex noster promptus" (no. 59), the elements give voice to the merely human woe that must speak its grief, although it ultimately yields to the celestial music. They lament the bloodshed of the Lamb and of his bride, herself a lamb—but this blood is shed at her wedding, it is the sign of consummation. Meanwhile, in a brilliant metamorphosis, the virgin martyrs have been transformed into something rich and strange—a necklace of pearls "from the matter of the Word of God," strangling the ancient serpent at the very moment when he thinks to have triumphed. For the *materia* compare "O splendidissima gemma" (no. 10).

65. **Cum vox sanguinis (B-R 55)**

Hymn to the 11,000 virgins.
D 169^{r}–170^{r}; R^{c} 477vb–478ra

This extraordinary hymn reveals Hildegard's deep grounding in the Bible and the exegetical tradition. In her antiphons and responsories she had told Ursula's story; in "O Ecclesia" she celebrated Ursula's marriage with the Lamb. "Cum vox sanguinis" presupposes a knowledge of the legend, which has disappeared almost totally from the hymn itself. It is an exercise in typology, a daring transposition through which Ursula takes the place of Christ as the antitype of all the Old Testament figures. Abraham's encounter with God at Mamre (Gen. 18:1–15), the substitution of the ram for Isaac (Gen. 22:13), the animal sacrifices of the Law (Lev. 1:1–5), and the vision in which Moses was allowed to see

God's back but not his face (Exod. 33:20–23) were commonly understood as types of the Trinity, the sacrifice of Christ, and the incompleteness of Hebrew revelation. The *Hoc sunt* of stanza 6 makes this exegetical framework explicit: the imperfect sacrifices of the Law and the veiling of God's face signify that before the Incarnation, God was known only by hearing and not yet by sight. Hildegard expresses this universal Christian understanding in *Scivias* I.5.5, where she perceives the expectant prophets waiting in Synagoga's womb, marveling from afar at the beauty of Ecclesia.

With the birth, death, and resurrection of Christ, all the prophecies are fulfilled and the mystical significance of Old Testament events becomes clear. In this hymn, however, the moment of fulfillment is not Christ's passion but Ursula's—or rather, her death is so totally identified with his that one can serve as a type of the other. The "narrative" of "Cum vox sanguinis," such as it is, describes a liturgical procession in heaven. As soon as Ursula and her troupe are martyred, Abraham steps forth—*prophetia* in line 4 is either an abstraction or a scribal error for *propheta*—and addresses all the saints: "This blood is touching us, now let us all rejoice!" Next the congregation of the Lamb—Isaac with all the patriarchs and prophets—says more or less the same thing. Moses and the Hebrew priesthood come forth in stanzas 5–7. All these priestly and prophetic voices are celebrating the triumph of martyrdom: the virgins' blood, united with Christ's, is a source of joy and praise among the blessed. But the difficult stanzas 7 and 9 reveal a further meaning in this particular martyrdom.

Stanza 7 echoes "Spiritui sancto" (no. 60) and "Favus distillans" (no. 62), which were probably sung on the same occasion. By gathering her virginal flock, the martyr has earned a change of name: she will no longer be called Ursula ("little bear") but rather Columba ("dove"), as a sign of her innocence. Stanza 8 reaffirms the parallel between Ursula and Ecclesia, developed in the preceding song. In the convoluted stanza 9, this particular flock of virgins becomes an exemplar of Mary's virginity, the miracle signified by the burning bush (Exod. 3:2). But Hildegard's exegetical zeal takes her even further: she will have this bush "planted in the primal root" of the human race, that is, in Adam and Eve. The grammar here is troubling, for the human being formed from clay must be Adam (Gen 2:7), yet the one meant to live "without the commingling of man" can only be Eve. In any case, the first parents lost their gift of virginity in the Fall, but Ursula and her maidens have regained it. Hence the prophets' festivity has a double theme: redemptive blood and redemptive purity.

The last lines of stanza 9 take up an allusion to Vulgate Psalm 44, which was introduced earlier in stanza 5: "The Queen"—Ecclesia—"stood at your right hand in golden vestments, clothed in many colors. . . . All the glory of the king's daughter is within, clothed round about in many colors, with golden borders" (Vulg. Ps. 44:10, 14–15). Queen Ecclesia's ornaments are fitting for her virgin train; thus in the *Book of Life's Merits* 6.43, Hildegard sees the glorified virgins in heaven clad in white robes woven with golden thread and decked with gems of every kind (Pitra 236). Later these many-colored gems are said to represent the works of the elect. At the end of "O Ecclesia" they became a necklace to strangle Satan; here they are finery for the people of God. By a last synesthetic fusion, the maidens' celestial gems are revealed to be one with their "cry"—of pain, or perhaps of intercession. Underlying the whole stanza is a logically or at least typologically clear train of thought, but it is quintessentially Hildegardian in its compression, allusiveness, and grammatical strangeness.

66. O virgo Ecclesia (B-R 56)
Votive antiphon for the dedication of a church.
D 170^{r}; R^{b} 405va; R^{c} 472^{rb-va}; V^{2} 156rb

The two full-length songs in honor of Saint Ursula lead directly into the last and briefest section of the *Symphonia,* which consists of four antiphons for the dedication of a church. The first two and the last two are paired. It is not possible to specify the precise church or churches for which they were composed. While the Rupertsberg and its daughter house at Eibingen are the most obvious possibilities, Hildegard could also have been approached with a commission from one of the many convents or monasteries where she had connections.

Like "O Ecclesia" (no. 64), all four antiphons personify the Church as bride of Christ. Medieval Latin, a language with no articles or capitals for proper names, made no orthographic distinction between the cosmic Ecclesia (the Church-as-bride) and the local ecclesia (a church congregation or building). This linguistic feature underscores Hildegard's already strong Platonizing tendency to see the universal embodied in the particular. Thus "O virgo Ecclesia," which alludes to an apparent schism, may refer either to the infighting of a local congregation or to some event that shook the universal Church. It is impossible to be sure. Hildegard was deeply vexed by the papal schism that Frederick Barbarossa initiated in 1159; but that schism did not end until 1177, and "Nunc gaudeant" (no. 67) celebrates the restoration of unity.

As I have argued elsewhere (*Sister of Wisdom* 237), the two antiphons may refer in veiled terms to Arnold of Brescia's revolt. Arnold was a populist firebrand who called for radical disendowment of the clergy, won support from the people of Rome, and drove Hildegard's first patron, Pope Eugenius III, out of the city. In Holy Week of 1155 a new pope, Adrian IV, resorted to the desperate measure of placing the whole populace of Rome under interdict until they expelled Arnold and returned to submission—which they promptly did. Arnold may be the "savage wolf" and the "cunning serpent" of this antiphon. In a letter to Adrian IV, Hildegard alluded cryptically to his battles with savage beasts (PL 197, 154a). The second half of the antiphon offers assurance that, even in the face of schism, Christ who married the Church with the dowry of his blood will not allow her sons to perish. The "King's standard" is of course the cross.

67. Nunc gaudeant (B-R 57)
Votive antiphon for the dedication of a church.
D 170^{r-v}; R^{b} 405va; R^{c} 472va; V^{2} 156rb

This antiphon, the sequel to "O virgo Ecclesia," celebrates the end of schism and the restoration of peace. Ecclesia rejoices because her children have returned to the fold, Satan or his agent is confounded, and the sacraments have been restored to those who lay under ban (l. 10). This is the last of Hildegard's compositions in D; the manuscript continues in a different hand with a text on exorcism.

68. O orzchis Ecclesia (B-R 67)

Votive antiphon for the dedication of a church; titled *Cantus ad Romam* in S.
R^b 405va; R^c 472va; S 28^r; V^2 156^{rb-va}

In the second book of Hildegard's *Vita* her hagiographer asks, "Who would not marvel that she composed chant of surpassingly sweet melody with amazing harmony, and invented letters never seen before, with a language hitherto unheard?" (PL 197, 101b). Many have "marveled" but no one has yet deduced the purpose of Hildegard's *Lingua ignota.* This glossary of faintly Germanic-sounding names for plants, animals, celestial beings, church furnishings, garments, tools, and so forth is preserved in two manuscripts, including R (a fragment is edited in Pitra, 496–502). But only in this single antiphon did Hildegard ever use words from her secret language in a literary context.

Evidently the language was of some importance to her, for she confided to no less a personage than Pope Anastasius IV (1153/54?) that God had inspired her to "form unknown letters, and utter an unknown language, and resound with melody in many tones" (PL 197, 152d). In the years of autonomy following her move, we know that she clothed her nuns in special visionary garb, wrote an exceptional play for them to perform, and taught them to sing her music. Did she teach them her "unheard language" as well, making her convent into the twelfth-century equivalent of a charismatic commune?

The five secret words in "O orzchis Ecclesia" are glossed in R^b and S as follows: 1 *orzchis*=immensa; 4 *caldemia*=aroma; *loifolum*=populorum; 6 *crizanta*=ornata (R^b) or uncta (S); 8 *chorzta*=choruscans (R^b) or chorusca (S). Even with glosses, however, the antiphon is cryptic in the extreme. The Church is acclaimed as bride and city (Apoc. 21:2) in terms fraught with double meaning. She is either girded or fortified with the armor of

God (Eph. 6:11–17). *Iacinctus* (jacinth or hyacinth) is a sky-blue gem or fabric associated with the priesthood (Exod. 28). Line 4 is a compressed, synesthetic image: the "wounds" of sin will become "fragrant" in the City of God because the Holy Spirit anoints them with the oil of mercy (cf. "O ignee Spiritus," no. 27, 12). I take the music and the anointing or robing of lines 6–8 to suggest a coronation rite in accord with the image of Ecclesia as queen, and with the ceremonies for consecration of a church.

69. O choruscans lux stellarum (B-R 68)
Votive antiphon for the dedication of a church (unlabeled in MS.)
R^c 472vb

This is Hildegard's version of Vulgate Psalm 44, the epithalamium for the royal bride. Ecclesia is not named, but she is obviously the "noble person" without spot or wrinkle (Eph. 5:27; *maculatam rugam* is Hildegard's eccentric version of *maculam aut rugam*). Stars allegorically represented saints, but the twinkling starlight is also an analogue for the flashing of gems the composer loved so well—possibly because it was the closest equivalent, in ordinary life, to the scintillating luminosity of her visions.

Lines 7–8 echo Ephesians 2:19 and Hebrews 12:22–24, the latter a description of the celestial Jerusalem where saints and angels pray together. But the "ancient destroyer's cave" is Hildegard's own invention, mentioned earlier in "O Ierusalem" (no. 49, 4b). Satan is not associated with caves in the Bible, so the image probably derives from her conceptions of pagan worship or of contemporary witchcraft and heresy.

O Verbum Patris
R^b 404va; V^2 155rb

This lyric celebrating divine prescience in creation belongs to the same thought-world as the first three *Symphonia* pieces and employs closely related language. The wheel is a classic symbol of eternity which Hildegard used frequently, as in her letter to the bishop of Bamberg on the Trinity: "In the Father eternity abides, that is, nothing can be taken away from the Father's eternity nor added to it, for eternity abides like a wheel that has neither beginning nor end" (PL 197, 168c). But the wheel is spinning, not static, for it denotes the vitality as well as the timelessness of God, charging all creation with a powerful energy (*divina vi,* l. 4).

O Fili dilectissime
R^b 405ra; V^2 155vb

This is the only Marian piece in which Hildegard employs direct speech, or *prosopopoeia,* and places words in the Virgin's mouth. The miscellany introduces Mary's prayer with a stage direction: "Ipsa enim ad filium suum sic de virginitate dicit" (She speaks thus to her son concerning virginity). "O Fili dilectissime" is followed by the two *symphonie* for virgins and widows (nos. 57–58), the prayer "O magne Pater" (no. 6), and the lyric "O factura Dei" (below). Together these pieces, comprising part (c) of the miscellany, seem to form one scene of a dramatic sketch about Eve, Mary, and the Church.

The image of the circling wheel in this piece and in "O Verbum Patris" serves to link creation and Incarnation. For the music in Mary's womb, compare "Ave generosa" (no. 17). If this lyric were indeed meant to be sung, "the flowers of the tones" would be self-referential for the chanting nuns.

O factura Dei
R^b 405rb; V^2 156^{ra-b}

A short lyric reminiscent of "O quam mirabilis" (no. 3). It is the promise of the Incarnation, "God in humanity," which renders the original creation holy.

O magna res
R^b 407ra; S 53^v–54^r; V^2 158ra; V^3 121^{r-v}

Because of its roughly parallel syntactic units and its resemblance to the sequence "O virga ac diadema" (no. 20), I have divided this admirable piece into paired strophes. Though briefer and less developed than the sequence, it traces a similar trajectory, evoking the eternal counsel of Wisdom (1a), the fortunate fall of Eve (1b–2a), the dawn of salvation in Mary (2b–3a), and her role as "sister of Wisdom" in giving birth to a new and fairer creation (3b). Only 1b is difficult, with its typically embedded relative clauses. God is the great king, Mary the dawn, and the "wise man" probably Solomon, the bridegroom of Sapientia (see the apocryphal Wisdom of Solomon 7). The wisdom that had remained concealed in the Old Testament prophecies and typologies has now been "mercifully revealed" through Mary. "O magna res" is a succinct and effective synopsis of Hildegard's sapiential thought.

Bibliography

I. Latin editions of Hildegard's works

Causae et curae, ed. Paul Kaiser. Leipzig, 1903.

Epistolarium, ed. Lieven Van Acker. *Corpus christianorum: Continuatio mediaevalis* [CCCM] 91-91a. Turnhout, 1991, 1993. Additional volumes forthcoming, ed. Monika Klaes.

Liber divinorum operum, ed. Albert Derolez and Peter Dronke. CCCM 92. Turnhout, 1996.

Liber vite meritorum, ed. Angela Carlevaris. CCCM 90. Turnhout, 1995.

Lieder, ed. Pudentiana Barth, M.-I. Ritscher, and Joseph Schmidt-Görg (musical edition; Latin and German). Salzburg, 1969.

Migne, J.-P., ed. *Hildegardis Opera omnia*. *Patrologia latina* vol. 197. Paris, 1855. Includes *Physica* and saints' lives.

Ordo virtutum, ed. and trans. Peter Dronke, in *Nine Medieval Latin Plays* (Cambridge, 1994): 147-84.

Ordo virtutum (musical edition), ed. Audrey Ekdahl Davidson. Kalamazoo, 1985.

Pitra, Jean-Baptiste, ed. *Analecta S. Hildegardis*: *Analecta sacra*, vol. 8. Monte Cassino, 1882. Includes *Expositiones evangeliorum*, 145 *Epistolae*, and other works.

Scivias, ed. Adelgundis Führkötter and Angela Carlevaris. CCCM 43-43a. Turnhout, 1978.

Sequences and Hymns, ed.Christopher Page (musical edition). Newton Abbot, Devon, England: Antico Church Music, 1983.

Symphonia harmoniae caelestium revelationum, ed. Peter Van Poucke. Peer, Belgium: Alamire, 1991. Facsimile of music from Dendermonde codex.

Vita Sanctae Hildegardis, ed. Monika Klaes. CCCM 126. Turnhout, 1993.

II. English translations

Book of Divine Works, with Letters and Songs, ed. Matthew Fox, trans. Robert Cunningham et al. (abridged). Santa Fe, 1987.

Book of the Rewards of Life, trans. Bruce Hozeski. New York, 1994.

Explanation of the Rule of Benedict, trans. Hugh Feiss. Toronto, 1990.

Hildegard of Bingen: Mystical Writings, ed. Fiona Bowie and Oliver Davies, trans. Robert Carver. New York, 1990.

Holistic Healing [*Causae et curae*], trans. Patrick Madigan. Collegeville, MN, 1994.

Letters of Hildegard of Bingen, trans. Joseph Baird and Radd Ehrman, 2 vols. Oxford, 1994, 1998. Additional volumes to appear.

Life of the Saintly Hildegard, trans. Hugh Feiss. Toronto, 1996.

Play of the Virtues, trans. Peter Dronke, in *Nine Medieval Latin Plays*. Cambridge, 1994.

Scivias, trans. Columba Hart and Jane Bishop, in Paulist Classics of Western Spirituality. New York, 1990.

Secrets of God: Writings of Hildegard of Bingen, trans. Sabina Flanagan. Boston, 1996.

III. General studies of Hildegard

Beer, Frances. *Women and Mystical Experience in the Middle Ages*. Woodbridge, Suffolk, UK, 1992.

Brück, Anton, ed. *Hildegard von Bingen, 1179-1979: Festschrift zum 800. Todestag der Heiligen*. Mainz, 1979.

Burnett, Charles, and Peter Dronke, eds. *Hildegard of Bingen: The Context of Her Thought and Art*. London, 1998.

Davidson, Audrey Ekdahl, ed. *The* Ordo Virtutum *of Hildegard of Bingen: Critical Studies*. Kalamazoo, 1992.

Dreyer, Elizabeth. *Passionate Women: Two Medieval Mystics*. New York, 1989.

Dronke, Peter. *Women Writers of the Middle Ages: A Critical Study of Texts from Perpetua († 203) to Marguerite Porete († 1310)*. Cambridge, 1984. Chapter 6 and Appendix.

Flanagan, Sabina. *Hildegard of Bingen, 1098-1179: A Visionary Life*. London,1989.

Forster, Edeltraud, ed. *Hildegard von Bingen: Prophetin durch die Zeiten*. Freiburg, 1997.

Fox, Matthew. *Illuminations of Hildegard of Bingen*. Santa Fe, 1985.

Gössmann, Elisabeth. *Hildegard of Bingen: Four Papers*. Toronto, 1995.

Gouguenheim, Sylvain. *La Sibylle du Rhin: Hildegarde de Bingen, abbesse et prophétesse rhénane*. Paris, 1996.

Gronau, Eduard. *Hildegard von Bingen, 1098-1179*. Stein-am-Rhein, Switzerland, 1985.

Lautenschläger, Gabriele. *Hildegard von Bingen: Die theologische Grundlegung ihrer Ethik und Spiritualität*. Stuttgart, 1993.

Liebeschütz, Hans. *Das allegorische Weltbild der hl. Hildegard von Bingen.* Leipzig, 1930.
Newman, Barbara. *Sister of Wisdom: St. Hildegard's Theology of the Feminine*, 2nd ed. Berkeley, 1997.
____, ed. *Voice of the Living Light: Hildegard of Bingen and Her World.* Berkeley, 1998.
Nolan, Edward Peter. *Cry Out and Write: A Feminine Poetics of Revelation.* New York, 1994.
Schipperges, Heinrich. *Hildegard of Bingen*, trans. Eva Jauntzems. New York, 1989.
Schrader, Marianna, and Adelgundis Führkötter. *Die Echtheit des Schrifttums der hl. Hildegard von Bingen.* Cologne and Graz, 1956.
Widmer, Bertha. *Heilsordnung und Zeitgeschehen in der Mystik Hildegards von Bingen.* Basel and Stuttgart, 1955.

IV. Studies of the Symphonia

Bent, Ian. "Hildegard of Bingen," in *New Grove Dictionary of Music and Musicians*, ed. Stanley Sadie (London, 1980): vol. 8, 553-56.
Bronarski, Ludwig. *Die Lieder der hl. Hildegard: Ein Beitrag zur Geschichte der geistlichen Musik des Mittelalters.* Leipzig, 1922.
Cogan, Robert. "Hildegard's Fractal Antiphon," *Sonus* 11 (1990): 1-19.
Dronke, Peter. "The Composition of Hildegard of Bingen's *Symphonia*," *Sacris Erudiri* 19 (1969-70): 381-93.
____. *Poetic Individuality in the Middle Ages: New Departures in Poetry, 1000-1150* (Oxford, 1970): 150-79.
____. "Tradition and Innovation in Medieval Western Colour-Imagery," *Eranos Jahrbuch* 49 (1972): 51-106; on Hildegard, 82-88.
Escot, Pozzi. "The Gothic Cathedral and Hidden Geometry of St. Hildegard," *Sonus* 5 (1984): 14-31.
Fassler, Margot. "Composer and Dramatist: 'Melodious Singing and the Freshness of Remorse,'" in Newman, ed., *Voice of the Living Light.*
Holsinger, Bruce. "The Flesh of the Voice: Embodiment and the Homoerotics of Devotion in the Music of Hildegard of Bingen," *Signs* 19 (1993): 92-125.
Martin, Janet, and Greta Mary Hair. "*O Ecclesia*: The Text and Music of Hildegard of Bingen's Sequence for St. Ursula," *Tjurunga* 30 (1986): 3-62.
Pfau, Marianne Richert. "Hildegard von Bingen's *Symphonia armonie celestium revelationum*: An Analysis of Musical Process, Modality, and Text-Music Relations." Ph.D. diss., SUNY at Stony Brook, 1990.
____. "Mode and Melody Types in Hildegard von Bingen's *Symphonia*," *Sonus* 11 (1990): 53-71.
Ritscher, Maria-Immaculata. "Zur Musik der hl. Hildegard von Bingen," in Brück, ed., *Hildegard von Bingen*, 189-210.
Schlager, Karlheinz. "Hildegard von Bingen im Spiegel der Choralforschung: Rückschau und Ausblick," in *De Musica et Cantu: Studien zur Geschichte der Kirchenmusik und der Oper*, ed. Peter Cahn and Ann-Katrin Heimer (Hildesheim, 1993): 309-23.

Schmidt-Görg, Joseph. "Zur Musikanschauung in den Schriften der hl. Hildegard," in *Der Mensch und die Künste: Festschrift für Heinrich Lützeler* (Düsseldorf, 1962): 230-37.

Walter, Peter. "Die Heiligen in der Dichtung der hl. Hildegard von Bingen," in Brück, ed., *Hildegard von Bingen*, 211-37.

____. "*Virgo filium dei portasti*: Maria in den Gesängen der hl. Hildegard von Bingen," *Archiv für mittelrheinische Kirchengeschichte* 29 (1977): 75-96.

V. Latin liturgy, hymnography, and music: primary sources

Abelard, Peter. *Hymnarius Paraclitensis*, ed. Joseph Szövérffy, 2 vols. Albany, NY, 1975.

Adam of St. Victor. *The Liturgical Poetry of Adam of St. Victor*, ed. and trans. D. S. Wrangham, 3 vols. London, 1881.

____. *Sämtliche Sequenzen: Lateinisch und deutsch*, ed. Franz Wellner. Munich, 1955.

Analecta hymnica medii aevi, ed. G. M. Dreves and Clemens Blume, 58 vols. Leipzig, 1886-1922.

Andrieu, Michel. *Les "Ordines Romani" du haut moyen âge*, 5 vols. Louvain, 1936-1961.

Aurelian of Réôme. *De musica disciplina*, ed. Lawrence Gushee. Nijmegen, 1975.

Barbera, André, ed. *Music Theory and Its Sources: Antiquity and the Middle Ages.* Notre Dame, 1990.

Corpus antiphonalium officii, ed. R.-J. Hesbert. *Rerum ecclesiasticarum documenta, series major. Fontes* 7-12. Rome, 1963-1979.

Guido of Arezzo. *Micrologus de disciplina artis musicae*, ed. Joseph Smits van Waesberghe. Nijmegen, 1955.

Hildebert of Lavardin. *Carmina minora*, ed. A. Brian Scott. Leipzig, 1969.

Johannes Affligemensis. *De musica*, ed. Joseph Smits van Waesberghe. Rome, 1950.

Liber usualis missae et officii. Rome, 1950.

Notker Balbulus. *Liber ymnorum*, ed. and trans. Wolfram von den Steinen. Bern, 1960.

Peter Damian. *L'opera poetica di S. Pier Damiani*, ed. Margareta Lokrantz. Stockholm, 1964.

Pontifical Romano-Germanique du dixième siècle, ed. Cyrille Vogel and Reinhard Elze, 3 vols. Rome, 1963-1972.

Scriptores ecclesiastici de musica sacra potissimum, ed. Martin Gerbert, 3 vols. St. Blasien, 1784; rpt. Milan, 1931.

Scriptorum de musica medii aevi novam seriem, ed. Charles Edmond de Coussemaker, 4 vols. Paris, 1864-1876; rpt. Hildesheim, 1963.

Strunk, Oliver. *Source Readings in Music History from Classical Antiquity through the Romantic Era.* New York, 1950.

VI. Latin liturgy, hymnography, and music: studies

Adey, Lionel. *Hymns and the Christian "Myth."* Vancouver, 1986.

Benton, John. "Nicholas of Clairvaux and the Twelfth-Century Sequence, with Special Reference to Adam of St. Victor,"*Traditio* 18 (1962): 149-80.

Blaise, Albert. "Latin," in *Sacred Languages*, ed. Paul Auvray et al., trans. S. J. Tester (New York, 1960): 121-70.

Bower, Calvin. "Natural and Artificial Music: The Origins and Development of an Aesthetic Concept," *Musica Disciplina* 25 (1971): 17-33.

Brinkmann, Hennig. "Voraussetzungen und Struktur religiöser Lyrik im Mittelalter," *Mittellateinisches Jahrbuch* 3 (1966): 37-54.

Cattin, Giulio. *Music of the Middle Ages*, vol. 1, trans. Steven Botterill. Cambridge, 1984.

Chamberlain, David. "Wolbero of Cologne (d. 1167): A Zenith of Musical Imagery," *Mediaeval Studies* 33 (1971): 114-26.

Crocker, Richard. *The Early Medieval Sequence.* Berkeley, 1977.

de Bruyne, Edgar. *Études d'esthétique médiévale*, 2 vols. Bruges, 1946. On musical aesthetics see 1: 306-38 and 2: 108-32.

de Ghellinck, Joseph. *L'Essor de la littérature latine au XIIe siècle*, 2 vols. Paris, 1946.

Diehl, Patrick. *The Medieval European Religious Lyric: An Ars Poetica.* Berkeley, 1985.

Dronke, Peter. *The Medieval Lyric.* London, 1968. On Hildegard, pp.75-78.

Fassler, Margot. *Gothic Song: Victorine Sequences and Augustinian Reform in Twelfth-Century Paris.* Cambridge, 1993.

Gérold, Théodore. *Les Pères de l'Église et la musique.* Paris, 1931.

Hammerstein, Reinhold. *Die Musik der Engel: Untersuchungen zur Musikanschauung des Mittelalters.* Bern and Munich, 1962.

Hiley, David. *Western Plainchant: A Handbook.* Oxford, 1993.

Hoppin, Richard. *Medieval Music.* New York, 1978.

Hughes, Andrew. *Medieval Manuscripts for Mass and Office: A Guide to Their Organization and Terminology.* Toronto, 1982.

____. *Style and Symbol: Medieval Music, 800-1453.* Ottawa, 1989.

Jonsson, Ritva, and Leo Treitler. "Medieval Music and Language: A Reconsideration of the Relationship," in *Studies in the History of Music*, vol. 1, *Music and Language* (New York, 1983): 1-23.

Leclercq, Jean. *The Love of Learning and the Desire for God: A Study of Monastic Culture*, trans. Catharine Misrahi. New York, 1961.

Liver, Ricarda. *Die Nachwirkung der antiken Sakralsprache im christlichen Gebet des lateinischen und italienischen Mittelalters.* Bern, 1979.

Mohrmann, Christine. *Études sur le latin des chrétiens*, 4 vols. Rome, 1961-1965.

____. *Liturgical Latin: Its Origins and Character.* Washington, 1957.

Norberg, Dag. *Introduction à l'étude de la versification latine médiévale.* Stockholm, 1958.

Pirrotta, Nino. "'Musica de sono humano' and the Musical Poetics of Guido of Arezzo," *Mediaevalia et Humanistica*, n.s. 7 (1976): 13-27.

Portnoy, Julius. *The Philosopher and Music.* New York, 1954. On medieval aesthetics, pp. 1-106.

Raby, F. J. E. *A History of Christian-Latin Poetry from the Beginnings to the Close of the Middle Ages*, 2nd ed. Oxford, 1953.

Reifenberg, Hermann. *Stundengebet und Breviare im Bistum Mainz seit der romanischen Epoche.* Münster, 1964.

Stevens, John. *Words and Music in the Middle Ages: Song, Narrative, Dance and Drama, 1050-1350.* Cambridge, 1986.

Szövérffy, Joseph. *Die Annalen der lateinischen Hymnendichtung*, 2 vols. Berlin, 1964-1965.

Vogel, Cyrille. *Medieval Liturgy: An Introduction to the Sources*, rev. and trans. William Storey and Niels Rasmussen. Washington, 1986.

von den Steinen, Wolfram. *Notker der Dichter und seine geistige Welt*, 2 vols. Bern, 1948.

Wright, Craig. *Music and Ceremony at Notre Dame of Paris (500-1550).* Cambridge, 1989.

Yardley, Anne Bagnall. "'Ful weel she soong the service dyvyne': The Cloistered Musician in the Middle Ages," in *Women Making Music: The Western Art Tradition, 1150-1950*, ed. Jane Bowers and Judith Tick (Urbana, 1986): 15-38.

Discography

This discography excludes the many CDs containing only one or two pieces from Hildegard's *Symphonia*, as well as New Age adaptations of her music.

Anonymous 4. *11,000 Virgins: Chants for the Feast of St. Ursula*, 1997. Harmonia mundi 907200.

Early Music Institute, dir. Thomas Binkley. *The Lauds of St. Ursula*, 1991. Focus 911.

Ensemble für frühe Musik, Augsburg. *Hildegard von Bingen und ihre Zeit: Geistliche Musik des 12. Jahrhunderts*, 1990. Christophorus 74584. Music of Hildegard and Abelard.

Ensemble Mediatrix, dir. Johannes Göschl. *Feminea Forma Maria*, 1996. Calig 50982. Marian songs of the Dendermonde codex.

Ensemble Organum, dir. Marcel Pérès. *Hildegard von Bingen: Laudes de Ste. Ursule*, 1997. Harmonia mundi 901626.

Norma Gentile. *Unfurling Love's Creation: Chants by Hildegard von Bingen*, 1997. Lyrichord LEMS 8027.

Gothic Voices, dir. Christopher Page. *A Feather on the Breath of God*, 1984. Hyperion CDA 66039. Sequences and hymns.

Instrumentalkreis Helga Weber, with Almut Teichert-Hailperin. *Geistliche Musik des Mittelalters und der Renaissance*, 1980, 1993. Christophorus CHE 0041-2. Music of Hildegard, Brassart, Dunstable, and Dufay.

Musica Sacra, dir. Richard Westenburg. *Monk and the Abbess*, 1996. BMG Catalyst 09026-68329-2. Music of Hildegard and Meredith Monk.

Ellen Oak. *The Harmony of Heaven*, 1995. Bison Tales 0001.

Oxford Camerata, dir. Jeremy Summerly. *Hildegard von Bingen: Heavenly Revelations*, 1994. Naxos 8.550998.

Schola der Benediktinerinnenabtei St. Hildegard, dir. M. I. Ritscher. *Gesänge der hl. Hildegard von Bingen*, 1979. Bayer 100116.

Catherine Schroeder et al. *O nobilissima viriditas*, 1995. Champeaux CSM 0006.

Sequentia, dir. Barbara Thornton. *Canticles of Ecstasy*, 1994. Deutsche Harmonia mundi 05472-77320-2.

Sequentia, dir. Barbara Thornton. *O Jerusalem,* 1997. Deutsche Harmonia mundi 05472-77353-2.

Sequentia, dir. Barbara Thornton. *Ordo virtutum* (2 disks), 1982. Deutsche Harmonia mundi 77051-2-RG. Re-recorded 1998. DHM 05472-77394-2.

Sequentia, dir. Barbara Thornton. *Symphoniae: Geistliche Gesänge*, 1985. Deutsche Harmonia mundi 77020-2-RG.

Sequentia, dir. Barbara Thornton. *Voice of the Blood*, 1995. Deutsche Harmonia mundi 05472-77346-2.

Sinfonye, dir. Stevie Wishart. *Symphony of the Harmony of Celestial Revelations*, Vol. 1, 1996. Celestial Harmonies 13127-2.

Tapestry, dir. Laurie Monahan. *Hildegard von Bingen: Celestial Light,* 1997. Telarc 80456. Music of Hildegard and Robert Kyr, with Notre Dame polyphony.

Viriditas, dir. Juliette Hughes. *Jouissance*, 1993. Spectrum/Cistercian Publications, ISBN 0-86786-344-7. Music of Hildegard and Abelard.

Voices of Ascension, dir. Dennis Keene. *Voices of Angels: Music of Hildegard von Bingen,* 1997. Delos 3219.